ΑΡΧΑΙΑ ΕΛΛΑΣ 1

ΑΡΧΑΙΑ ΕΛΛΑΣ

MONOGRAPHS ON ANCIENT GREEK HISTORY
AND ARCHAEOLOGY

EDITED BY SARA B. ALESHIRE

VOLUME 1

J.C. GIEBEN, PUBLISHER

AMSTERDAM 1995

THUCYDIDES' PENTEKONTAETIA
AND OTHER ESSAYS

W. KENDRICK PRITCHETT

EMERITUS PROFESSOR OF GREEK IN THE
UNIVERSITY OF CALIFORNIA, BERKELEY

J.C. GIEBEN, PUBLISHER
AMSTERDAM 1995

No part of this book may be translated or reproduced in any form, by print, photoprint, microfilm, or any other means, without written permission from the author.

© by W.K. Pritchett, 1995 / Printed in The Netherlands / ISBN 90 5063 487 7

CONTENTS

ACKNOWLEDGMENTS	vii
CHAPTER	
I. THUCYDIDES' PENTEKONTAETIA	1
1. THUCYDIDES 1.101.2: SYNTAX	5
2. 1.101.2: EARTHQUAKE	12
3. 1.103: NUMERAL	24
4. 1.103: NAUPAKTOS	62
5. NAXOS, THASOS, AND THEMISTOKLES' FLIGHT	81
6. DRABESKOS	94
7. 1.107–108: ATHENIAN LONG WALLS	122
II. THUCYDIDES 1.61.3–5	133
III. DIODOROS' PENTEKONTAETIA	163
IV. THE SOLAR YEAR OF THUCYDIDES	173
V. AETIOLOGY SANS TOPOGRAPHY	205
1. KENCHREAI AND THE BATTLE OF HYSIAI	207
2. THYREATIS AND THE BATTLE OF CHAMPIONS	228
3. PHIGALEIA AND THE ORESTHASIANS	263
4. THE ITHOMAIA AND THE MESSENIAN WARS	268

ACKNOWLEDGMENTS

In addition to my wife who for more than fifty years has loyally read proof of my manuscripts, without the assistance of three scholars this work would not have seen the light. Professor Barbara Saylor Rodgers, chairperson of a Classics department, to whom I dedicated *Topography* V in 1985, has continued to assist me by transforming onto a floppy disk my not always legible manuscript. The formatting of camera-ready copy is the work of Dr. Sara B. Aleshire, who generously took time from her own research and her editorial work with *SEG*. To John McK. Camp II, retiring as Mellon Professor of Classical Studies in the American School of Classical Studies, now Director of the Agora excavations, I owe a debt which goes beyond the ability of any words to acknowledge. He traveled with me to the various sites which are discussed in this volume. The two of us project a work which will be titled "An Archaeological and Topographical Commentary on Thucydides," the completion of which, however, will require several years and lies very much in the lap of the gods. In addition, I have had the benefit of discussing with Ronald Stroud in the seminar room at Berkeley various problems which are treated in this volume. J.C. Gieben of Amsterdam, without resorting to the delays created by copy-editors, has in the most friendly spirit undertaken the publication of the text.

I

THUCYDIDES' PENTEKONTAETIA

INTRODUCTION

I T IS WITH THE DEEPEST OBLIGATION to Professor E. Badian and his recent book on Thucydides' Pentekontaetia (*From Plataea to Potidaea. Studies in the History and Historiography of the Pentecontaetia* [Baltimore 1993]) that I offer an opinion in defence of the Greek historian. The occurrence of alleged errors in Thucydides is always a subject that stirs me to rebellion, and prompts me to take the other side. Thucydides is a magisterial writer; whether he is also a scrupulous historian depends on how often he gets things right. He certainly professes a concern for accuracy. Topography and archaeological discoveries, including epigraphy, offer an opportunity to check some part of the record.[1] In some circles, his critics have accused him of discrep-

---

[1]E. A. Freeman, Regius Professor at Oxford, who spent three long sojourns in Sicily between 1886 and 1890, following in the steps of A. Holm (1870), says (*The History of Sicily* 2.419), "That Thucydides had stepped out every inch of the battleground of Syracuse, I feel as sure as that I have done so in his steps." H.-P. Drögenmüller, *Syrakus* (*Gymnasium* Beiheft 6 [1969]), offered a study with sketch-maps and photographs sustaining the Thucydidean record. Dover responded in *Phoenix* 25 (1971) 282–285; cf. *HCT* 4 (1970) 461–484. Drögenmüller, in turn, returned to the subject in *RE* Suppl. 13 (1973) 815–836. Involved are the size of the ancient city and the location of Trogilos. For recent bibliography on Syracuse, see R. S. Stroud, *Chiron* 24 (1994) 302 n. 74. I spent ten days in Syrakuse, but soon realized that early scholars had opportunities of investigation denied to a traveler a hundred years later. Dover believes that the early chapters on the colonization of Sicily were probably a digest of Antiochos' *History of Sicily*. For a collection of bibliography and appraisals of Thucydidean topography up to 1980, the work of G. Schepens, "L' 'Autopsie' dans la méthode des historiens Grecs du Vᵉ siècle avant J.-C.," *Verhandelingen*

2 THUCYDIDES' PENTEKONTAETIA

ancies by extracting a nucleus of fact from the floscules of Diodoros, scholiasts, Plutarch, Ktesias, and the like; and he stands forth in their opinion as an historian whose conscience is warped to the extent of suppressing the truth, then as an artist who cares for nothing but rhetorical effect, and even a pedantic professor who manipulates events for the sake of his political philosophy.

The excursus known as the Pentekontaetia (1.89–118.2) is a bare narrative of events, with no mention of significance, the subject of which is the growth of Athenian power. Many believe that Thucydides was aware of events that he omits, although the number of such events has been reduced by M. Chambers' redating of IG I³.11 and the debate over Attic script. Thucydides states in 1.97.2 that the only one who had touched upon this period was Hellanikos in his *Atthis*, but that he had treated it βραχέως τε καὶ τοῖς χρόνοις οὐκ ἀκριβῶς.[2] Since it is generally held that the *Atthis* of Hellanikos, to whom Thucydides refers in 1.97.2, was not published until after 407/6 B.C. (*FGrH* 323a frgs. 25 and 26), some scholars hold that the Pentekontaetia was not composed until after that date.[3] Others follow Schwartz in believing that 1.97.2, where Thucydides gives his view that Hellanikos' work was chronologically inaccurate, was a late insertion into a context at

---

van de Koninklijke Academie voor Wetenschappen, Letteren en Schone Kunsten van België 42 (1980) No. 93, pp. 130-208, is a major contribution, superior in my judgment to Andrewes and Dover.

[2] I pass over the problem of composition, on which scholars such as Gomme and Andrewes/Dover do not agree. Involved are the problems of the date of the publication of the *Atthis*, and whether copies were circulated prior to final publication, etc. A priori, the latter might seem unlikely; but a passage in Herodotos was known in Athens (whether orally or in writing) long before the publication of his extant work: Immerwahr, *CHCL* 1 (1985) 427. For a summary about the composition of the Pentekontaetia, see Immerwahr, ibid. 443. Hellanikos also published the "Priestesses of Argos" (Jacoby, *FGrH* 4 frgs. 74–84) which apparently contained a chronological framework for history.

[3] See, for example, Immerwahr, *CHCL* 1 (1985) 443.

I. THUCYDIDES' PENTEKONTAETIA 3

variance with his statement, and that Thucydides did not live to revise his record.

Serious scholarly debate over the chronology of the Pentekontaetia, to judge from Classen's 1879 edition, began with the work of the eminent Greek grammarian K. W. Krüger, *Historisch-philologische Studien* 1 (Berlin 1837), and has not altered much over the decades, since, apart from the quota-lists, and Babylonian documents on the dates of Persian kings, the readings and significance of which have been disputed, there has been relatively little new evidence. Elaborate investigations were made independently by W. Pierson, *Philologus* 28 (1869) 40–69, 193–220. Krüger's position was examined by A. Schäfer, *Disputatio de rerum post bellum Persicum* (1865). This was in turn assailed by Krüger in his *Kritische Analecten* (Berlin 1867). Classen, in his early editions, followed Krüger. In a posthumous publication, the views of early scholarship were examined in *AJP* 7 (1886) 325–343, by C. D. Morris, professor with Gildersleeve at Johns Hopkins, who had published an edition of book 1. As early as 1841, Clinton (*Fasti* 2.44) had computed that Xerxes' death was in 465 B.C.[4] The episode of Ithome remained a central issue.

Even without 1.97.2, it would seem likely that an historian in giving a bare-bones sketch of a lengthy period would record the events in chronological order. Indeed, it is beyond dispute that the vast majority of passages is in chronological sequence. The

---

[4]To judge from Clinton's tables, he deduced from Thucydides 4.50 that Artaxerxes died in the winter months of 425/4 B.C. In this Thucydides coincides with Diodoros 12.64, who mentions the death of Artaxerxes as occurring in the archonship of Stratokles, and says that he had been on the throne for 40 years. This last statement Diodoros makes also in 11.69, where he says that Xerxes died after a reign of over 20 years (ἔτη πλείω τῶν εἴκοσι), and that Artaxerxes succeeded him and reigned 40 years. If one accepts these statements, Xerxes must have died in 465 B.C. Not all investigators did, and one argument was advanced that the numerals are corrupt, since Ktesias and Diodoros give slightly different figures.

4   THUCYDIDES' PENTEKONTAETIA

framework is chronological. When Gomme published volume 1 of *HCT* (1945) and the editors of *ATL* their volume 3 (1950), both offered tables (394–396, 408 and 175–179, respectively), holding that the events were recorded in chronological order, although they disagreed sharply about individual passages.

We have at least one important piece of evidence about the chronology which was not known to the editors of *ATL*. M. E. White (*JHS* 84 [1964] 142 n. 13) noted for classical scholars that a Babylonian legal agreement had been published which showed that news of Artaxerxes' accession had reached Egypt by January 2, 464. Actually, the date was deduced by Clinton and seems to have been known to Gomme (1.397), although he does not give his source. In any case, M. W. Stolper, *JHS* 108 (1988) 196–198, has shown that this text was misread; but he publishes an astronomical text which gives the date for Xerxes' death as August 4–8, 465 B.C. We assume that the astronomer who added that bit of information to his observation about an eclipse in Babylon, as with other additions, was correct. Thucydides' report, then, of Themistokles' arrival in Asia Minor must be after this date.

Our purpose is to focus on the text of our primary source Thucydides, where his accuracy has been impugned, in support of the position that events were given in chronological order. Only later do we turn to the record in Diodoros and later sources. If at any point Thucydides failed to make his account chronologically accurate, that is something that must be proved against him. Our concern is only with what we believe are the real cruxes which come with Drabeskos, the Ithome episode, the settlement at Naupaktos, the flight of Themistokles, the Athenian long walls, problems where topography is often a factor. There is considerable merit in the quotation attributed to R. H. Tawney in the *TLS*, "What historians need is not more documents but stronger boots."

We treat these cruxes in the following order. Since some of the sections are of some length, it has been convenient to start each section with footnote 1.

I. THUCYDIDES' PENTEKONTAETIA

1. Thucydides 1.101.2: Syntax
2. 1.101.2: Earthquake
3. 1.103: Numeral
4. 1.103: Naupaktos
5. Naxos, Thasos, and Themistokles' flight
6. Drabeskos
7. 1.107–108: Athenian Long Walls

For the order of events, the reader may wish to consult the table in Gomme, *HCT* 1.394–396.

SECTION 1

THUCYDIDES 1.101.2: SYNTAX

In 1.101.2, a passage which follows a statement about the siege of Thasos, Thucydides says that the Thasians appealed to the Lakedaimonians to help them by invading Attika. The Lakedaimonians promised to do so and they intended to keep their promise, διεκωλύθησαν δὲ ὑπὸ τοῦ γενομένου σεισμοῦ, ἐν ᾧ καὶ οἱ Εἵλωτες αὐτοῖς καὶ τῶν περιοίκων, Θουριᾶται τε καὶ Αἰθαιῆς ἐς Ἰθώμην ἀπέστησαν, thus bringing on the Third Messenian war.[1]

The crux of the passage is the meaning of the aorist participle in the first attributive position. It is maintained that the meaning must be, "which had previously happened." Badian writes (92–93):

> It was the singular merit of Raphael Sealey, in an unpretentious note <*Historia* 6 (1957) 368–371>, to draw attention to Thucydides' phrase, that the Spartans were prevented from carrying out their promise ὑπὸ τοῦ γενομένου σεισμοῦ. Sealey showed, by analysis of Thucydides' usage, that this must mean "by the earthquake

---

[1]For ἐν ᾧ, see Schwyzer 2.640. Cf. Hammond, *Historia* 4 (1955) 376.

6 THUCYDIDES' PENTEKONTAETIA AND OTHER ESSAYS

which had (previously) happened" — the obvious prima facie meaning for (say) an elementary student of Greek, but rejected by his betters because they preferred to know what Thucydides "must have" meant. Indeed, the application of standard philological method to the phrase thirty years ago, which would normally have been accepted as decisive, has in this case been largely ignored, or even rejected with arguments that illustrate the victory of prejudice over method and linguistic training. ... Suppressing the well-known immediate consequence of the great earthquake helps to give the impression that the development of the Ithome war was indeed something new and unexpected, sufficient to account for the fact that the Spartans evidently did *not* aid Thasos, and yet making the report of the promise to do so (and the positive preparations implied) acceptable to those who wished to believe. That those who did not know the facts (or Greek grammar) might also be misled into thinking that the earthquake itself intervened, and that the withdrawal of the helots and their allies to Ithome was in fact its immediate consequence, would (if he ever considered it) be irrelevant to what he wanted to convey — or might be all to the good.

As one who has had linguistic training in my high school days and later in the syntactical seminar at Johns Hopkins, I must respond that I have always taught the condemned usage, and that not out of prejudice. Accordingly, I would differ about the position that rejects Thucydides' story of the promise to help Thasos, and would respectfully disagree with my friends on their interpretation of the Greek aorist participle. It is well known that γίγνεσθαι, to become, turn out, prove, behave, was used in tenses other than the present system for the missing tenses of "to be," εἰμί. See LSJ⁹ 349; P. Chantraine, *Dictionnaire etymologique* 221.[2] Gildersleeve (*SCG* 60) classifies εἰμί and γίγνομαι as two forms

[2] For γίγνεσθαι in Thucydides, see J. G. A. Ros, *Die Metabole (Variatio) als Stilprinzip des Thukydides* (Amsterdam 1968) 335.

1. THUCYDIDES' PENTEKONTAETIA

of the copula. Furthermore, our school texts remind us that Thucydides uses γίγνεσθαι as a passive of ποιεῖσθαι.

In answering the question, "Why did Thucydides write ὑπὸ τοῦ γενομένου σεισμοῦ and not ὑπὸ τοῦ σεισμοῦ?" I would respond that we are dealing with a common use of γενόμενος. The aorist participle is often used of the phenomena of nature, ὕδωρ, βρονταὶ καὶ ἀστραπαί, σεισμός, ἡμέρα, νύξ. In Thucydides, cf. 2.5; 2.77; 3.87; 4.75; 6.70; 8.41.[3] The genitive absolute, ἡμέρας γενομένης, mentioned by Spieker (p. 327), is common. E. Powell in his *Lexicon* classifies 32 examples in Herodotos of what he calls the "redundant" use of γίνομαι: ἐν τῇ πρὸς Μεγαρέας γενομένη στρατηγίῃ; κατὰ τὴν ὁμολο‑ γίην τὴν πρὸς Μεγακλέα γενομένην; ἡ εὐτυχίη ἡ κατὰ τοὺς πολέμους γενομένη; etc. In English translation, the word is usually otiose or translated by a form of to be.

We are concerned here with the aorist participle γενόμενος. Gildersleeve states the well-known rule (*SCG* 329): "The participle as a verbal adjective is chiefly used in the present, aorist, and perfect tenses. The temporal relation is that of the kind of time. The sphere of time depends on the context." In his famous review, "Notes on Stahl's Syntax of the Greek Verb," (= *AJP* 29.257–279, 389–409; 30.1–21), published separately as a mono‑ graph in 1909, he noted (389) that Stahl, in his massive volume, used the definitions of Zeitart and Zeitstufe, which he rendered as "kind of time" and "sphere of time." I believe that students of linguistics often use the term "aspect" for "kind of time." The aorist of the side moods indicate a momentary 'phenomenon,' simply a thing attained, an "upshot aorist" (*SCG* 238), classified as ingressive, total negation, etc. When the present participle is used, the sphere of time can be determined as often contempo‑ raneous with the action of the main verb; when the aorist, the sphere of time is often prior. But the action of the aorist partici‑ ple is often coincidental, especially when the main verb is aorist,

[3]See also Nordheider, in Snell, *Lexicon* Lief. 10.149, section B.

8 THUCYDIDES' PENTEKONTAETIA AND OTHER ESSAYS

and Gildersleeve gives half a page of examples in *SCG* 345.[4] J. L. Rose, "The Durative and Aoristic Tenses in Thucydides," *Language* 18 (1942) Suppl. 1, collects a host of examples. He writes (34–35):

> The significant thing is not whether the present participle is contemporary with, the aorist participle prior to, the main verb, but the fact that the former denotes continuance, the latter attainment. This is clearly seen when the aorist participle expresses time contemporaneous with or subsequent to, the present participle time prior or subsequent to, that of the main verb. Consider the following examples of the aorist participle:
>
> 4.81.1 γενόμενον (subsequent); 8.50.2 (ἐπιστείλας (contemporary); 7.23.1 ληφθέν (contemporary); 8.73.4 διαφθαρέντας (contemporary); 6.61.2 προελθοῦσα (contemporary); 3.20.1 ἐπιλιπόντι (contemporary).
>
> Other instances of the aorist participle expressing contemporary or subsequent action are 1.3.4 ὕστερον κληθέντες; 71.4 ἐσβαλόντες; 2.25.5 ἐκλιπόντες; 49.4 λωφήσαντα; 4.32.3 λαβόντες; 6.4.4 ὀνομάσαντες κτλ.; 34.9 τολμήσαντες; 8.87.3 ἀφείς.
>
> Occurrences of the present participle denoting action prior to that of the leading verb are 1.2.1 οἰκουμένη; 4.3.2 οὔσῃ; 5.32.4 πράσσοντες; 6.6.3 ἀκούοντες; 53.2 ξυλλαμβάνοντες.

The student of Greek will find many sentences where the main verb has dependent upon it participles in different tenses where the sphere of time is the same. The aorist participle expresses

---

[4]Gildersleeve's study of the participle in *AJP* 9 (1888) 137–157, gives references to dissertations on the subject. That of G. M. Bolling, "The Participle in Hesiod," was published in the *Catholic University Bulletin* 3 (1897) 421–471. Much information on the tenses is contained in the article of my teacher, C. W. E. Miller, "The Imperfect and Aorist in Greek," *AJP* 16 (1895) 139–185. I offered a study on the force of the moods in the conditional sentence against the conventional classification of Goodwin in *AJP* 76 (1955) 1–17.

only attainment; the sphere of time can only be deduced from the context. An earthquake occurred. There is no implication of previous time, and no justification to support the interpretation that the earthquake in question occurred many years previous to the action of the main verb. De Romilly translates: "Sparte, à l'insu des Athéniens, le leur promit, et elle allait le faire: elle en fut empêchée par le tremblement de terre qui eut lieu, et au cours duquel les hilotes, ainsi que les périèques de Thouria et d'Aithaia se révoltèrent et s'établirent sur l'Ithome." It is hard to understand why anyone would construe the phrase to mean, "They were prevented in c. 465/5 by an earthquake which occurred in c. 469/8."

Of the Badian translation "which had previously happened," Hornblower, in his commentary on the passage, writes (1 p. 157), "There is no doubt that their translation is correct." The only references given by Sealey to our grammars to sustain his interpretation were Goodwin, *M&T* 48–49, and Schwyzer 2.390. In section 150 p. 52, Goodwin writes, "An aorist participle denoting that in which the action of a verb of past time consists may express time coincident with that of the verb, when the actions of the verb and the participle are practically one." The reference to Schwyzer is to a section giving various attendant circumstances in relation to the main verb: condition (μή), cause, means, etc., including time. These are modern categories, constituting what the modern reads into the context, and may be found in Goodwin 832ff. Such categories are useful to English and German readers who use the participle only for the sphere of time and often employ such words as if, when, because, etc. Gildersleeve in the *SCG* disregarded such categories which are a matter of modern interpretation, and editors often differ except when μή is used. To the Greek, the only relation was the kind of time (aspect).[5] One understands an initial blunder, but it is surprising that such a

---

[5]Professor Sealey recognizes the aspectual nature of the participle in his *The Justice of the Greeks* (Ann Arbor 1994) 46.

10 THUCYDIDES' PENTEKONTAETIA AND OTHER ESSAYS

"howler" should be repeated, and that without checking the references.[6] In the preceding sentence, Kühner-Gerth (1.199) cite the two aorist participles as clear examples of the zeitlose Natur of the participle.

In a note to a statement (p. 80) about Thucydides, an author, Badian claims, "on whom very little of the basic grammatical and stylistic work has yet been done, even though books have appeared in plenty," we read (p. 205 n. 15):

> That general books on Thucydides appear at the rate of about one a year does not require demonstration. As in many other cases, it is easier to write another book of general interpretation than to do detailed and laborious work, which alone would make such interpretations genuinely valid and useful. That there is a dearth of work of the latter kind is unfortunately easy enough to demonstrate, in one striking instance. Nearly a century ago, Friedrich Hultsch (editor, grammarian, and metrologist) published a series of major studies entitled *Die erzählenden Zeitformen bei Polybios* (ASAW 13 [1893] 1–210, 347–468; 14 [1894] 1–100: occasionally obtainable bound together as a book). It is a classic of stylistic investigation and an essential tool for understanding Hellenistic prose — presumably helpful for Classical prose as well, since superficial observation confirms the existence of some of the phenomena he noted but there is still no such work on Thucydides, whose "erzählende Zeitformen" are often cheerfully interpreted in its absence by those who write about him.

[6]Oddly, after Lewis rejected Badian's interpretation of the participle in *CAH* 5[2], Badian replied in an Appendix (p. 105): "He rejects the linguistically correct translation of Thucydides' phrase introducing the first mention of the (obviously known) earthquake (see n. 32 with text, above) as 'not a likely interpretation of Thucydides': unfortunately, for purposes of discussion, he, unlike some other scholars, cautiously avoids giving us his own interpretation. In the circumstances, it is methodologically necessary to accept Sealey's until it is refuted by argument."

1. THUCYDIDES' PENTEKONTAETIA

The passage seems incongruous in a publication by the Johns Hopkins Press, which for fifty-five years published the *American Journal of Philology* under the editorship of Basil L. Gildersleeve, usually regarded as America's greatest Hellenist, and his successor, C. W. E. Miller. The latter devoted a forty-six page critique to Hultsch's work in the *AJP* 16 (1895) 139–185. Gildersleeve devoted one year of his four-year cycle of seminars to Thucydides, and his articles and "Brief Mention" are replete with references to the grammar, vocabulary, and style of Thucydides, from which I quote one aphorism (*AJP* 28 [1907] 356), "He who does not know the syntax of Thukydides does not know the mind of Thukydides." Parenthetically, we do endorse the final relative clause in the above quotation. In one of his last Brief Mentions, Gildersleeve wrote (*AJP* 37 [1916] 119) of Lamb's book:

> The chief object of his book is a vindication, or, if you choose, the appreciation of Thukydides as a stylist. The subtitle is *A Study of Prose-form in Thucydides*, a subject which has formed the staple of my seminary work in Greek Historiography, once every Olympiad, for many years. Much of the work was conducted on syntactical lines, and Thukydides' syntax, or as some would say, lack of syntax, proved a useful organon in studying the stylistic stratification of the great work, and in quickening the appreciation of Thukydides' power of personation, a power denied to him by Dionysios. Etc.

Gildersleeve believed that the study of style should be grounded in ancient literary criticism, a field in which we have attempted a modest contribution for Thucydides in our *Dionysius of Halicarnassus: On Thucydides*.

Any "elementary student of Greek" who follows "standard philological method" by consulting the rich grammatical literature may dismiss the meaning "which had previously happened."

12 THUCYDIDES' PENTEKONTAETIA AND OTHER ESSAYS

SECTION 2

THUCYDIDES 1.101.2: EARTHQUAKE

Having dealt with the aorist participle, we move on to the problem of the conflicting dates given for the earthquake. Since they cannot be reconciled, the matter is one of evaluation of our sources. Essentially, the question is do we believe Thucydides and Pausanias, or Diodoros and the scholiast to Aristophanes *Lysistrata*, although various scenarios have been put forward in defense of one or the other dates.[1]

1. Thucydides 1.101.1–2 writes:

> Θάσιοι δὲ νικηθέντες μάχῃ καὶ πολιορκούμενοι Λακεδαιμονίους ἐπεκαλοῦντο καὶ ἐπαμύνειν ἐκέλευον ἐσβαλόντας ἐς τὴν Ἀττικήν. οἱ δὲ ὑπέσχοντο μὲν κρύφα τῶν Ἀθηναίων καὶ ἔμελλον, διεκωλύθησαν δὲ ὑπὸ τοῦ γενομένου σεισμοῦ, ἐν ᾧ καὶ οἱ Εἵλωτες αὐτοῖς καὶ τῶν περιοίκων Θουριᾶταί τε καὶ Αἰθαιῆς ἐς Ἰθώμην ἀπέστησαν.

2. Pausanias 4.24.5 (Loeb):

> The Messenians who were captured in the country, reduced by force to the position of serfs, were later moved to revolt from the Lacedaemonians in the seventy-ninth Olympiad, when Xenophon the Corinthian was victorious. Archimedes was archon at Athens. The occasion which they found for the revolt was this. Certain Lacedaemonians who had been condemned to death on some charge fled as suppliants to Taenarum; but the board of ephors dragged them from the altar there and put them to death. As the Spartans paid no heed to their being suppliants, the wrath of Poseidon came

---

[1]Herodotos (9.35) places the events at Ithome between the battles of Dipaia and Tanagra. Plutarch has much to say in *Kimon* 16.4ff., but gives no specific date. Cf. Pausanias 7.25.3; Aelian *Var. Hist.* 6.7; Polyainos 1.41.3.

I. THUCYDIDES' PENTEKONTAETIA

upon them, and the god razed all their city to the ground. At this disaster all the serfs who were of Messenian origin seceded to Mount Ithome.

Archimedes is considered as a corruption for Archidemides (Diodoros and Dionysios, 464/3); so von Schoeffer, *RE* s.v. Archontes 585.

3. Diodoros (under the year 469/8) 11.63.1–11.64.4 (in part. Loeb):

> When Phaeon was archon in Athens, in Rome the consulship was taken over by Lucius Furius Mediolanus and Marcus Manilius Vaso. During this year a great and incredible catastrophe befell the Lacedaemonians; for great earthquakes occurred in Sparta, and as a result the houses collapsed from their foundations and more than twenty thousand Lacedaemonians perished. And since the tumbling down of the city and the falling in of the houses continued uninterruptedly over a long period, many persons were caught and crushed in the collapse of the walls and no little household property was ruined by the quake. And although they suffered this disaster because some god, as it were, was wreaking his anger upon them, it so happened that other dangers befell them at the hands of men for the following reasons. The Helots and Messenians, although enemies of the Lacedaemonians, had remained quiet up to this time, since they stood in fear of the eminent position and power of Sparta; but when they observed that the larger part of them had perished because of the earthquake, they held in contempt the survivors, who were few. Consequently they came to an agreement with each other and joined together in the war against the Lacedaemonians. The king of the Lacedaemonians, Archidamus, by his personal foresight not only was the saviour of his fellow citizens even during the earthquake, but in the course of the war also he bravely fought the aggressors. For instance, when the terrible earthquake struck Sparta, he was the first Spartan to seize his armour and hasten from the city into the country, calling upon the other citizens to follow his exam-

14 THUCYDIDES' PENTEKONTAETIA AND OTHER ESSAYS

ple. The Spartans obeyed him and thus those who survived the shock were saved and these men King Archidamus organized into an army and prepared to make war upon the revolters. ... At this time, it may be explained, the Lacedaemonians had finally overcome both the Helots and Messenians, with whom they had been at war over a long period, and the Messenians they had allowed to depart from Ithomê under a truce, as we have said, but of the Helots they had punished those who were responsible for the revolt and had enslaved the rest.

4. Diodoros (under the year 456/5) 11.84.8 (Loeb):

And the Helots, revolting in a body from the Lacedaemonians, joined as allies with the Messenians, and at one time they were winning and at another losing. And since for ten years no decision could be reached in the war, for that length of time they never ceased injuring each other.

5. Scholia in the Codex Ravennas of *Lysistrata* 1138–1144, c. 1000 A.C. Marginal scholia in small uncials. We print the scholion as it appears in the left margin of folio 125ᵛ, not reproducing the ligatures but separating the words. We do not insert material from the right margin according to line numbers, as in Dübner (1877). At the time of writing, D. Holwerda's projected edition of the scholia of the *Lysistrata* has not appeared, so far as we are aware.

ταῦτα καὶ οἱ συντεταχότ τ ατείδ ἱστοροῦσιν περι
τ λακεδ μονι· ὁ δὲ φιλόχορ φη καὶ τὴν ἡγεμονι τ
ἀθηναί λαβεῖν, δια τ κατασχ σας τὴν λακεδ μον
συμφοράς· ; σει μέγα ὁ Ποσειδων σεισμοὶ γὰρ
συχνοὶ ἐγένοντο ὅτε ὁ πόλεμ συνειστήκει κίμ
μετὰ τὴν ἐν Πλαταεαῖς μ χ ιβ ἔτει ὑστερ ταυτ ἦν
ἐπὶ θεαγενίδ · καὶ γὰρ τ ταΰγέτ τί παρρεράγη
ὑπὸ τ σεισμῶν καὶ τὸ ωδι καὶ ἕτερα καὶ οἰκίαι
πλεῖστ κτλ.

I. THUCYDIDES' PENTEKONTAETIA 15

We may translate: The compilers of Atthides also relate these matters concerning the Lakedaimonians. Philochoros says that the hegemony of the Athenians resulted from the calamities which befell Lakedaimon. Great earthquakes: Poseidon. There were frequent shocks of earthquakes while the war was in progress. Kimon: These things were in the twelfth year after the battle of Plataiai in the archonship of Theagenides (468/7). For some part of Taygetos and the Odeion and other buildings and very many houses were thrown down by the earthquakes, and the Messenians revolted and made war, and the helots rebelled until Kimon came and saved them through supplication.[2]

The scholiast gives two lemmata, σείων and Κίμων, after the quotation from Philochoros. The commentaries of Didymus and Symmachos on Aristophanes, for example, were independent books, not annotated editions, from which notes were made. Our editor followed no discoverable principle of selection; his choice seems to have been fortuitous. The information conveyed in the scholia is often incomplete, and the language in which it is expressed is sometimes incoherent. It would be a mistake, therefore, to postulate that the scholiast took these two hypomnemata from Philochoros. One may claim that an earlier commentator had used Philochoros or some other source. The problem of marginalia in general is discussed by G. Zuntz, *An Inquiry into the Transmission of the Plays of Euripides* (Cambridge 1965) 272–275, with reference to his more detailed study in *Byzantion* 14 (1939).[3] Extracts from ancient learned commentaries were combined with schoolmastery exposition.

[2]Since the Odeion is otherwise unattested, L. Ziehen, *Hermes* 68 (1933) 232 n. 3, says ᾠδεῖον is probably an error for γυμνάσιον.

[3]Cf. J. W. White, *The Scholia in the Aves of Aristophanes* (Boston 1914) lxxiii–lxxiv. For the meager scholia in the Ravennas in comparison with the Venetus, see lxxviii. J .van Leeuwen, in his Praefatio to the Ravennas facsimile, notes (p. x) that in the Venetus MS., there are subscriptions which state that

16 THUCYDIDES' PENTEKONTAETIA AND OTHER ESSAYS

We select leading sentences from a few of the diverse studies which deal with the scholia.[4] W. G. Rutherford (1896) wrote that the scholiast was mistaken about the date, referring to G. Meiners, *Dissertationes Philologicae Halenses* 11 (1890) 366–368, who in his study *Quaestiones ad scholia Aristophanea historica pertinentes* (pp. 217–402) conveniently collects the scholia on Herodotos, Thucydides, Xenophon, Philochoros, Aristotle, Olympiads, et al. Meiners regards the name of the archon as an added note, not taken from Philochoros.

Kolbe, *Hermes* 72 (1937) 251 n. 3:

> Im schol. Arist. Lys. 1144 muß das Zahlreichen ‚ιβ' verderbt sein. Das Erdbeben soll danach im zwölften Jahre nach der Schlacht bei Plataiai stattgefunden haben, was sowohl der Rechnung nach attischen Archonten — wie nach spartanischen Königsjahren widerspricht. Das nachfolgende ταῦτα ἦν ἐπὶ Θεαγενίδου ist ledeglich ein interpretierender Zusatz.

---

material was taken from Heliodoros (*Nubes*), Phaeinos and Symmachos (*Pax*), and Symmachos and others (*Aves*). The name of Philochoros appears sixteen times in the Ravennas scholia: *Ran.* 219, 693, 1033, 1196; *Aves* 556, 1106; *Pax* 466, 477, 605, 665; *Lysistrata* 835, 1138, 1141; *Ach.* 220; *Vespae* 210; *Eccl.* 193. In *Pax* 605, the scholiast cites Philochoros for what Platnauer regards as confused and inaccurate things about Perikles. The scribe used alphabetic numerals, regularly citing the books of Herodotos, Thucydides, and Theopompos. For Homer, the alphabet was used.

[4]Hammond, *Historia* 4 (1955) 371–381, uses an eclectic method in an attempt to reconcile all sources. This results in having Thucydides calculate the duration of the war as a whole from an earlier Messenian revolt which he has failed to record. P. Deane, *Thucydides' Dates* (Ontario 1972) 15–30, deals with the scholia as part of his argument that Thucydides' dates are out of chronological order.

I. THUCYDIDES' PENTEKONTAETIA

Gomme, *HCT* 1 (1945) 407–408:

> The other view is that of Kolbe, p. 251.3, and of Jacoby (given to me in conversation). Accepting, of course, Thucydides' implied date for the Helot revolt and Kimon's expedition against Ithome, they think it impossible that the *Atthis* could have got the dates wrong, and accordingly infer that originally it had μετὰ τὴν ἐν Πλαταιαῖς μάχην ιϛ ἔτει ὕστερον (464–463 B.C., or ιε, 465–464), which was at some time misread as ιβ ἔτει, as it now appears in schol. *Lys.* 1144 (above, p. 402, n. 2), and that the scholiast or his immediate source added, from the archon-list, ταῦτα ἦν ἐπὶ Θεαγενίδου ("lediglich ein interpretierender Zusatz", Kolbe). Jacoby adds that in schol. *Lys.* 1138, ταῦτα καὶ οἱ συντεταχότες τὰς Ἀτθίδας ἱστοροῦσιν περὶ τῶν Λακεδαιμονίων. ὁ δὲ Φιλόχορός φησι καὶ τὴν ἡγεμονίαν τοὺς Ἀθηναίους λαβεῖν διὰ τὰς κατασχούσας τὴν Λακεδαίμονα συμφοράς, the disasters to Sparta must be the earthquake and revolt (this is hardly consistent with Κίμων ἔσωσεν αὐτούς of the scholion on 1144, but is nevertheless probable enough). Diodoros' date, then, which is 469–468, not 468–467 — it does not 'confirm' the scholiast's date — will only be one of his many unaccountable errors.

Jacoby, *FGrH* 3b Suppl. 1 (1954) 459–460:

> But the main point is that probably no Atthidographer at all told of the earthquake or of the Messenian revolt *suo anno*. ... It would be wrong to assume that an Atthidographer delimited a period of Athenian history by the Xerxes War on the one side and the Spartan misfortunes on the other, instead of by an Athenian event made possible or caused by those misfortunes and their consequences which eventually changed the relations between Sparta and Athens finally. We know from Thukydides himself that there was an interval of some length (*i.e.* at least one year) between those two events: Λακεδαιμόνιοι δέ, ὡς αὐτοῖς πρὸς τοὺς ἐν Ἰθώμηι ἐμηκύνετο ὁ πόλεμος. I therefore propose to change ιβ to ιη (an easy change palaeographically): the period delimited by

18 THUCYDIDES' PENTEKONTAETIA AND OTHER ESSAYS

Ph. comprises the eighteen years 479/8–462/1 B.C. (both terms included, as is usual in such statements). If further confirmation is needed it is furnished by Aristotle who, most probably taking his dates from Androtion, tells us that ἔτη δὲ ἑπτακαίδεκα μάλιστα μετὰ τὰ Μηδικὰ διέμεινεν ἡ πολιτεία προεστώτων τῶν Ἀρεοπαγιτῶν .... ἔπειτα τῆς βουλῆς ἐπὶ Κόνωνος ἄρχοντος (462/1) ἅπαντα περιεῖλε (*scil.* Ἐφιάλτης) τὰ ἐπίθετα κτλ. It is no surprise for us either that Ph. agrees with Androtion, or that both define the period primarily from the point of view of home politics. Only primarily, not wholly, as Aristotle does, who is writing an Ἀθηναίων πολιτεία, not an Ἀτθίς: the expression which Ph. uses (there is not the least reason to distrust the scholion on *Lysistrata* 1138, where he is cited) refers to the leadership which Athens won by the misfortunes of Sparta, an absolute leadership not qualified by τῆς θαλάττης or even τῶν συμμάχων.

Reece, *JHS* 82 (1962) 116: "It is on the whole more likely that Philochoros would have given a date from Kimon's expedition to Ithome than for the outbreak of the revolt, which as an event of purely Spartan history was not relevant to his subject." We may add that the hypomnema giving the date was under the lemma for Kimon.

P. J. Rhodes, *A Commentary on the Aristotelian Athenaion Politeia* (Oxford 1981) 310:

Jacoby in his commentary on Phil. 328 F 117 argued that schol. Ar. *Lys.* 1144 is derived from Philochorus, irresponsibly emended a dating of the Spartan earthquake and the outbreak of the Third Messenian War from the 12th year after Plataea = 468/7 to the 18th year = 462/1, and deduced from this that Androtion (reflected in *A.P.*) and Philochorus both regarded the period of the Aeropagus' supremacy as a distinct era in Athenian history.

I. THUCYDIDES' PENTEKONTAETIA   19

J. Henderson, 1987 edition of *Lysistrata* p. 201:

> The great earthquake of 464 (cf. *Ach.* 510–11) was followed by
> helot revolt. The rebels fortified Mt. Ithome in the Messenian plain
> and were besieged by the Spartans, who appealed for help to mem-
> bers of the alliance against Persia formed in 481, including Athens.
> Kimon, Spartan proxenos and leader of the conservative democrats
> (1144 n.), persuaded the Athenians (over objections from Ephialtes
> and the radical democrats) to honour the Spartan request. Kimon
> himself set out with a substantial hoplite force (Th. 1.102.1 πλήθει
> οὐκ ὀλίγῳ) and after an unsuccessful attempt to reduce Ithome by
> assault was ignominiously dismissed (late 463 or early 462, see
> below). This incident ended Kimon's career (he was ostracized in
> 462/1) and his policy of joint Spartan-Athenian hegemony, and it
> was a milestone in the history of enmity between the two states
> (Th. 1.102.3 διαφορὰ ἐκ ταύτης τῆς στρατείας πρῶτον
> Λακεδαιμονίοις καὶ ᾿Αθηναίοις φανερὰ ἐγένετο, cf. De Ste.
> Croix 180–3). For these events see Hdt. 9.35, Th. 1.101–3, D.S. 11.64.4,
> 15.66.4, Plu. *Kim.* 17.2. ... For the dates see *HCT* i.401–8. Σ[R] at 1144 is
> a scholarly note (probably drawing on Philochoros, as at 1138 = 328
> F 117), giving the standard Atthidographic date of 468/7 for
> earthquake and revolt, distinguishing between helots and
> Messenians.

Thucydides was in a position to collect information from the
survivors of the Ithome episode, which the Atthidographers were
not. The latter had no fasti for events, but computed their dates.
The problem of how chronographers computed their dates is
addressed by A. A. Mosshammer in his important book, *The
Chronicle of Eusebius and Greek Chronographic Tradition* (1979),
which J. Mansfeld reviews in detail in *Mnem.* 36 (1983) 202–207.
Following Jacoby, he examines how Apollodoros and his predecessors including Philochoros established synchronisms between
events, sometimes giving absolute dates, but with these not always
agreeing with each other. In examining the chaotic material,

20 THUCYDIDES' PENTEKONTAETIA AND OTHER ESSAYS

Mosshammer focuses in the final chapter on the chronographic tradition for dates of the tragedians and their plays. He argues that for Apollodoros an acme method was used, and other dates were computed from these. We extract a few sentences: "All the dates of our sources prior to the Peloponnesian Wars are, in varying degree, products of reconstruction." "There is a difference between chronology and history, between archons as eponyms and archons as archons, between lists and their contents — a difference as fundamental as that between the yardstick and the line." "The possibility of using different generational lengths could certainly have produced different absolute dates from the same genealogically based information." "Greek chronography developed as a mixture of remembered tradition, literary and documentary evidence, and arithmetical construction." "It would be pointless to attempt to account for every easily corruptible numeral in every text. One could, for example, debate endlessly about the origin and purport of the *vita*'s statement on Sophocles (127 West) that he was 17 years younger than Aeschylus and 24 years older than Euripides."[5]

It is well known that Jacoby's two-volume 3b Supplement to the *FGrH* is in great part an attempt to reconcile the divergent dates deduced from the various Atthidographers on events in Athenian history, for example, between Herodotos and the Atthidographers on the building program of the Alkmeonids (3b.1 p. 453), between Philochoros and Aristophanes/Ephoros about the cult statue of Athena (p. 490), between divergencies

---

[5]In *Hermes* 103 (1975) "Themistocles' Archonship in the Chronographic Tradition," 222–234, Mosshammer presents a well-argued paper in which he posits than in 1.93.1, Thucydides was rejecting an Atthidographic tradition found in Apollodoros and ultimately derived from Hellanikos. We note that on *Pax* 605, the Ravennas scholiast cites Philochoros as giving a date for the great chryselephantine statue of Athena as the archonship of Theodoros, whereas Heliodoros gives the date as the archonship of Pythodoros, seven years later.

I. THUCYDIDES' PENTEKONTAETIA

concerning the distribution of corn in 445/4 (462–463), etc. ad infinitum. Many of his arguments have been seriously challenged, particularly about the political bias of Androtion and others,[6] but the principle is sound. We do not extract a flosculus in the form of a date without weighing many other factors, including the general credibility of the author in question.

As Gomme notes, the received texts of our sources give us three different dates for the earthquake: 469/8 (Diodoros), 468/7 (Ravennas), and apparently 464/3 (Pausanias). One who believes that Thucydides recorded events in chronological order can accommodate the date given in Pausanias, an author whose reliability in the use of his historical sources has been dramatically enhanced since the strictures of Pearson and Starr. I find attractive the hypothesis of Jacoby that the Atthidographers reconstructed the past from the standpoint of home politics, and that the Spartan earthquake was a computed date. I would follow many scholars who believe that the archon date in the Ravennas is the notation of a late scholar after the numeral had been mistranscribed.[7] We shall treat the matter of numerals in the next section. While one concedes that numbers written out as words, demanding more space and greater trouble, might be regarded as more dignified than the use of numerals and less liable to misunderstanding or alteration, hence the practice, we are assured, that schoolmasters in Egypt insisted on the use by their pupils[8] of

---

[6] See P. Harding, "Atthis and Politics," *Historia* 26 (1977) 148–160.

[7] For the various forms of the digamma, see Tod, *BSA* 45 (1950) 135.

[8] Publishing in 1933, J. G. Winter, *Life and Letters in the Papyri* (Ann Arbor) 239, wrote: "Like most of the historians of antiquity, Herodotus suffered from the efforts of writers in a degenerate age to reproduce him in "tabloid" form, as is shown by a portion of a vellum codex of the fourth century A.D., which gives an epitome of Book vii.148–152 and 163. While no Ptolemaic text of Thucydides has yet appeared, his popularity in Roman times is sufficiently attested by twenty-three published texts, mostly from Oxyrhynchus and ranging from the first to the sixth century in date." He added, "It is a surprise, too, that the

22 THUCYDIDES' PENTEKONTAETIA AND OTHER ESSAYS

cardinals/ordinals in historical texts, nonetheless, many errors in numbers can only be explained by faulty transmission. In *Tyche* 8 (1993) 77, W. Liesker, "Tax Documents from Socnopaiou Nesos," publishes a papyrus which uses both numerals (K, Γ, K) and cardinals for the same figures, apparently to avoid any misunderstanding. There is no commentary, and I assume the practice was common. Jacoby (3b Suppl. 1 p. 12) writes of Hellanikos:

> I am not prepared to believe in four (or even five) volumes on the strength of F 7 where I regard the $\overline{\Delta}$ as an evident error of a scribe for δευτέρωι — as easy and almost as frequent a mistake as the dittography of an ι after the ἐν τῆι of a quotation which would give twelve books to the *Atthides* of Kleidemos and Androtion.

We find no difficulty in supporting an emendation in the *Lysistrata* scholion. Indeed, since acrophonics were earlier used at Athens for all purposes of counting and enumeration, we would assume that they would also be used for ordinals. In the light of a theory that acrophonic numeral signs were not used for ordinals,[9] which we will study in the next section, it is enough to note here that in one of the most famous historical papyri, Aristotle *Ath. Pol.*, alphabetical numerals were used for both cardinals and ordinals: 43.2 (5), 44.4, 47.2, 47.4, 50.2, 51.1 (2), 51.2 (2), 55.2, 61.5, 63.3, 68, and frg. 3.

---

popular historians of the fourth century B.C., Philochorus and Androtion, have not come to light." What we do not learn from Oxyrhynchus is what was written in texts offered for sale. From Libanius in the fourth century, we infer that there were expensive texts of Thucydides written in majuscules and others written in uncials with abbreviations. W. Jaeger is quoted as saying that, with regard to Plato, the critical time was in the first generation after publication. The chancery style of decrees affords no reliable clue; numerals were not uncommon in other types of epigraphical texts.

[9]See *ATL* 3.162 n. 19.

I. THUCYDIDES' PENTEKONTAETIA   23

Turning to the flat-footed Diodoros, we note that he alone records the earthquake, as well as all the events at Ithome, under the archonship of Φαίων at Athens, which by his sequence is 469/8 B.C. The name is not attested in Kirchner, *PA*, nor in Pape-Benseler. Nor is it adopted for the name of the archon of 469/8 in any archon table known to me, including that of A. E. Samuel. The Parian marble (A. 56) has ᾿Αψηφίονος. Diogenes L. (2.44) refers to this same archonship according to Apollodoros, a fragment published by Jacoby, *FGrH* 244 frg. 34. H. S. Long, in the Teubner text of Diogenes, gives the form as ᾿Αφεψίωνος, and is followed by Jacoby. The old text of Huebner and the Loeb Diogenes have it ᾿Αψεφίωνος. The codices of Plutarch *Kimon* 8.8, according to Ziegler, give the form ᾿Αφεψίων, which has been emended by editors to ᾿Αψεφίων. We may easily say that the error is a scribal one, but it is not beyond the realm of possibility that Diodoros placed the events of Ithome under the wrong archonship. A. H. M. Jones, *Sparta* (Oxford 1967) 59, says that events described in 11.50, a few chapters earlier, are recorded under the wrong year.[10]

Diodoros recorded the entire record of the Ithome episode under the year 469/8, and then later under the year 456/5 writes of the conclusion of the war, which had lasted ten years, "at this time" (κατὰ τὸν αὐτὸν χρόνον). The focus of Diodoros' account in 11.63–64 is on the activities of the Spartan king Archidamos. In *Kimon* 16.4, Plutarch places the earthquake in the fourth year of this king's reign: τέταρτον ἔτος ἐν Σπάρτῃ βασιλεύοντας. Woodward, who has no axe to grind, in the

---

[10]Jacoby, *FGrH* 3b Suppl. 2.366 n. 8, writes: "The archon of 469/8 B.C. is called Φαίων in ch. 63.1, the true name is ᾿Αψεφίων (*P.A.* 2805). I cannot help suspecting that Φαίων is not due to a mere copyist's error, but that Diodoros had in mind the archon Φαίδων of 476/5 B.C., his first (wrong) year for Archidamos (11, 48, 1/2), and that he transferred him to 469/8, the year of the earthquake which is again wrong. Perhaps this contributes to the explanation of the muddle."

24 THUCYDIDES' PENTEKONTAETIA AND OTHER ESSAYS

Oxford Classical Dictionary s.v., would place Archidamos' accession to the throne ca. 469. W. G. Forrest, *A History of Sparta* (London 1968) 101, writes, "Archidamos was presumably in theory reigning from the time of his grandfather Leotychidas' exile in 476 but in practice may not have become influential before Leotychidas' death in 469. There is nothing in the evidence to connect Archidamos with a change in Sparta's policy, but there is no doubt that it is from about 470 that the story takes on a different colour." Gomme, in my opinion, has a satisfactory treatment of the two contradictory passages in Diodoros (*HCT* 1.403–407), which is endorsed by *ATL* 3.176 n. 58. In any case, the detailed and rhetorical treatment of Spartan history given by Diodoros reads like nothing in the fragments of the Atthidographers, as studied by L. Pearson in his book, *The Local Historians of Attica*. The position that we can extract a phrase or a date from Diodoros and claim that it has preference in veracity over Thucydides, and that without examining Diodoros' account of the Pentekontaeteia *in toto*, is a cardinal error in the evaluation of our source material. We do not look for gold nuggets in a compost heap.

SECTION 3

THUCYDIDES 1.103.1: NUMERAL

If we maintain chronological order and place the Messenian settlement at Naupaktos after the affair at Thasos, scholars have observed that the numeral δεκάτῳ in the phrase οἱ δ ἐν 'Ιθώμῃ δεκάτῳ ἔτει of 1.103.1 must be wrong: Οἱ δ ἐν 'Ιθώμῃ δεκάτῳ ἔτει, ὡς οὐκέτι ἐδύναντο ἀντέχωιν, ξυνέβησαν πρὸς τοὺς Λακεδαιμονίους ἐφ' ᾧ ἐξίασιν ἐκ Πελοποννήσου

I. THUCYDIDES' PENTEKONTAETIA 25

ὑπόσπονδοι καὶ μηδέποτε ἐπιβήσονται αὐτῆς.[1] Here we must take our cue first from those who have collated the manuscripts and attempted to establish the complete text, not from those who thump the table on the basis of one passage. As indicated in *Essays* p. 1, we do not attribute to Thucydides the text of 5.2.2, found in all manuscripts. In endorsing the insertion of a single word into the text of 4.8.6 (*Essays* 168–169), where Thucydides is describing a battle in which I believe he participated, we reviewed the opinions of Gomme, Dover, and de Romilly about the textual tradition, quoting de Romilly's maxim, *non auctoritate sed judicio*. Some scholars propose that there have been sizable interpolations into the text. See, for example, Kopff, *GRBS* 17 (1976) 23–30; Smart, *GRBS* 18 (1977) 33–42; Calder, *CQ* 78 (1984) 485–486.

The transmission of numerals, like the transmission of proper names, falls into a separate category, and requires special treatment. J. P. Mahaffy, "The Arithmetical Figures Used by Greek Writers during the Classical Period," *Essays and Studies Presented to William Ridgeway* (1913) 195–197, arguing that Thucydides did not use the "lapidary script universal in the Parthenon accounts," but "certainly wrote the literary symbols," proposed emendations in several passages. Sterling Dow, in *TAPA* 92 (1961) 66–80, collected opinions about the corruptions of numbers in the MSS. of Thucydides, including two dissertations which touched on the subject by David Lewis and M. Chambers (non vidi), as well as the work of B. Hemmerdinger, *Essai sur l'histoire du texte de Thucydide* (Paris 1955). Any definitive study would be extended to the transmission of numerals in all texts, geographical, palaeographical, and papyrologi-

---

[1]Cf., for example, Gomme, *HCT* 1.402–408. C. R. Rubincam, *AJAH* 4 (1979) 77–95, discusses phrases qualifying numerals in Thucydides. R. Develin, "Numerical Corruption in Greek Historical Texts," *Phoenix* 44 (1990) 31–45, treats eight passages with numerals in Thucydides. V. Hanson, *CSCA* 23 (1992) 213 n. 10, collects examples of μυριάδες.

26   THUCYDIDES' PENTEKONTAETIA AND OTHER ESSAYS

cal, to examine the general nature of scribal corruptions. We stress the fact, which is beyond all cavil, that Polybios assigned what he regards as errors in numerals in Ephoros not to the author, but to the scribe (γραφεύς): 12.4a.4–6. The arithmetical error was real.

In his review of Mme de Romilly's Book 1 in the Budé, Gomme wrote (CR 69 [1955] 156):

> Sometimes all our present knowledge proclaims a text corrupt, but no correction certain, as 57.6, μετ᾽ ἄλλων δέκα στρατηγοῦντος; Mme de Romilly is surely wrong to put τεσσάρων in her text, with a reference to Hermann's δύο in the apparatus, instead of †δέκα† in the text and an explanatory note. On δεκάτῳ ἔτει, 103.1, the critical note should be *dubitaverunt multi*, rather than 'τετάρτῳ Krueger', as though 'four' were the only possible correction of a corrupt 'ten'. (For the same reasons, in ii.2.1, ἔτι δύο μῆνας should be marked as corrupt, for an Athenian archon must have had at least three, more probably four, months to serve after 'the beginning of spring'; whereas μηνὶ ἕκτῳ, ibid., should have only *dubitaverunt multi* in the apparatus.) In her note on 103.1 Mme de Romilly defends δεκάτῳ, on the ground that Thucydides could anticipate in concluding a brief narrative of an event which did not immediately concern Athens; but this is here an inadequate defence, for the event did concern Athens directly, the Messenians being settled at Naupactus (103.3), and the defence ignores the strongest argument for another figure, ἕκτῳ or πέμπτῳ or τετάρτῳ, that Philochorus says and Diodorus implies that the war ended in 460 or 459, i.e. just where its end would be placed if Thucydides is here writing chronologically.

Mme de Romilly referred to the criticism in Book 2 p. 86.

M. N. Tod gave us a series of articles on Greek numerals in epigraphy: "The Greek Numeral Notation," *BSA* 18 (1911/2) 98–132; "Three Greek Numeral Systems," *JHS* 33 (1913) 27–34; "Further Notes on the Greek Acrophonic Numerals," *BSA* 28

I. THUCYDIDES' PENTEKONTAETIA

(1926/7) 141–157; "The Greek Acrophonic Numerals," *BSA* 37 (1936/7) 236–257; "The Alphabetic Numeral System in Attica," *BSA* 45 (1950) 126–139; "Letter-Labels in Greek Inscriptions," *BSA* 49 (1954) 1–8. Bibliography may be found in M. Guarducci, *L'epigrafia Greca* (Rome 1987) 87–88. A plethora of examples will be found in her references to W. Larfeld. For Attic epigraphy, the study of Athenian numerals by L. Threatte, *The Grammar of Attic Inscriptions* 1 (1980) 110–119, now supersedes earlier studies. He finds that by Roman times, the alphabetic numeral system, although rarely found early (p. 117), had superseded the acrophonic which, he says, had been used only for cardinals. He writes, "The alphabetic numerals had a much more extensive usage than the earlier acrophonic ones. They could be used for ordinal as well as cardinal numerals, and were thus frequently used in dates." Letter-labels occur early, including digamma for the sixth letter. T. L. Shear Jr. finds that the alphabetic labels were in use in Athens about 350 B.C.: *Hesperia* 39 (1970) 167. Wyatt and Edmonson, *AJA* 88 (1984) 135–167, report their use in 460–420 B.C. M. Lang, "Numerical Notation on Greek Vases," *Hesperia* 25 (1956) 5, writes, "The use of alphabetic numerals in the third quarter of the 5th century is not unprecedented in Athens." The evidence is assembled by R. Hackl, "Merkantile Inschriften auf attischen Vasen," *Münchener Archäologische Studien dem Andenken Adolf Furtwänglers Gewidmet* (Munich 1909) 1–106, esp. 76ff. Lang's reference is to an earlier work by the same author: *Graffiti und Dipinti auf attischen Vasen* (1906). The notations on the vases are in Ionic script; the signatures in Attic. However, it is to be noted that these notations using alphabetic numerals are taken by Amyx to be prices: *Hesperia* 27 (1958) 287ff.[2] A. W. Johnston, *Trademarks on Greek Vases* (1979), in his

---

[2]Although not concerned primarily with numerals, there is much information in G. E. M. de Ste. Croix, "Greek and Roman Accounting," *Studies in the History of Accounting*, ed. by A. C. Littleton and B. Yamey (London 1956) 14–

28   THUCYDIDES' PENTEKONTAETIA AND OTHER ESSAYS

chapter on numerals (26–31), gives a catalogue which distinguishes Ionic and acrophonic numerals. The use of Ionic numerals declined with the emergence of Athens as a leading power. Other systems are noted.

In addition to cardinals (εἷς, δύο) and ordinals (πρῶτος, δεύτερος), the Greeks generally used either a so-called 'acrophonic' or 'initial' class of numeral notations (Ι = 1, Γ πέντε = 5, Δ δέκα = 10, Η ἑκατόν = 100, Χ χίλιοι = 1,000, Μ μύριοι = 10,000), or a class of signs of the ordinary 24 letters of the alphabet plus wau (6), koppa (90), and sampi (900), (α = 1, ια = 11, κ = 20). Heath and Toomer, in OCD^2 741, refer to the latter as "the 'alphabetic' or 'Milesian' system, probably originating in Ionia and the older of the two." Other systems are attested for individual city-states. J. W. Graham, "X = 10," *Phoenix* 23 (1969) 347–358, assembles the evidence for numerals at Olynthos with considerable bibliography, denying that any numerals there were acrophonic in origin. Rather, an alphabetic system was used based on the last four letters of the alphabet. An inscribed fragment of a tile of the mid-fifth century B.C., found in the excavations at Aianes in the nomos of Kozani in Makedonia, displays two rows of acrophonics: G. Karametrou-Menteside, *To Archaiologiko Ergo ste Makedonia* 4 (1990) 82 and fig. 25. The author notes that the text is among the earliest inscriptions of Makedonia. Tod notes in his initial article that outside of Attika we find a free use of non-acrophonic elements. Myceneans used ideograms which stand for a definite word meaning (Ventris, *Documents in Mycenean Script*[2] [1973] 30), in which the "decimal system was in vogue (as) shown by the fact that in no case does the repetition of a single figure exceed nine" (Evans, *Scripta Minoa* 256). The use may derive from the fingers. In the Pseudo-Aristotle *Problems*, a product of the Peripatetic School, the author writes (15.3.910b, with Loeb tr.):

---

74. The author observes that conclusions have been drawn from literary texts rather than from the much more common documentary texts.

I. THUCYDIDES' PENTEKONTAETIA 29

Διὰ τί πάντες ἄνθρωποι, καὶ βάρβαροι καὶ Ἕλληνες, εἰς τὰ δέκα καταριθμοῦσι, καὶ οὐκ εἰς ἄλλον ἀριθμόν, οἷον β´, γ´, δ´, ε´, εἶτα πάλιν ἐπαναδιπλοῦσιν, ἔν πέντε, δύο πέντε, ὥσπερ ἔνδεκα, δώδεκὰ οὐδ᾽ αὖ ἐξωτέρω παυσάμενοι τῶν δέκα, εἶτα ἐκεῖθεν ἐπαναδιπλοῦσιν ἔστι μὲν γὰρ ἕκαστος τῶν ἀριθμῶν ὁ ἔμπροσθεν καὶ ἔν ἢ δύο, καὶ οὕτως ἄλλος τις, ἀριθμοῦσι δ᾽ ὅμως ὁρίσαντες ἄχρι τῶν δέκα.

Why do all men, both foreign and Greek, count in tens, and not in any other numbers? For instance, they might count 2, 3, 4, 5, and then repeat one five, two five and so on as now they say eleven, twelve and so on. Or they might stop at a number beyond ten and repeat it. For each number is made by putting one, two and so on before it, and hence another number is formed, but they all count from ten as a limit.

He then asks, ἢ ὅτι πάντες ὑπῆρξαν ἄνθρωποι ἔχοντες δέκα δακτύλους᾽

The alphabetic system is found in Attika, as we have noted, in markings on early vases using the Ionic script,[3] as well as on a mysterious Athenian inscription dated in the third quarter of the fifth century: IG I³ 1387 (= I² 760), which uses digamma ("More Milesiorum certe, e.g. 14 scribitur ΙΔ")[4] The system is thought to have been invented at Miletos. It is studied by J. G. Smyly in *Mélanges Nicole* (1905) 515–530, who shows how alphabetical numerals were used in multiplication, division, subtraction, and addition by geometricians and mathematicians such as Archimedes, Apollonios, Theon, and Eutocius. Examples are

[3]One of the vases is illustrated in J. Kirchner, *Imagines Inscriptionum Atticarum²* (1948) no. 23. Cf. Beazley, *AJA* 31 (1927) 349.

[4]Cf. Tod, *BSA* 45 (1950) 137.

30 THUCYDIDES' PENTEKONTAETIA AND OTHER ESSAYS

collected by W. Larfeld in *Handbuch der griechischen Epigraphik* 1 (Leipzig 1907) 424–427. An early use of the alphabetic system is found in a West Lokrian inscription: Tod *GHI* no. 24. See, also, Haussoullier, *BCH* 4 (1880) 295ff.; Keil, *Hermes* 29 (1894) 265ff.;[5] A. Rehm, *Didyma* 2(1958) 13 n. 1.[6] For our purposes, it is important to note that Edwin Mayser, *Grammatik der griechischen Papyri aus der Ptolemäerzeit* 1.51, begins his account of 'Zahlzeichen' with the statement: "Das alexandrinische 27ziffrige Zahlensystem ist durchweg verwendet sowohl für Kardinal- als für Ordnungszahlen. Zahlzeichen sind die geläufigen 24 Buchstaben des Alphabets, außerdem als ἐπίσημα die alten Zeichen στίγμα (= 6), κόππα (= 90), σαμπῖ (= 900)." This 'Alexandrian' system of 27 numerals is identical with what the epigraphist calls the 'Milesian', or Ionic system. We conclude, therefore, that if a scribe in Ionia or at Alexandria used numerals for either cardinals or ordinals through Ptolemaic times, his system was an alphabetic one of 27 letters.

Throughout studies on Thucydidean chronology, we are repeatedly told that acrophonic numerals did not represent ordinals in Attika. Ordinals are relatively rare in fifth-century Athenian texts in stone, being written out in *IG* I³ 4.20/21, 46B.43, 237.12, 259–289 (with ἀρχή), and repeatedly in dates with πρυτανεία. They become common in decrees, particularly prescripts; but ordinals are by no means as common as cardinals. What we are not told is that alphabetic numerals used as ordinals in non-Attic epigraphical texts seem to be equally rare in the classical and Hellenistic periods. Cardinals are used in thousands of documents, including inventories and catalogues, but ordinals

[5]Writing in 1890 (*Hermes* 25.319), Keil said that the last use of acrophonics occurred in the inscription more recently published as *IG* II² 2336.

[6]J. and L. Robert in the *Bulletin épigraphique* in *REG* regularly reported on numerals in new texts, and their Index volumes under the word 'chiffres' will lead the reader to this material. P. Lévêque and P. Vidal-Naquet, *Clisthène l'Athénien* (Paris 1964) 95–96, discuss the early history of the two systems.

I. THUCYDIDES' PENTEKONTAETIA   31

are rare outside of prescripts giving dates. L. Threatte (*Grammar* 1.115–116) cites no example of alphabetical numerals used as ordinals before Augustan time, after which they became not uncommon. It is well recognized that in Athens in documents on stone, acrophonic numerals were used extensively for sums of money. But, if an Athenian counted the number of sheep and goats, he recorded the number with acrophonics (Attic Stelai). Acrophonics were used for the number of bushels of wheat, of amphoras, of roof-tiles. The number of victories or prizes in contests was recorded with acrophonics: *IG* I³ 1386. In *IG* II² 1541 (356/5), II² 1534A, II² 1534B, we have a mixture of acrophonic and written-out numbers. The acrophonic system was used for the gaming-table or abacus; see Pritchett, *CSCA* 1 (1968) pl. 4. In short, when the Athenian school-boy learned to count, he used acrophonics. By contrast, the Milesian or Alexandrian would have learned to count with the alphabetical system. The fact that numerals are not found for ordinals, used primarily in prescripts in epigraphical texts, does not mean that in other types of writing numerals for ordinals were prohibited.

The book trade presents a different medium. We assume that Thucydides would probably have written in a script with capitals, like epigraphical texts. H. Immerwahr has published articles about scenes on Attic vases containing book rolls: *Classical, Mediaeval, and Renaissance Studies Presented to B.L. Ullman* (Rome 1964) 1.17–48, and *Antike Kunst* 16 (1973) 143–147. The series of vases seems to begin about 500 B.C. One realizes how ponderous writing must have been. E. G. Turner, *Athenian Books in the Fifth and Fourth Centuries B.C.* (London 1952) 13, states that early books lacked punctuation and accents. He suggests (p. 21) that they were sold in establishments which employed slaves. I quote this note from W. G. Rutherford, *A Chapter in the History of Annotation* (London 1905) 5:

> The faultiness of books sold in the shops is often noted, as are also βιβλιωπῶλαι γραφεῦσι φαύλοις χρώμενοι καὶ οὐκ ἀντιβάλ-

32   THUCYDIDES' PENTEKONTAETIA AND OTHER ESSAYS

λοντες, as Strabo describes them 13 609. Galen frequently speaks of the untrustworthiness of the βιβλιογράφοι in his own days and in the past. Here is his advice to a reader who finds a passage obscure: K 18 (2) 321 ἐπίσκεψαι μὲν πρῶτον εἰ μὲν τὸ βιβλίον ἡμάρτηταί σου παραβάλλων τε καὶ ἀντεξετάζων τοῖς ἀξιοπίστοις ἀντιγράφοις· εἶτ' ἂν ὀρθῶς ἔχειν φαίνηται δεύτερόν τε καὶ τρίτον ἀνάγνωθι τὴν αὐτὴν λέξιν προσέχων ἀκριβῶς αὐτῇ τὸν νοῦν. Cp. ib. 363.

The complexity of the manuscript tradition of Thucydides is illustrated in D. Lewis' review of A. Kleinbogel in *Gnomon* 38 (1966) 135–138. For a detailed analysis, see O. Luschnat, *RE* Suppl. 13 (1971) s.v. Thukydides 1299–1323. A. W. Spratt, in his Introduction to Book 3 p. xi, writes:

> The grammarians themselves call attention to the existence of two distinct classes of διφθέραι, the one, carefully written in large letters, so heavy as to be carried by slaves, and only to be acquired at great cost. Of the second kind we find mention in the pages of Libanius, a sophist of the fourth century A.D., who speaks of a MS. of Thucydides possessed by himself, written in small letters, and quite a pleasure to carry: i.e. an edition written, with contractions, in minuscules. Both Galen and Libanius speak of σημεῖα used by those who write εἰς τάχος. Here, says Cobet (Miscell. Gr. p. 159), we may trace a triple source of error in misreading the minuscules, confusing the contractions, or attempting to supplement the deficiencies of the well-thumbed volumes by the insertion of notes and comments of readers. Few indeed of this high-priced class of MSS. have come down to us; but Cobet questions their superior literary merit.

Gomme (*HCT* 1.209) believes that early copyists would have used abbreviations. There are many studies on the Greek brachygraphic and stenographic systems, relating to the so-called σημειογράφοι (*POxy.* 724); see, for example, H. Boge, *Klio* 51

(1969) 89–115; J. and L. Robert, 1970 no. 38. Plutarch (*Cato Minor* 23) writes:

> This is the only speech of Cato which has been preserved, we are told, and its preservation was due to Cicero the consul, who had previously given to those clerks who excelled in rapid writing instruction in the use of signs, which, in small and short figures, comprised the force of many letters; these clerks he had then distributed in various parts of the senate-house.

A. F. Norman, "The Book Trade in Fourth-century Antioch," *JHS* 80 (1960) 122–126, republished in the *Wege der Forschung* volume (1983) on Libanios, sheds interesting light on the virtually untouched subject of copyists, from which we extract a few quotations:

> He himself usually got his books by presentation rather than by purchase, and in any case he maintained his own copyist. His fellow rhetors, Acacius and Demetrius, did the same, and the lending of a text for the purpose of taking a copy was normal practice (e.g. or. 54,68). There was, however, in addition to the demand which these private copyists satisfied in the establishments of professional sophists or the wealthy families, some market for books for which the professional copyist catered. That there was also some traffic in second-hand books is indicated by Libanius' account of the repeated attempts to burgle his library and of the theft and subsequent misadventures of his prized text of Thucydides. This turned up in the possession of a freshman who had purchased it on the open market (or. 1,148). The ordinary student found the purchase of books a necessity, and Libanius reproves those parents who keep their sons so short of money that they are unable to buy the texts they need (e.g. ep. 428.3). ... They <copyists> seem to form part of the households of the very wealthy or the dilettanti alone. They were regularly maintained, either as slave or as free men, in the sophistic establishments, as is only to be expected; Libanius,

34 THUCYDIDES' PENTEKONTAETIA AND OTHER ESSAYS

both as a student in Athens and at the beginning of his career in Constantinople, had a Cretan as his personal βιβλογράφος (or. 1,43). Later in his life, he records the deaths of slaves who acted as copyists for him (or. 1.184–185), and of his secretary, whose handwriting, he notes, was much better than his own (or. 1,232). ... Concerning the technique of the copyist, Libanius allows us a few incidental remarks which have some importance. He records that, just after A.D. 350, he and his friend Aristaenetus had come to the conclusion that the standard of writing, with regard to presentation and appearance, had declined, as compared with that of an earlier time, and he laments the absence from it of κάλλος γραμμάτων (ep. 580,2). In A.D. 371, he regards his text of Thucydides, which was stolen from his library, as irreplaceable. He describes it as easy to carry and the lettering as small and neat. This fashion of writing seems to belong, in fact, to a time early in the preceding century. On the other hand, big lettering is mentioned in A.D. 362 (ep. 798). As for the differences in handwriting, Libanius has mentioned his own as compared with that of his secretary (or. 1,232), but even more interesting is the claim which he makes to be able to identify the handwriting of one of his friends at a glance, even when the signature is hidden (ep. 44,7–8). This is one of the few comments upon an individual's style of handwriting to be found in Greek. No fixed limit can be assigned to the life of his texts. His Thucydides was clearly quite an old copy, perhaps 150 years old.

Ten copyists were employed for the distribution of Libanios' panegyric throughout the cities (*Or.* 1.113). In the case of Thucydides, the problems of composition and publication are always with us, since his work was unfinished. W. K. Prentice, "How Thucydides Wrote his History," *CP* 25 (1930) 117–127, for example, postulated that Thucydides wrote on flat sheets of papyrus and that his original manuscript consisted of loose sheets with alterations and insertions, these sheets being transposed to rolls after his death. He does not speculate whether Thucydides

I. THUCYDIDES' PENTEKONTAETIA

used contractions and abbreviations. The fact that there were different traditions in antiquity about the number of books (R. J. Bonner, "The Book Divisions of Thucydides," *CP* 15 [1920] 73–82) suggests that our division may not have been made by Thucydides, for, if it had been, others would hardly have obtained currency. Whereas Libanios complained about one copy in which many of his expressions had been deliberately changed, Thucydides apparently did not live to check the work of early scribes for his complete text, and we are left to guess whether the slaves who made early copies were as careless or ignorant as many of the Byzantine scribes. We have no leading MS. to which we can refer as authoritative as in the case of Aischylos or Demosthenes, and, if we apply the rule of Jaeger, it may be that corruptions came early. Moreover, in contrast with the soil and climate of Egypt, papyrus did not last forever in Greece and Ionia.

With regard to numerals in Greek palaeography, Sir E. M. Thompson, *An Introduction to Greek and Latin Palaeography* (Oxford 1912) writes (p. 91):

> In Greek MSS. we find two systems of expressing numbers by signs, both being taken mainly from the alphabet. The older system employs the initial letters of the names of certain numbers as their symbols, as Γ for 5, Δ for 10, H (aspirate) for 100, X for 1,000, M for 10,000. The numerals from one to four are represented by units, from six to nine by Γ with added units; multiples of tens and upwards are expressed by repetitions or differentiations of the several symbols. This has been called the Herodian system, after the name of the grammarian who described it. It is seen in use in the papyri, especially in the stichometrical memoranda of the numbers of the lines contained in them; and such notes are also found transmitted to vellum MSS. of the middle ages.
>
> The other system was to take the first nine letters of the alphabet for the units, and the rest for the tens and hundreds, disused letters

36 THUCYDIDES' PENTEKONTAETIA AND OTHER ESSAYS

> being still retained for numeration, viz. *digamma*, for 6, ... This
> system was in full use in the third century B.C. The numerals were
> usually distinguished from the letters of the text by a horizontal
> stroke above: thus $\overline{a}$. To indicate thousands a stroke was added to
> the left of the numeral.[7]

In Aristotle *Ath. Pol.*, where numerals are used for both cardinals and ordinals, the scribe at 44.4 wrote the ordinal as μετὰ
τὴν ϛ´ instead of writing out μετὰ τὴν ἕκτην (πρυτανείαν). If
an Athenian scribe of the pre-Augustan period had used a numeral, he would have written μετὰ τὴν ΓΙ. At different times
and in different places, Greek scribes and stonecutters used different systems, and corruptions could occur in either system in
transmission or in switching from one system to the other.
Indeed, in a fifth-century B.C. inscription from Halikarnassos
(*SIG*³ 46), both systems of notation are used in the same text: K A
= 21, NE = 55, ΔΔΔΔΓΙΙΙ = 48. The same is true of a much later
Athenian inscription of the first century B.C., a subscription list
for the cult of Pythian Apollo; see Tod, *BSA* 45 (1950) 131. In the
same genre, our text of Pseudo-Skylax (iv B.C.) in the *Periplous*
has alphabetical numerals throughout; Agatharchides (ii B.C.)
spelled out all numbers; whereas the anonymous author of the
Periplous ponti Euxini used a mixture of the two. Our texts of

---

[7]Although Thompson gives no reference, Herodian's work on Numbers is
published by H. Stephanus in his appendix to volume 8 (1865) of Dindorf's
TLG cols. 345ff. Herodian says that he had seen in Solon's laws acrophonic
numerals denoting fines which might be inflicted. One who wishes to pursue
the subject may find of interest the eleventh-century work of Psellus, Περὶ
ἀριθμῶν, published by Tannery in *REG* 5 (1892) 343–347. See also the important
work of Priscian (vi A.C.), *De figuris numerorum quos antiquissimi habent
codices*, published by H. Keil, *Grammatici Latini* 3 (1859) 406–417. All attest the
use of the acrophonic system in codices and imply the difficulties scribes had
with a system with which they were not familiar. Rules deduced from Attic
epigraphy do not apply to codices.

I. THUCYDIDES' PENTEKONTAETIA   37

Strabo spell out numbers; yet the *Chrestomathiae* (ix A.C.), or summaries, of Strabo, published in Müller, *GGM* 2.529–636, usually substitute alphabetical numerals (scores of examples), but with a scattering of cardinals in adjacent passages. One does not expect ordinals in geographical authors. We may be reminded that today scholars write Arabic and Roman numerals, adopting various conventions for their use. Readers of reviews will know that errors are not uncommon, the most frequent one being 'p. 000' (e.g. *The Liar School* p. 240: 000 for 111). Most have no palaeographical explanation (e.g. *Topography* 8.104, 155 for 157). Although the final page proof of *The Liar School* had a Table of Contents, this page was lost in the printing.

Instructive would be a collection of examples of numbers illustrating disagreement among scribes of the same author. Thus, in 1.74.1, the correct reading is judged to be τετρακοσίας; but one of the principal codices, according to de Romilly, has τριακο‾ σίας. In 5.57.2, we have both πεντακόσιοι and τετρακόσιοι. In comparing 1.57.6 with 1.116.1, Mme de Romilly believes that Δ in the Attic system (= acrophonics) was confused with Δ in the Milesian system (= alphabetic); in other words, at some stage in the transmission to the exemplar of our MSS., a non-Athenian scribe was at work. De Romilly's statement is in accord with the independent conclusion of Hemmerdinger in *Studi ital. filol. class.* 25 (1951) 91: "Les chiffres Milesiens dans le texte de Thucydide." In Herodotos 2.5.2 and 6.14.2, the MSS. vary between δέκα and ἕνδεκα. In Aristotle *Ath. Pol.*, an unintelligible δε has been variously emended to δ΄ = τέτταρας or Δ = δέκα. In the publication summarized in *SEG* 41.1753, we find confusion between A and Δ, ε and θ by the stonemason.

We have an interesting example from Latin palaeography of the corruption of numbers. F. W. Shipley, *Certain Sources of Corruption in Latin Manuscripts* (New York 1904), compared the readings of the codex *Puteanus* of the fifth century, which contains the third decade of Livy's history, with a ninth-century copy (*Reginesis*) made from it by monks. Shipley writes (p. 47):

38   THUCYDIDES' PENTEKONTAETIA AND OTHER ESSAYS

"There were in all thirty-two cases of corruption involving numbers; and were it not for the fact that in P many of the numbers are not represented by symbols, but are expressed in full, corruptions of this nature would have been much more numerous."[8]

In the Introduction to the Strabo Budé Book 1, Lasserre writes (p. xcii): "On s'en servira tout particulièrement pour les corrections de chiffres, à l'exemple des précédents éditeurs de Strabon. La confusion de λ´ avec ν´ est la plus fréquente (voir W. Aly, *De Strabonis* ..., 245)." This must mean that at some early stage, numeral signs were used where our texts now have cardinals. We make no effort to catalogue the differences in manuscripts or the alleged corruptions. We find in 2.1.40.93 ἐννακισχιλίων (Budé) corrupted into πεντακισχιλίων, where one codex has ε´κισχιλίων, a type of corruption in compounds which Griffith denied for Demosthenes on the basis of papyrological practice, and Hornblower for Thucydides.[9]

It would be useful to have a collection of errors in papyrology, particularly those which are not obviously palaeographical. Thus, in vol. 1 of *POxy*, the editors write, p. 95, "ἔτους β is a mistake for ἔτους γ"; p. 107, "β has apparently been omitted by mistake";

---

[8]Damokrates of Athens (c. A.C. 50) is known to have written his medical recipes in iambic verse in order to avoid corruption; see M. Wellmann in *RE* s.v. Damokrates no. 8 (1901) 2069. Galen *De antidotis* 1.31–32 (Kühn, vol. 14 pp. 31–32, 44) has a lengthy passage on the corruption of numerals in medical writers. He refers to Menekrates who wrote a work with the title Ὁλογράμματα ("written at full length").

[9]In a decree of 325/4 B.C. (*IG* II² 260 lines 9 and 68), πεντέδραχμος is expressed by a combination of the symbol Γ and the written word: L. Threatte, *Grammar* 1.111. In M. Avi-Yonah's collection of *Abbreviations in Greek* (ed. A. N. Oikonomides, Chicago 1974) 42, the numbers of the Greek alphabet are occasionally joined to denote words, ΑΕΔΡΟΥ = πρωτοπροέδρου, etc. In Lysias 30 *Nikomachos* 8, all MSS. read τριακοσίων ... τρισχιλίων, where modern editors read τετρακοσίων ... πεντακισχιλίων.

I. THUCYDIDES' PENTEKONTAETIA 39

p. 226, "the number ought to be 9 not 8." In A. A. Mosshammer, *The Chronicle of Eusebius and Greek Chronological Tradition* (1976), there are a number of numerals which are judged to be corrupt: p. 191, "the interval was corrupted from 108 years to 88, an easy error in Greek (PH to ΓH)"; p. 231, "Either the text is corrupt (XXIX instead of XXXIX) or Solinus made the common error of confusing an Apollodoran birth date with the acme"; p. 236, "the emendation of Aristotle's text must be accepted" (the reference is to *Pol.* 5.1315b.22, an error in palaeography, first detected in Röper, *Philologus* 20 [1863] 722–723); p. 277, "the numeral is a corruption of the Apollodoran birthdate in Olympiad 49 (M̄Ē instead of M̄Θ̄)"; etc. W. Lapini, "Tucidide e il sistema numerale acrofonico," *Prometheus* 17 (1991) 19–28, proposes to emend πολλὰ (τάλαντα) in 6.31.5 to ΓΔΔΔΔ, which he strangely and mistakenly claims are acrophonic numerals corresponding to ὀγδοήκοντα ("... ὀγδοήκοντα, nel sistema acrofonico usato ai tempi di Tucidide, si scriveva ΓΔΔΔΔ, quasi uguale a ΠΟΛΛΑ.").

If Demosthenes wrote the alleged eight copies of Thucydides attributed to him, it is easy to believe that he wrote εἰς τάχος and used σημεῖα. Texts with different readings circulated in antiquity. We cannot endorse the statement of Unz, *CQ* 80 (1986) 75 n. 32:

> Soon after Thucydides' history was 'published' (i.e. copied out in large numbers and generally circulated), every significant public or private library would have had its own copy of such an important and influential work. After this (unless the *original* scribe had made an error in all his copies), textual corruptions could not have widely entered the tradition again until the Middle Ages or later.

In our *Dionysius of Halicarnassus: On Thucydides* (1975) xvii–xviii, we noted that a number of readings found in Dionysios are judged to be correct against the MSS. In separate works of Dionysios, he reproduces different texts for the same passage of

40 THUCYDIDES' PENTEKONTAETIA AND OTHER ESSAYS

Thucydides, although in both cases he claims that he is quoting word for word (κατὰ λέξιν): *De Thuc.* 26 and *Ep. II ad Amm.* 2–6.

In the Attic Orators, we note the following passages where editors have found difficulties with numerals:

Antiphon 6 *Choreutes* 44; Blass, in the critical apparatus of the second edition, suggests corruptions because of alphabetical numerals. By using this passage with restored dates in *IG* I² 324 (= I³ 369), Meritt has attempted to assign a date to this oration and has been followed by others, incorrectly in my view.

Deinarchos 1 *Demosthenes* 89: N and A read τετρακόσια, whereas A² has τέτταρα, an emendation accepted by Blass and others.

Isaios 2 *Menekles* 4: Q and editors read ἔτει ἢ πέμπτῳ whereas A, the other codex, reads ἔτει. It is conjectured that A was copying a text with ἢ ε ΄.

5 *Dikaiogenes* 5: Kaibel conjectures that δ ΄ (τετάρτη) has fallen out after δέ.

8 *Kiron* 7: Dobree substituted δ ΄ (τέτταρας) for τριάκοντα (= λ ΄) of MSS.

11 *Hagnias* 42: A wrote τριακόσιαι which A² altered to τρεῖς αἳ. Blass reads τριακόσιαι ἃ.

Lysias 19 *Aristophanes* 21: For δέκα dropping out after δέ, see the Budé edition.

22 *Corn-dealers* 8: For τέτταρες as the correct text where the codd. have δύο (δ ΄), see the Budé edition.

32 *Diogeiton* 20: Gernet reads τετρακισχιλίας for ἑπτακισχιλίας of codd.

These are but samples to illustrate that editors believe that numeral signs were used in the archetype of our MSS. of several authors.

I. THUCYDIDES' PENTEKONTAETIA 41

The text of Pseudo-Plutarch *Lives of the Ten Orators* requires 45 pages in the Budé 1981 edition of M. Cuvigny; that of Thucydides' Pentekontaetia 18 pages in de Romilly's edition. In the case of the *Lives*, we have much evidence to check the figures. Consulting Cuvigny's critical apparatus and his Notes complémentaires, we note the following numerals which are regarded as erroneous or questionable:

		CODICES
835B	ὀκτώ	ἑκατόν
835C	ὀγδοηκοστῆς	ὀγδοηκοστῆς καὶ δεύτερος
835D	τριάκοντα	ἑξήκοντα
835E	τριακοσίων	τριῶν
836A	"650 talents" (Durrbach)	"250 talents"
842F	"1200 talents" judged to be enormous	
846	Cuvigny uses angular brackets for three clauses containing	numerals to indicate errors or omissions
851	Figure of "500 talents" questioned	

The codices of the *Lives* are said to be derived from a minuscule archetype earlier than the ninth century. More significant that the alleged errors are the divergent readings derived from a common text:

842	ἑξήκοντα and ἑξακοσίων
852B	ἐνακόσια and ἑξακόσια
852B	ἑξακόσια and διακόσια

With this very sketchy background of the use of numerals and their corruption, before taking up the numerals in 1.103.1, we offer a limited collection of twenty examples where the readings of numerals in the MSS. of Books 1–4, with one addition from

42 THUCYDIDES' PENTEKONTAETIA AND OTHER ESSAYS

Book 5, have been regarded as corrupt by major commentators. The list is not exhaustive; indeed, we believe that the numeral in 8.44.4 must be emended. Our examples are largely drawn from the excellent and level-headed "Notes Complémentaires" of Mme de Romilly, a series which might serve as a profitable propaedeutic for all who attempt to treat the text of Thucydides, not merely with regard to numbers, but throughout. We offer no solution to many, nor a complete bibliography, but merely indicate that serious editors, familiar with the manuscript tradition, believe that tradition is very faulty with regard to the transmission of numerals, particularly those resulting in a δέκα. I would like to lay to rest such simplistic pronouncements on the numeral of our passage as "When you change a number you lose a possible link with Thucydides and gain only your own sayso; you have not won Thucydides' support for your theory" (M. Lang, "A Note on Ithome," *GRBS* 8 [1967] 269) in an article which Badian applauds in his indictment of Thucydides. The nearest we can get to a control of what Thucydides wrote is a careful study of the manuscript tradition, in the context of whatever other evidence can be adduced about a particular reading. I do not believe that Thucydides wrote Kolophon in 5.2.2, and I hope that my disbelief amounts to more than my "sayso."

1. **1.29.1.** In giving the Korinthian force sent to what resulted in a naval battle off Aktion, the codices read ἑβ-δομήκοντα ναυσὶ καὶ πέντε δισχιλίοις τε ὁπλίταις. Mme de Romilly emends δισχιλίοις to τρισχιλίοις. We learn from 1.27 that of the 75 ships, 30 were Korinthian ones; the rest furnished by the allies, of which it hence appears that the Eleians furnished some. When Thucydides refers to the 30 ships being prepared by the Korinthians, the text gives the figure for the hoplites as 3,000. Any corruption must be early, since the scholiast notes the discrepancy and says the thousand were left behind in contempt of the Kerkyreans!

I. THUCYDIDES' PENTEKONTAETIA   43

Gomme (*HCT* 1.163) writes, "We can easily imagine reasons why eventually only 2,000 were sent, but not why Thucydides should not have explained the discrepancy," and he offers explanations of how palaeographically a mistake might be made according to various types of numbers. Since the ships were sent, one would expect the same complement of hoplites. Hornblower is quite confused, referring to the ships as "Corcyrean," does not debate Gomme's claim that the hoplites were not epibatai, nor examine Thucydides' not infrequent use of ναῦς = warship.[10] He concludes, however, with the observation: "But note that Lewis (*Towards a Historian's Text*, 54) showed an easy way in which the present manuscript reading could have been corrupted from '70 ships and 5000 hoplites'."

2. **1.57.6.** All MSS. read μετ᾽ ἄλλων δέκα στρατηγοῦντος. This number, however, would give eleven στρατηγοί here, though the regular number was only ten, and with five mentioned in 1.61.1, sixteen in all this year. Krüger, therefore, conjectured that we should read τεσσάρων here, supposing that δ´ = 4, may have been mistaken for the first letter of δέκα. Classen supposes that δ may have stood for δύο, who remarks that three στρατηγοί for 30 ships and 1,000 hoplites corresponds very well with the five in 1.61 for 40 ships and 2,000 hoplites. The significant feature is that, whatever the explanation, δέκα is a sure candidate for corruption.[11]

---

[10]For the use in Herodotos, see B. Jordan, *The Athenian Navy* (Berkeley 1972) 7.

[11]On the 1.57.6 passage, Hornblower cites Griffith (*HM* 2.529) to the effect that four and ten were not liable to be confused, but Griffith's strictrures, following Turner, apply to what are called well-written Greek manuscripts of

44 THUCYDIDES' PENTEKONTAETIA AND OTHER ESSAYS

3. 1.74.1. In the statement of the Athenian envoys about the number of ships at Salamis, the text reads, ἐς τὰς τετρακοσίας (v.l. τριακοσίας) ὀλιγῷ ἐλάσσους τῶν δύο μοιρῶν. Herodotos (8.48) gives the total number of the Greek fleet as 380 exclusive of 5 pentekonters; Aischylos (*Persai* 339) gives 310; Demosthenes (18 *Crown* 238), 300. It is interesting that the number given in Demosthenes 14 *Symm.* 29 is 200 in the best MSS.[12] The Athenian contingent according to Herodotos was 180, or, with the twenty furnished to the Chalkidians (8.1), 200. Demosthenes states it in the former passage to have been 200, in the latter 100. The conventional Athenian number was 200, as evidenced by the "Themistokles decree": Meiggs and Lewis, no. 23. Steup and Poppo read τριακοσίας. Editors believe that Thucydides follows Herodotos, not Aischylos, but gives a round number for the precise one of Herodotos, and that the speaker allows himself an exaggeration of the Athenian contingent. For bibliography on the number of ships at Salamis, see H. Wankel, *Demosthenes Kranzrede* 2 (Heidelberg 1976) 1056–1057. Hornblower discredits the article of Walters

---

classical literature in Egypt. Turner states of the composite word δεκαδαρχία, "if abbreviated this could in Harpocration's time have been written Ι᾽αρχιαν, in IV B.C. it might have been written δ᾽αρχιαν," and reports that numerals are very common in Christian texts and in documentary papyri. See above n. 9. In the running texts of inscriptions from Miletos and Kos, the number of the day, for example, was regularly given by numerals. Inventories of all states regularly used numerals. As indicated above, Polybios believed that scribes made errors in numerals. J. Gow, "The Greek Numerical Alphabet," *Journal of Philology* 12 (1883) 278–286, states that alphabetic numerals were used in Alexandria early in the third century B.C. and became common thereafter.

[12]Papanikolaou, *RM* 114 (1971) 220 n. 5, disagrees with other scholars in claiming that the reference is not to Salamis, but this seems unlikely.

I. THUCYDIDES' PENTEKONTAETIA   45

devoted to the Thucydidean passage (*RM* 124 [1981] 199–211).

4. **1.76.2.** In the phrase ὑπὸ τῶν μεγίστων νικηθέντες, τιμῆς καὶ δέους καὶ ὠφελίας, H. Weil, *RPh* 2 (1878) 92, suggests that τριῶν has dropped out of the text before τῶν, referring to 1.74.1 and 3.40.2. He is followed by Hude.

5. **1.107.3.** For the phrase Ἀθηναῖοι ναυσὶ περιπλεύσαντες, "the Athenians had sailed around with their fleet and were intending to block their way," Hornblower writes:

> Lewis (*Towards a Historian's Text*, 180 n. 82) suggests the insertion of πεντήκοντα, 'fifty', before ναυσί, making an Athenian fleet of fifty ships, which is what Diodorus specifies at xi.80.1. (In a manuscript the abbreviation for this number would be ν´, so it is easy to see how an original ν´ ναυσί could be copied as ναυσί.)

Those who adopt this reading must believe that alphabetic numeral signs and not cardinals were used at some stage in our archetype.

6. **2.2.1.** The phrase ἔτι δύο μῆνας for the length of time remaining in Pythodoros' archonship when the Thebans attacked Plataiai is tied to the important problems of Thucydidean seasons and the date for the commencement of the war. The bibliography is large, but scattered. In addition to Gomme, we single out the article of J. D. Smart in *Past Perspectives* (Cambridge 1986) 24–27, which is criticized by Hornblower (1 pp. 235–241) who follows Andrewes and Wenskus, who, in turn, were criticized by me in *ZPE* 62 (1986) 205–211 and *Topography* 8

46 THUCYDIDES' PENTEKONTAETIA AND OTHER ESSAYS

(1992) 55–57. We note in passing that Smart's calendar has the year of Euthydemos begin on the new moon before the solstice, which is counter to the calendar schemes of Dinsmoor and Meritt, based in part on the date on the Milesian parapegma.

7   2.2.1. Following the passage above, our MSS. read μηνὶ ἕκτῳ καὶ ἅμα ἦρι ἀρχομένῳ for the interval between the battle of Poteidaia and the attempt on Plataiai. J. H. Lipsius, *Leipziger Studien* 8 (1885) 161ff. and Wilamowitz, "Thukydideische Daten," *Hermes* 20 (1885) 484ff., both supported the insertion of καὶ δεκάτῳ after ἕκτῳ and before καὶ ἅμα. Steup, in vol. 2, devoted a lengthy note in his Anhang (pp. 283ff.) to a discussion of early views. Hude endorsed the addition of δεκάτῳ. Gomme (*HCT* 1.421ff.), in reviewing the events which fall in the period (1.63–88, 118–125: the Athenian wall on the north side of Poteidaia, χρόνῳ ὕστερον Phormio's despatch from Athens with 1,600 hoplites, his march on the road [κατὰ βραχὺ προιών], the wall south of Poteidaia, the meeting of the allies at Sparta, the Spartan mission to Delphi, the second meeting at Sparta, etc.), as well as the problem of the beginning of spring, argued that ἕκτῳ must be emended to δεκάτῳ or ἐνάτῃ; cf. de Romilly, 2 p. 86. In *Hermes* 96 (1969) 216–232, W. E. Thompson devotes an article to the defense of ἕκτῳ. The two emendations are rejected by Hornblower, who promises a full treatment in an appendix to his forthcoming volume 2. The problem cannot be resolved without determination of the epoch date of the archon's years, a complicated problem involving Meton's calendar, *IG* I³ 364 and 365, and Thucydides' use of summers and winters. See Essay IV below.

I. THUCYDIDES' PENTEKONTAETIA   47

8. 2.7.2. Our codices give the number πεντακοσίων for the intended total of all Lakedaimonian ships. Both Gomme (*HCT* 2 p. 7) and de Romilly (2 pp. 87–88) argue that the number is impossible.

9. 2.13.3–8. In giving the financial and military resources of Athens, our MSS. give the figure ἑξακοσίων ταλάντων for the annual income from the tribute, τριακοσίων ἀποδέοντα μυρία for the maximum amount of the reserve, τεσσαράκοντα τάλαντα for the value of gold from the statue of Athena, and ἑξακισχιλίων καὶ μυρίων for the number of defense forces at home. All have been challenged and as vigorously defended by many authorities. Up-to-date bibliography on the subject of the financial resources of Athens is given in Lisa Kallet-Marx, *Money, Expense, and Naval Power in Thucydides' History* 1–5.24 (Berkeley 1993) 98ff., who, I believe, works on the principle that the numbers are sound. Discussion about the numbers will be found in Gomme, *Historia* 2 (1953) 1–21. Rhodes, in his edition of Book 2 (1988), offers one emendation. We limit ourselves to the comment that if the Thucydidean numbers are correct, several in other sources are incorrect.

10. 2.20.4. In this example, which was the starting point of S. Dow's article, Thucydides says that the hoplitai of the deme Acharnai were 3,000 in number. A recent and good discussion of the corruption is D. Whitehead, *The Demes of Attica* (Princeton 1986) 397–399. Hornblower, in his commentary (p. 274), writes, "There is a good possibility that Th. wrote not ὁπλῖται but πολῖται." Given a choice between corruption in a numeral and that in a noun, I would certainly choose the former. In any case, there is corruption.

48 THUCYDIDES' PENTEKONTAETIA AND OTHER ESSAYS

11. **2.65.12.** The MSS. apply the phrase τρία μὲν ἔτη to the number of years the Athenians held out against their enemies after the disaster in Sicily. Gomme (*HCT* 2.196–197), de Romilly (2 p. 101), as well as Rhodes and Hornblower, believe the numeral "is obviously wrong." Steup and Gomme favor ὀκτώ.

12. **2.75.3.** The word ἑβδομήκοντα is applied to the number of days the Lakedaimonians spent in building a ramp at Plataiai. Gomme (*HCT* 2.207–208) compares other constructions, the labor force, and the length of other campaigns, and finds the figure much too large, as does de Romilly. Stahl suggested an original θ´ (= 9) for MSS. ο´ (= 70). Parenthetically, W. G. Rutherford, *A Chapter in the History of Annotation* (1905) 56, notes that Galen (K 17 [1] 794) commented on the confusion between Θ and Ο. The loss of ever so tiny a fibre of the papyrus might involve the loss of the stroke across the theta. Even if no fibre had gone from the stroke, the stroke in itself even from the first may have been so faint as to disappear altogether in time. Again in K 18 (2) 778, Galen comments on the misreading of faint or blurred letters and the filling in of accidental lacunae. Rutherford says that the best account of errors arising from confusion of letters is C. G. Cobet's in *Oratio de Arte interpretandi* (1847). Steup devotes a lengthy note in his Anhang, suggesting ἑπτακαίδεκα. There is a similar passage in Livy 5.19.10–11.

13. **3.16.3.** The number of ships ravaging the Peloponnesian coast is reported in the phrase αἱ περὶ τὴν Πελοπόννησον τριάκοντα νῆες τῶν Ἀθηναίων. Editors have argued that the number of thirty ships cannot be reconciled with 3.7.2–3, where Asopios sent back eighteen of thirty ships, and 3.13.3–4, where at the

I. THUCYDIDES' PENTEKONTAETIA 49

time of the Olympic festival Asopios was on the Lakonian coast. The ravages announced at this time could not have been committed by the thirty ships of Asopios, for their passage along the Lakonian coast could not have lasted so long. The most recent editor, Hornblower, retains the MSS. reading, explaining in part in italics, "The mistake was Th.'s own or was a Spartan misapprehension correctly reported by him." J. de Romilly writes, "Ces trente vaisseaux, semble-t-il, reviennent d'Acarnanie en deux groupes ou après avoir fait leur jonction." Gomme devotes a long note, concluding, "Since the number should be 18, not 30, perhaps τριάκοντα should still be bracketed." The matter is involved, and Steup in his Anhang devotes more than three pages of small print to the problem, rejecting the reading of 30, which had been defended by H. Müller-Strübing, *Thuk. Forschungen*, 1881, 109ff. The passage appears in *POxy* 3891, of the second century, published by Haslam in 1990. The papyrus reads τριάκοντα, but deletes the καί after ἠγγέλοντο. Haslam comments, "Steup proposed the deletion of τριάκοντα, identifying these ships with the fleet of 100. The presence of καί, if retained, seems to me a severe obstacle to this solution. The papyrus removes the obstacle, but at the same time it reinforces the authority of τριάκοντα." Cagnetta refers to this papyrus in an appraisal of the manuscript tradition: *RFIC* 121 (1993) 195–204.

14. 3.26.1. In giving the number of Peloponnesian ships intended for Mytilene, the MSS. read τὰς ἐς τὴν Μυτιλήνην δύο καὶ τεσσαράκοντα ναῦς. J. de Romilly and Hornblower believe the number should be emended. Since in previous mentions of this fleet, reference to which is indicated by the article, the number of ships is only forty (3.16.2; 3.25.1), as likewise in the

50 THUCYDIDES' PENTEKONTAETIA AND OTHER ESSAYS

further account till the union with Brasidas (3.29.1; 3.69.1), the number forty-two can hardly be correct here. Some editors have bracketed δύο καί on the assumption that some interpreter added to the forty ships the two mentioned in 3.5 and 3.25. Gomme believes that no commentator would have been so stupid and opts for a different solution. Stahl would bracket all three words. Diodoros (12.53) mentions 45.

15. 3.50.1. The number of the instigators of the Mytilenaean revolt who were put to death is given as ὀλίγῳ πλείους χιλίων. Schutz and Mahaffy, who argue that the island of Tenedos (3.35), which is described as being 80 stadia in circumference, was too small to accommodate such a crowd and their guards and that the population of Mytilene was only 5,000, hold that Λ ΄ (30) was corrupted into ΄Α (1,000), which de Romilly favors. Holzapfel, *RM* 37 (1882) 448–464, Stahl, *Gött. gel. Anz.* 1882 99ff., Herbst, *Philologus* 42 (1882) 707ff., and Steup, in his Anhang, argued the matter at length. Gomme debates the reading of the MSS., which is accepted by Hornblower, citing Wilson, *Historia* 30 (1981) 147–148, who adds nothing to Gomme. Examples of massacres were collected in *War* 5.218–219. No humanistic sentiment was involved, and we can dismiss H. Müller-Strübing's theory (*Thuk. Forschungen* [1881] 154ff.) that the passage was the "interpolation eines blutdürstigen Grammatikers." The Mytileneans sent by Paches to Athens consisted (3.35) partly of the πράξαντες πρὸς τοὺς Λακεδαιμονίους μάλιστα τῶν Μυτιληναίων (3.28.2), who on the entry of the Athenians had fled to the altars and then been transferred to Tenedos, where they could be more easily watched (cf. 3.2.3); partly of any others that seemed to Paches responsible for the revolt. It is argued that the language of this second class

I. THUCYDIDES' PENTEKONTAETIA 51

(3.35) suggests only a small number: καὶ εἴ τις ἄλλος αὐτῷ αἴτιος ἐδόκει εἶναι τῆς ἀποστάσεως. It is then maintained that the πράξαντες group was only a small part of the oligarchs, since the dominant oligarchical party had with the demos made an agreement with Paches (3.28.1) and would not have taken refuge at the altars. A major consideration is the allotment of land and the income derived from the rental (3.50.2), studied by P. Gauthier at length, who concludes (*REG* 79 [1966] 80), "1000 paraît un chiffre trop élevé." There are other considerations in the long debate. L. D. Reynolds and N. G. Wilson, *Scribes and Scholars*[3] (Oxford 1991) 223, state, "Since numerals were represented by letters in both languages they were often incorrectly transmitted, a fact which is a serious hindrance to students of economic and military history." Among three pages of confusions, they include our passage of 3.50.1: "χιλίων MSS.; but this number seems too large for the ringleaders of a revolt in Mytilene, and τριάκοντα has been suggested instead. χιλίων would be written ͵Α (in uncials), τριάκοντα Λ ΄ (cf. A (ii) above)."

16. **3.68.2.** Our MSS. date an alliance between Athens and Plataiai ἔτει τρίτῳ καὶ ἐνενηκοστῷ before the destruction of Plataiai in 427 B.C., which gives us a date in 519/8 B.C. Editors of the text of Thucydides retain the reading of the MSS.; but some historians place the alliance ten years later and would read ὀγδοηκοστῷ. Grote, in a lengthy note in chapter 31, argued that the alliance could not take place until after the expulsion of Hippias. Macan, in his commentary on Herodotos 6.108.1, writes:

> Thuc. 3.68,2 dates the alliance ninety-two years before the destruction in 427 B.C. That date brings us to 519 B.C. Grote, in

52 THUCYDIDES' PENTEKONTAETIA AND OTHER ESSAYS

an unanswerable note (vol. iii. p. 583, ṗt. ii. c. xxxi.), has proved that this date is highly improbable. It is not, however, necessary to suppose that Thucydides in this case committed a blunder. Let it be granted that a copyist added one Δ too many (ϜΔΔΔΙΙΙ for ϜΔΔΙΙΙ) in an uncial MS. of Thucydides, and the error is traced to the likeliest source. (This is the suggestion of the late Professor A. von Gutschmid, cp. Busolt, *Die Lakedaimonier*, i. 307 n.) The date of the alliance is 509 B.C. if the application to Kleomenes was made on the occasion of his second expedition into Attica: cp. 5.72 *supra*.

In turn, Mahaffy, in *Essays Presented to William Ridgeway* (1913) 196, suggested that $\overline{OΓ}$ was mistaken for $\overline{QΓ}$. Both How-Wells and A. W. Lawrence, on the Herodotean passage, support the emendation. Hornblower provides more recent bibliography.

17. 3.70.1. We are told that 250 Kerkyraian captives at Korinth were set free on bail at the sum of ὀκτακοσίων ταλάντων pledged by their proxenoi. Gomme writes, "But 800 tal. seems impossibly large, twice the annual revenue of the Delian League, and over 3 tal. each ... Eighty talents, instead of 800, would mean 20 minae per man, and must be near the maximum likely sum; 800 minae is possible." 800 mnai equals 80,000 drachmai. The large sum has its defenders, particularly since the transaction was a fictitious one; but in *War* 5, in collecting examples of ransom, I favored (pp. 257–258) the emendation to ὀγδοήκοντα which, not noted by Gomme, was the reading of Valla. As indicated there, B. Hemmerdinger (*Essai* p. 58) had defended other read-

I. THUCYDIDES' PENTEKONTAETIA

ings in Valla,[13] but he does not discuss our passage. Bloomfield claimed that in a cursive script the numeral pi (80) might appear as omega (800) if the top of the letter faded away.

18. **4.13.2.** Our MSS. give the number of Athenian ships which arrived at Pylos from Zakynthos as τεσσα-ράκοντα. Mme de Romilly observed:

> Le chiffre de quarante navires, donné par les manuscrits, est manifestement impossible; la flotte athénienne en comportait quarante à l'origine (2.2); sur ce nombre, il faut en retrancher trois (les cinq de 5.2 moins les deux de 8.3); mais, inversement, il faut ajouter les secours mentionnés à 13.2, secours qui comportent, en plus des navires athéniens, quatre navires de Chios.
>
> D'autre part, le chiffre adopté ici (cinquante) est justifié par le fait qu'à 23.2 un renfort de vingt navires porte le chiffre de la flotte à soixante-dix.

Gomme, too, noted the difficulty and reported that most editors follow the inferior and later MSS. in reading πεντήκοντα. He added that Steup and Wilamowitz would emend to ἑπτὰ καὶ τεσσαράκοντα to account for Demosthenes' three in the later total of seventy. The reading of "40" is old, going back to Portus.

19. **4.116.2.** The sum τριάκοντα μνᾶς (bis) is given as the amount (= 3,000 dr.) paid to the soldier who was the first to mount the wall of a temple at Lekythos. Gomme comments, "a remarkably large sum to be promised a

---

[13]As noted by R. Pheiffer, *History of Classical Scholarship* (Oxford 1976) 38, Valla spent four years on his translation of Thucydides into Latin, and his text is evidence for the manuscript he was using.

54 THUCYDIDES' PENTEKONTAETIA AND OTHER ESSAYS

soldier (who might earn 1 dr. a day, so this is equal to 3,000 day's pay) in an enterprise that we cannot believe to have been either desperate or of the first importance." Mahaffy (*Hermathena* 3.458) and Hemmerdinger suggest Δ (4) for Λ (30). We collected examples of the use of scaling-ladders in *Topography* 8.129–138, with a few examples of awards of aristeia on pp. 140–141, including one of 100 mnai. The question is whether Brasidas would have had such a large sum to dispense.

20. 5.25.3. For the period of time the two powers observed the armistice, the MSS. read ἐπὶ ἓξ ἔτη μὲν καὶ δέκα μῆνας. Mme de Romilly emends to ἑπτὰ ἔτη, writing (p. 189), "Le chiffre a été corrigé, parce que celui des manuscrits (six ans dix mois) était impossible; mais le correction adoptée n'est nullement certaine," with a long note explaining her position.

With this general background of the alleged corruption of numerals, we turn to our passage in 1.103.1, where we are told that the Messenians surrendered to the Lakedaimonians: οἱ δ' ἐν Ἰθώμῃ δεκάτῳ ἔτει (codices). We offer two quotations from scholars who at the time of writing believed the passage was in chronological order.

B. Hemmerdinger, *Essai sur l'histoire du texte de Thucydide* (Paris 1955) 25–26:

> Diodore de Sicile en 11,64,6, présente la même erreur que Thucydide. M. G. Klaffenbach raisonne comme s'il avait affair, non à Diodore, mais à sa source principale pour la Pantékontaétie, Éphore, dont l'oeuvre est perdue. Dans ce cas, l'erreur serait antérieure à 340 avant J.-C., date à laquelle Éphore achève son histoire. Mais, on l'a vu, cette erreur résulte de l'adoption à Athènes d'une édition de Thucydide présentant des chiffres ioniens, et cette conjoncture est inconcevable avant la fondation de la bibliothèque

I. THUCYDIDES' PENTEKONTAETIA

d'Alexandrie. Si, en revanche, on traite le passage de Diodore, non comme de l'Éphore, mais simplement comme du Diodore, il n'y a plus de difficulté chronologique: Diodore aura utilisé, non seulement un Éphore, mais aussi un Thucydide, au texte duquel il aura emprunté la faute en question. La *Bibliothèque historique* de Diodore de Sicile étant parue à Rome vers 30 avant J.-C., cela constitue pour cette faute un *terminus ante quem*.

After citing what he regarded as two errors of "10" for "4" in Herodotos, he continued:

> Le fait qu l'ensemble des manuscripts médiévaux de Thucydide présente à plusiers reprises Δ «4» pris pour Δ «10» est essential pour l'histoire du texte, car il implique que l'ensemble des manuscrits médiévaux de Thucydide procède du même exemplaire athénien de l'édition d'Aristophane de Byzance.
>
> Les chiffres sont en toutes letters dans les papyrus de Thucydide, dont aucun n'est antérieur à notre ère.
>
> Au IIe siècle de notre ère, seuls les plus anciens des manuscrits d'Hippocrate consultés par Galien ne présentent pas les nombres en toutes lettres:
>
> Ἔνια μὲν τῶν ἀντιγράφων προσγεγραμμένα τὸ τετάρτῃ, τινὰ δὲ τὸ τεταρταῖοι, τὰ δὲ τούτων ἔτι παλαιότερα τὸ Δ γράμμα ὃ μεῖζον τῶν ἄλλων γραμμάτων ἐστίν, ἔνια δ' οὐδ' ὅλως οὐδὲν ἔχει προγεγραμμένον. (Galien, ed. Kühn, XVII, 1, p. 730). On notera l'indication paléographique: les lettres symbolisant des nombres n'étaient distinguées des autres lettres ni par un trait horizontal ni par un trait oblique, mais parce qu'elles étaient plus grandes que les autres. Certes, Galien ne parle ici que de chiffres ioniens. Mais, si les suscriptions sont souvent ornées de fioritures dans les papyrus d'Égypte (plus accessibles et en moins mauvais état que ceux d'Herculanum), les chiffres attiques des indications stichométriques n'y présentent ni trait horizontal ni trait oblique.

56 THUCYDIDES' PENTEKONTAETIA AND OTHER ESSAYS

In his review of Hemmerdinger in *CR* 71 (1957) 24–25, Dover writes:

> Many numbers in Thucydides are demonstrably corrupt, and in some cases (not all) the assumption of visual error or misunderstanding in the transcription of numerals suggests a plausible emendation. From the standpoint of sense alone, there are usually equally plausible alternatives; and if we give preference to an alternative dictated by an assumption, we cannot then use it to prove the truth of the assumption. If we add to the known corruptions of numbers the large number which must be corrupt but are unquestioned because we have no grounds for questioning them, we may conclude that that proportion of the whole which is constituted by cases which seem positively to demand explanation as confusion between Attic and Milesian numerals is no higher than chance makes it. Numbers are liable to corruption because alternative numbers make sense in a way in which other alternatives do not. In 'twenty pigeons flew out of the trees' the sense inhibits the corruption of 'pigeons' to 'pigs' and helps to restore the original if the mistake has been made; but no such consideration inhibits the corruption of 'twenty' to 'thirty' or arouses suspicion in a subsequent editor, so that the mistake, once made, is incorrigible.

David M. Lewis, *Historia* 2 (1953) 415–416:

> What stood in Thucydides' manuscript must remain uncertain. The three possibilities are τετάρτῳ, πέμπτῳ, and ἔτκῳ. 1. I cannot believe in the most popular view, that there has been a mechanical corruption in which δ ´ (τετάρτῳ) has been taken as Δ (δεκάτῳ), because there is simply no evidence that acrophonics could represent ordinals, and, since this appears to be so, I do not see how any Athenian scribe could have made the mistake. The authors of ATL play with the notion that he could, unwisely, I think, but at least they recognise the difficulty and draw attention to it for the first time. 2. Even if one believes that Thucydides used

I. THUCYDIDES' PENTEKONTAETIA   57

aspirates, Gomme's preferred ἕκτῳ (Ηεκτοι read as Δεκατοι) is not particularly attractive palaeographically, if one thinks of the epigraphic character of fourth-century handwriting. 3. πέμπτῳ, his second string, seems to me not only preferable historically, for ἕκτῳ gives us a tight fit and τετάρτῳ somewhat too loose a one, but to be far the most likely to be corrupted. As an example to support his suggestion that ε´ may have dropped out before ἔτει we should note Athenaeus 506 A, where we should read οἱ ε´ ἔτει πρότερον τελευτήσαντες for οἱ ἔτι πρότερον τελευτήσαντες, as Casaubon saw.

That the alleged rule that the Athenians did not use acrophonics for ordinals should be supported by the Princeton-Oxford school of epigraphy ("no evidence that acrophonics could represent ordinals," Lewis citing *ATL* 3.162) seems remarkable in the light of Meritt's explanation of attested errors for ordinals in calendar equations. In *The Athenian Year*, Meritt writes: (p. 112) "Instead of holding that 23 was mistakenly written for 13, possibly ΔΔΙΙΙ read incorrectly for ΔΙΙΙ, I would suppose that 23 was mistakenly written for 18, ΔΔΙΙΙΙ, possibly, for ΔΓΙΙΙ."; (p. 161) "I would suggest ... that the scribe (or copyist) had in his notation of the date by prytany the numeral ΔΔΙΙ which he mistakenly cut on the stone as ἑβδόμει καὶ δεκάτει,"; (p. 93) "However specious the argument that a scribe might have mistaken ΔΔΓΙΙΙΙ for ΔΓΙΙΙΙ (so Mommsen, *Chronologie*, p. 466), and that therefore this was the probable error, it must be said that error, by its very nature, often defies rational explanation." Meritt, accordingly, assumed that the error was in the day by month, 11 for 1. Most editors assume that δεκάτηι was inscribed by error for εἰκοστῆι in *IG* II² 351 + 624. There are also errors in the calendar equations in giving the name of the month which defy palaeographical explanation unless the stonecutter was given a copy with acrophonics, as we today use Arabic numerals. In Meiggs and Lewis, *SGHI* no. 71, an acrophonic numeral was inscribed for the sum of drachmai, then subsequently erased, and

58 THUCYDIDES' PENTEKONTAETIA AND OTHER ESSAYS

the corresponding cardinal inscribed. This suggests that the mason had a copy with an acrophonic, which was subsequently changed in accordance with epigraphical practice.

So far as Thucydides' chronology is concerned, Lewis' (and Gomme's) reading of ἕκτῳ or ε′ might be acceptable, but this does not explain how palaeograhically δεκάτῳ became the reading in our codices. I follow the hypothesis of Hemmerdinger and de Romilly that a scribe might transcribe a Δ in the text that he was copying as δεκάτῳ; in short, that Δ standing for τεττάρτῳ (in Ionic or Alexandrian) might be expanded to δεκάτῳ, according to the nationalities of the scribes who were doing the transcribing. Thucydides' history was circulated in places other than Athens, and, if we take our cue from Turner, slaves other than Athenians might do the copying. I regard as absurd any rule that a scribe who used numerals for cardinals must spell out ordinals when he came to them, and it is enough to refer to the examples in Aristotle *Ath. Pol.* and to Mayser's statement about the practice in palaeography with regard to what he calls the 'Alexandrian' system. Since all scholars, including Lewis and Hornblower, believe that at some stage alphabetical numerals were used in our pre-archetype, we have no difficulty in assuming that a scribe, who used the acrophonic system for purposes of counting, mistook a Δ for "tenth" in 1.103.1 and transcribed δεκάτῳ. That Herodian and Priscian wrote treatises explaining in detail the acrophonic system illustrates the fact that texts with different systems were in existence. Shipley explains the errors in the *Reginensis* of Livy as due, not merely to carelessness on the part of scribes, but to ignorance of certain of the numerical signs and methods of notation.

In short, the Athenians in the classical and Hellenistic periods learned to count with acrophonic numerals, the Milesians and Alexandrians with alphabetical ones. In Attic epigraphy, acrophonics are extremely common in inventories and as monetary units. Ordinals are much rarer than cardinals, and in inscriptions are found for dates, primarily in prescripts, where the legal con-

I. THUCYDIDES' PENTEKONTAETIA 59

vention was to avoid abbreviations and spell out the numbers. In the book-trade, if a classical or Hellenistic Athenian scribe wished to abbreviate, he used the system he was taught, namely acrophonics. It is utterly absurd to invoke a rule that an Attic scribe could not use acrophonics, which is tantamount to saying that he could not abbreviate. Meritt's method of explaining errors in Attic epigraphy was sound. On the other hand, if a Milesian or Alexandrian scribe used abbreviations, he employed alphabetical numerals, which became common by the Roman period, although there is literary evidence that old codices still existed in which acrophonics were found. Probably the best known historical papyrus, the *Ath. Pol.* of about 80 A.C., used abbreviations for cardinals and ordinals. In the oldest commentary we have on Thucydides Book 2 (*POxy* 853 p. 124), the scribe used an alphabetical numeral in his lemma for 2.15.4, where our codices have an ordinal. A lemma is normally a reproduction of the text the scribe was using.

With one statement of Bede (*Opp.* 1.149, ed. J. A. Giles), who speaks of the work of scribes of his day, we can all agree: "numeri ... negligenter describuntur et negligentius emendantur."

We append a few words on a numeral in Diodoros. After describing (11.63–64) the earthquake and the so-called Third Messenian war under the year 469/8 ἐπ' ἄρχοντος Φαίωνος (sic), and stating that it lasted ἐπὶ ἔτη δέκα, Diodoros concludes the war (11.84.8) under the year 456/5 B.C. Scholars who discredit the theory of chronological sequence in Thucydides profess that they have found a nugget of gold in the numeral δέκα in 11.64.4, which confirms the corrupt δεκάτῳ in Thucydides 1.103.1.

The minimum standard of scholarship requires that before we extract a phrase from the compilations of this undistinguished Sicilian historian of the mid-first century B.C., we present his entire record of the Pentekontaetia in contrast with that of Thucydides. Here, we are concerned only with the numeral.

60 THUCYDIDES' PENTEKONTAETIA AND OTHER ESSAYS

According to the edition of Vogel-Fischer, we possess for Book 11, covering the years 480–451 B.C., in addition to fifteenth- and sixteenth-century codices, the Codex Patmius of the tenth or eleventh century. We are told in 11.19.6 that the total of the army of Mardonios, which was left behind in Greece, was οὐκ ἐλάττων τῶν τετταράκοντα μυριάδων (400,000), in 11.28.4 πλείους τῶν εἴκοσι μυριάδων (200,000), and in 11.30.2 εἰς πεντήκοντα μυριάδας (500,000). In 12.38.2, Diodoros gives a figure of 8,000 (τάλαντα σχεδὸν ὀκτακισχίλια); yet in 12.40.2 and 12.54.3, the same sum has become 10,000 (τῶν μυρίων ταλάντων). The ἔτεσι δυσί (2) of Diodoros 12.68.2 is ἑνὸς δέοντι τριακοστῷ ἔτει (29) in Thucydides 4.102.3. In 11.55.2, we are informed that the Athenian law of ostracism required an exile of only five years (πενταετῆ). Of the number who perished at Korinth, Diodoros (12.65.6) gives the figures τῶν Ἀθηναίων εἰς ὀκτώ, τῶν δὲ Κορινθίων πλείους τῶν τριακοσίων, whereas Thucydides (4.44.6) writes Κορινθίων δώδεκα καὶ διακόσιοι, Ἀθηναίων δὲ ὀλίγῳ ἐλάσσους πεντήκοντα. In 12.5.2, we learn that Krison of Himera won the stadion in 448/7, and in 12.23.1 that he again won in 444/3; yet in 12.29.1 he won the same race τὸ δεύτερον in 440/39. Either Diodoros was very muddled, or there are copyists' errors in numbers; probably both.

In 12.35, we are told that Archidamos died in 434; yet later he is leading an army into Boiotia (12.47.1) and invading Attika in 426 (12.52.1). In 12.1.5, Diodoros claims that Aristotle and Isokrates and his school, as well as Miltiades, Themistokles, Aristeides, and Kimon, flourished in 450–400 B.C. The guest-friend of Themistokles is called Lysitheides in 11.56.5, but Plutarch (*Themistokles* 26) calls him Nikogenes; see *RE* s.v. Lysitheides 2 (1928) 67. The Roman names of military tribunes in 12.60.1 are badly confused. The exploits of Kimon (11.60) are compressed from ten years into one; those of Themistokles from the origin of his downfall to his death are given under the archonship of 471/0. His confusion over Tanagra and Oinophyta is well known.

4. SETTLEMENT AT NAUPAKTOS

We attribute no chronological significance to the numeral δέ-κα in 11.64.4. It may be nothing but a numerical corruption before the 10th century. Or possibly, some scribe/scholar took it from the corrupted text of Thucydides. The oft-repeated claim that the figure was in Ephoros, or that Diodoros' numeral goes back ultimately to the Atthidographers, receives no credence from those who believe that Thucydides followed chronological order.

I share the opinions of A. Scheer, *Diodors* XI (Bottrop 1933) and W. Kolbe, *Hermes* 72 (1937) 241–269, that Diodoros contributes remarkably little to the knowledge of the period covered by Thucydides himself.[14]

SECTION 4

SETTLEMENT AT NAUPAKTOS

The difficulty of dealing with the Ithome episode is that much was going on in Athens which has found its way into sources five

---

[14]The position is somewhat different for the succeeding centuries, when he had more works on which to draw. *POxy* 13.1610 (= Jacoby, *FGrH* 2A 70 frg. 191), an Ephoros papyrus, shows remarkable *verbal* agreement with Diodoros for the history of the fifth century. Grenfell and Hunt (p. 113) comment, "Ephorus ... was not a great historian, and to judge by 1610 it may be doubted whether in his treatment of the fifth century b.c., which brought him into frequent conflict with Thucydides, many of the novelties were of real historical value. The servility of Diodorus, who, as it now appears, followed Ephorus almost blindly through that period, and was practically incapable of original composition, has probably prevented us from losing very much when Books X–XV of the older historian perished." Jacoby suggests that it was an epitome of Ephoros used by Diodoros. Africa, *AJP* 83 (1962) 86–89, finds the papyrus a caricature of Ephoros, and suggests it may be an epitome of Diodoros.

62 THUCYDIDES' PENTEKONTAETIA AND OTHER ESSAYS

hundred years later; and the attempts to synchronize this record with Thucydides' brief narrative has resulted in much chronological debate. Mme. J. de Romilly in her chapter of "The Point of View of Thucydides," in her *Thucydides and Athenian Imperialism* (English tr. Oxford 1963), has elegantly reminded us that Thucydides made no attempt to judge events on the home front. He neglected all the features which linked imperialism to Athenian political life in general, passing over in silence matters such as Kimon's ostracism, the reforms of Ephialtes, etc.

Our aim is first to examine the record of Thucydides to see whether his narrative presents any chronological difficulties in the light of geography, military practices, and contemporary politics, particularly as gleaned from contemporary epigraphical documents. The chief criticism has been that Thucydides' narrative calls for "a remarkably early intrusion by Athens into the Corinthian Gulf,"[1] a periplous to Naupaktos, it is claimed, which accords better with a later one of Tolmides, as recorded in Diodoros. The charge is also made that Thucydides' statement that the Athenians made an alliance with Naupaktos after transplanting the Messenians is "an anticipation and not in sequential order."[2]

We again cite the passage about the settlement of the Messenians with its context, giving the Loeb text and translation (1.103.1-4):

Οἱ δ' ἐν Ἰθώμῃ δεκάτῳ ἔτει, ὡς οὐκέτι ἐδύναντο ἀντέχειν, ξυνέβησαν πρὸς τοὺς Λακεδαιμονίους ἐφ' ᾧ ἐξίασιν ἐκ Πελοποννήσου ὑπόσπονδοι καὶ μηδέποτε ἐπιβήσονται αὐτῆς· ἢν δέ τις ἁλίσκηται, τοῦ λαβόντος εἶναι δοῦλον. ἢν δέ τι καὶ χρηστήριον τοῖς Λακεδαιμονίοις Πυθικὸν πρὸ τοῦ, τὸν ἱκέτην τοῦ Διὸς τοῦ Ἰθωμήτα ἀφιέναι.

---

[1] D. Lewis, *CAH* V² (1992) 500.

[2] P. Deane, *Thucydides' Dates* (Ontario 1972) 32.

I. THUCYDIDES' PENTEKONTAETIA

ἐξῆλθον δὲ αὐτοὶ καὶ παῖδες καὶ γυναῖκες, καὶ αὐτοὺς οἱ Ἀθηναῖοι δεξάμενοι κατὰ ἔχθος ἤδη τὸ Λακεδαιμονίων ἐς Ναύπακτον κατῴκισαν, ἣν ἔτυχον ᾑρηκότες νεωστὶ Λοκρῶν τῶν Ὀζολῶν ἐχόντων. προσεχώρησαν δὲ καὶ Μεγαρῆς Ἀθηναίοις ἐς ξυμμαχίαν Λακεδαιμονίων ἀποστάντες.

In the tenth year the rebels on Ithome found that they could hold out no longer and surrendered to the Lacedaemonians on condition that they should leave the Peloponnesus under a truce and should never set foot in it again; and if any of them should be caught there, he was to be a slave of his captor. Moreover, before this time the Lacedaemonians also received a Pythian oracle, which bade them let go the suppliant of Ithomean Zeus. So the Messenians left the Peloponnesus, themselves and their children and wives; and the Athenians received them, in consequence of the enmity to the Lacedaemonians already existing, and settled them at Naupactus, which they happened to have lately taken from its possessors, the Ozolian Locrians. And the Megarians also entered into alliance with the Athenians, revolting from the Lacedaemonians.

The numeral δεκάτῳ was discussed above.

We treat the settlement of the Messenians at Naupaktos under the following headings:

1. Geography of Ozolian Lokris
2. Epigraphical evidence for early Naupaktos
3. Reconstruction of Thucydides' scenario
4. The adverb νεωστί
5. Tolmides' campaign
6. Athenian alliance with Naupaktos
7. The Ozolian hostages of 1.108.3

64 THUCYDIDES' PENTEKONTAETIA AND OTHER ESSAYS

1. GEOGRAPHY OF OZOLIAN LOKRIS

The Aitolians are named in the Homeric Catalogue (*Iliad* 2.639-640) with five sites, Pleuron, Olenos, Pylene, Chalkis, and Kalydon.[3] The Aitolians occupy that part of Aitolia which was known to Strabo (10.2.3.450) as "Old Aitolia." W. J. Woodhouse, in his study of the Aitolian tribes (chap. 7) in *Aetolia* (1897), established that the western and eastern limits are the Acheloos and Mount Klokova (= Varassova, pl. 9b of Hope Simpson and Lazenby). For the territory between the great massif of Varassova and the Gulf of Itea (= Ozolian Lokris), we are dependent upon L. Lerat, *Les Locriens de l'ouest* (1952). If one consults the large fold-out map of Hope Simpson in *BICS* Suppl. 16 (1965), one sees that Mycenaean settlements are attested in only four places, including the sites of Chaleion and Oianthea,[4] on the long stretch of coast between Mount Varassova and the Gulf of Itea. The westernmost site, one east of Naupaktos, is a chamber-tomb found east of ancient Eupalion.[5] From the literature before Thucydides, we learn nothing of Ozolian Lokris.

One important modification must be made in the northern boundary of Ozolian Lokris as earlier postulated by Woodhouse and Oldfather.[6] L. Lerat, *Les Locriens de l'ouest* 1.76-77, has

[3]See Hope Simpson and Lazenby, *The Catalogue of Ships in Homer's Iliad* (Oxford 1970) 107-109.

[4]More recent bibliography for these two sites may be found in S. Lauffer's *Griechenland Lexikon* (Munich 1989).

[5]Cf. *Topography* 7.55.

[6]The numerous articles of Oldfather, who traveled in 1914, in the *RE* are not the equal of those of Bölte, E. Meyer, and others. J. and L. Robert, *REG* 53 (1940) p. 204, write, "Les articles de Oldfather sur les Lokrides font tache." Cf. L. Robert, *Études épigraphiques et philologiques* 240-241. G. Daux, *Delphes* (1936) 631, states, "compilation plus abondante que judicieuse, qui ne doit être consultée qu'avec prudence." Lerat is very critical throughout, stating on 1 p. xvii, "Il a manqué surtout d'esprit critique."

I. THUCYDIDES' PENTEKONTAETIA 65

established the line of the frontier between Aitolia and Western Lokris, one part of which we reproduce:

> L'identification du site de la ville étolienne de Poteidania par G. Klaffenbach a montré une fois de plus qu'il est dangereux de déterminer *a priori* une frontière politique en se fiant aux lignes tracées par la nature. C'est in 1933 que ce savant a découvert auprès d'une chapelle située à une demi-heure au Sud-Est du village de Kambos, accroché aux pentes du Vigla, une pierre portant le texte de deux affranchissements par vente à la déesse Athéna Pyrgia de Poteidania. Le site de la ville était donc aux environs de Kambos, comme l'affirmait la tradition locale. On a parfois affirmé que cette cité était d'origine locrienne; mais nous savons qu'elle était étolienne dès le Ve siècle et l'est toujours demeurée depuis lors et l'hypothèse reste gratuite. Cette localisation confirme l'impression qui se dégageait du récit de l'expédition de Démosthène par Thucydide: la Locride se réduisait à cet endroit à une bande côtière fort étroite de sept out huit kilomètres de profondeur. C'est à peu près la même que nous avons constatée à Longa, et Skala et Kambos sont situés sensiblement sur une même ligne.

In tracing Demosthenes' campaign of 426 B.C. in *Topography 7* chap. 3, we photographed the inscription (pl. 62) which determines the site of Poteidania, one of the towns named as Aitolian by Thucydides in 426 B.C. At Poteidania, Aigition, and Longa, we have Aitolian sites located within seven or eight kilometers of the coast. The site of Poteidania is particularly revealing; see *Topography 7* fig. 4.[7] Above the harbor of Monasteraki, where

---

[7]In exploring the region in the late 1980's, we noted (*Topography 7* p. 51) that along the ridge extending from the temple site at Poteidania southwards, there is a long series of recently excavated tombs placed on either side of a road about four meters in width (pls. 63, 64), as well as an unpublished inscription (n. 7). Publications run many years behind excavations. We also reported on an

66 THUCYDIDES' PENTEKONTAETIA AND OTHER ESSAYS

Demosthenes landed, the land rises roughly in the shape of an amphitheater, near the apex of which is Poteidania. The entire stretch of coast of Ozolian Lokris from Naupaktos to our candidate for Oineon was in clear view of the Aitolians. The western part of the territory of Ozolian Lokris was a narrow stretch of coastline. The "wild tribes" of the Aitolians were in visual contact and literally breathing down the backs of the Lokrians. If we wish to look for an explanation for why the Eastern Lokrians strengthened their colony at Naupaktos, or why the Naupaktians may have given over their town without a do-or-die struggle, one factor must have been relief from the menace of the Aitolians.

Naupaktos, the important town of Ozolian Lokris, is said to have derived its name from the Herakleidai having here built the fleet with which they crossed over to Peloponnesos: Strabo 9.4.7.426; Pausanias 10.38.10; Apollodoros 2.8.2. It was probably chosen as a site because of its strong hill (a triangular slope with a citadel at the apex), fertile plains, and copious supply of water, as well as the small harbor which played so great a figure in ancient history; Leake, NG 2.608. One would like to know the date of the earliest occupation at Naupaktos. The thriving modern town, with a good Class B hotel on the waterfront, is built over the ancient site. We have at least one excavation which establishes occupation at least as early as the beginning of the fifth century B.C. In 1972, part of a Classical cemetery containing five unplundered graves was excavated. One grave contained nearly thirty vases and a bronze mirror disk. Iphigeneia Dekoulakou has published the vases, including many impressive black-figured lekythoi: ADelt. 28 Chr. 1973 (1977) 391-393 with pls. 345-349.[8] Comparing

---

impressive Kastro (80-81; pls. 91-95), which becomes our candidate for Livy's Apollonia (fig. 4), that had escaped the notice of previous investigators.

[8]In ADelt. 17.B (1961/2) 183-184 with pls. 210-211, Mastrokostas published many other vases from Naupaktos, but offers no dates. A more recent report of rescue operations, conducted in 1987 and published in ADelt. 42 (1987 [1992])

I. THUCYDIDES' PENTEKONTAETIA 67

the lekythoi with those published by Haspels, Beazley, and others, she dates eleven of the vases to the first quarter of the fifth century and eight to the second quarter. One vase is inscribed (*SEG* 27.150). Tombs 2 and 4 are dated in the first, and Tomb 3 in the second quarter of the fifth century. The site was occupied by about 500 B.C., and we see no reason not to attribute the occupation to the Ozolian Lokrians, erstwhile East Lokrians.[9]

2. EPIGRAPHICAL EVIDENCE FOR EARLY NAUPAKTOS

We have four inscriptions relating to Naupaktos and the region dated to the first half of the fifth century. Three are conveniently published by C. D. Buck in his *Greek Dialects* (Chicago 1955) 248-257.

1. No. 57, an inscription found at Galaxidi (= Chaleion, a number of whose citizens participated in the enterprise, lines 46–47). Also published as Tod, *GHI* no. 24; Meiggs and Lewis, *SGHI* no. 20 ("Law of the Eastern Lokrians relative to their Colony at Naupaktos: ? 500-475 B.C."). The most detailed presentation of the text and bibliography is that of Klaffenbach, *IG²*.IX.1.3.718. This inscription offers an early example of alphabetical numeral signs, A -Θ (1–9).

Buck writes (p. 250), "Law governing the relations between the Eastern Locrian colonists at Naupactus and the mother country. This law does not refer to the founding of Naupactus, which was

---

Chr. 169-175, refers to walls partly of polygonal masonry and including a rectangular tower (pl. 85). Part of a classical city wall was found outside the medieval fortifications.

[9]Concerning the division of the Lokrians, J. A. O. Larsen, *Greek Federal States* (Oxford 1968) 49, writes: "How the division of the Locrians into two parts came about remains a matter of conjecture. Their dialect was Northwest Greek and they — or those among them who brought in the language — belong to the same group of invaders as the Phocians, but it is likely that the Locrians came first and that their division was due to the later invasion of the Phocians."

68 THUCYDIDES' PENTEKONTAETIA AND OTHER ESSAYS

much earlier." Tod states (p. 33) "The object of the colony is not indicated, but may have been to strengthen the Locrian hold upon a position of great strategic importance." Larsen, *Greek Federal States* (Oxford 1969) 49, states, "When early in the fifth century Naupactus, near the western extremity of Western Locris, was in trouble, the Eastern Locrians sent a colony to strengthen the city." L. Lerat, *Les Locriens de l'ouest* 2.30, concurs, "Le but de l'enterprise devait être de renforcer la population de Naupacte." Meiggs-Lewis, no. 20 date the text to "? 500-475 B.C.".

There is agreement that the text has to do, not with the "establishment" of a colony at Naupaktos, but with the strengthening of one.

2. No. 58, also found at Galaxidi, the site of ancient Chaleion, is republished by Tod no. 34 and, in greater detail, by Klaffenbach as IG^2.IX.1.3.717. The bronze tablet in early Lokrian script contains a treaty between Oianthea and Chaleion for the protection of foreigners visiting either city from reprisals. Chaleion is in the southern part of the Bay of Itea; Oianthea is to the west at Vitrinitsa, renamed Tolophon.

3. No 59 (= Meiggs and Lewis no. 13), written boustrophedon, fits into the general picture, being the enactment of an unknown town envisaging the possibility that their community might be forced to call in as settlers 200 men at arms. The script is of the Ozolian Lokrians (so Jeffery, *LSAG* 104-105). Unfortunately, the provenance of the inscription is debated. The bronze plaque was given to the museum at Thermon by a doctor. Buck, citing Chatzes, reports that it was probably found near Amphissa. Meiggs and Lewis, citing Lerat, report that it was "said by different informants to have come from Psoriani in Aetolia or the neighbourhood of Naupaktos." Psoriani is the modern name of a district, not a town, on the left bank of the Evenos a considerable distance east of Thermon. Because of the script and the mention of an Apollonion, which is attested for Naupaktos, Meiggs and Lewis associate it with Naupaktos.

I. THUCYDIDES' PENTEKONTAETIA 69

4. The fourth inscription is known only from the notice of E. Mastrokostas in *ArchDelt*. 19 B (1964) 295, which I reproduce in full:

Ναύπακτος

Εἰς τὴν Παπαχαραλάμπειον Βιβλιοθήκην κατετέθησαν τὰ ἐν τῷ αὐτόθι Γυμνασίῳ καὶ τῷ Μουσείῳ Πατρῶν φυλασσόμενα ἀρχαῖα (*AD* 17 (1961/2): Χρονικά, 183), αἱ ἀπελευθερωτικαὶ ἐπιγραφαὶ Lerat, *Les Locriens de l'Ouest*, I 92, ἀριθ. IIa (ὕψ. 0,18, πλ. 0,49, πάχ. 0,51 μ.) καὶ IIb (ὕψ. 0,152, πλάτ. 0,635, πάχ. 0,56 μ.), ὡς καὶ ἀπότμημα ἐξ 29 στίχων σπουδαιοτάτης ἐπιγραφῆς εἰς στοιχηδὸν φορὰν (ὕψ. 0,54, πλάτ. 0,11 – 0,59, πάχ. 0,16 μ.) ἔξω τῆς ἄνω ἀκροπόλεως εὑρεθὲν παρὰ τοῦ κ. Γεωργίου Ἰω. Κυριαζῆ. Χρονολογεῖται περὶ τὰ μέσα τοῦ 5ου αἰῶνος, εἰς τοὺς πρώτους χρόνους τῆς ἐγκαταστάσεως τῶν Μεσσηνίων ἐν Ναυπάκτῳ, τὴν ὁποίαν πρὸ ὀλίγου εἶχε κυριεύσει ὁ Ἀθηναῖος ναύαρχος Τολμίδης (Θουκ. I 103, Διοδ. XI 84,7). Εἶναι συμπολιτεία Μεσσηνίων καὶ Ναυπακτίων. Ἀναγράφει τὴν φράσιν *γυναῖκας καταβιβάσαι* ἐκ τῶν ὀρεινῶν περιχώρων δηλ., ὅπου θὰ εἶχον καταφύγει οἱ Ναυπάκτιοι καὶ ὁρίζει διὰ τοὺς παραβάτας τῆς συμφωνίας τὴν ἐπιβολὴν χρηματικοῦ προστίμου, τοῦ ὁποίου τὰ χρήματα θὰ εἶναι ἱερὰ τῆς Ἀθάνας τῆς Πολιάδος. Ἀναφέρει ἐπίσης καὶ *σφυρηλάτους ἀνδριάντας*. Τὸ ἱερὸν τῆς Ἀθηνᾶς Πολιάδος γίνεται τὸ πρῶτον γνωστόν.

70 THUCYDIDES' PENTEKONTAETIA AND OTHER ESSAYS

We stress that Mastrokostas has called the document a sympoliteia,[10] the Messenians and Naupaktians shared civic rights. We infer that the Athenian settlement of the Messenians at Naupaktos was not attended by the customary brutality of the victor over the conquered; at least the children and women were not sold into slavery, and the males later joined with the Messenians in warfare against a common enemy. We have two epigraphical documents of the fifth century which apparently attest the later collaboration of the Messenians and the Naupaktians. Both are important monuments from Delphi and Olympia. The Delphic monument consists of a bronze statue on a base of inscribed marble. For the bibliography, see Tod 1 p. 147; SEG 19.392 and 32.550. Here, the word Ναυπάκτιοι is restored: [Μεσ]σάνιο[ι καὶ Ναυπάκτιοι] ἀνέθ[εν]. The Olympic mon-

---

[10]Klaffenbach, in his Fasti to IG IX².1.3 (1968), put the matter succinctly: "Neque autem Naupactios expulsos esse docent et communis dedicatio Messeniorum et Naupactiorum Olympiae facta (nr. 656; cf. Lerat II 35) et titulus adhuc ineditus, e quo apparet sympolitiam quandam inter utrumque populum initam esse. Eodem titulo certiores fimus summam deam ᾿Αθάναν τὰν Πολιάδα fuisse." The Messenians and the male Naupaktians reached an agreement that the women, who had fled to the neighboring mountains when the Athenians took the city, were to be brought back and a monetary fine was to be inflicted on any transgressor to this action. The money was to be consecrated to Athena Polias. Apparently, no mention was made of the Athenians as an occupying force, which suggests that they withdrew completely as soon as the Messenians were brought in. One would like to know how the Naupaktians who entered into the sympoliteia with the Messenians were referred to in the opening lines of Mastrokostas' text. A letter to Dr. Mastrokostas brought the response, "Διὰ τὴν ἐπιγραφήν, ποὺ μοῦ γράφετε, δὲν εἶμαι ἕτοιμος ἀκόμη." Writing under the title "19 Χρόνια," Matthaiou, Horos 1 (1983) 84, commented on the long delay in publication of the text of the inscription. In 1995, the appropriate title would be "31 Χρόνια." The interpretation of the inscription in connection with Tolmides' campaign by D. Lewis, CAH V² 118–119, is in my opinion not satisfactory.

I. THUCYDIDES' PENTEKONTAETIA 71

ument is the base which supported the famous Nike of Paionios. Here, the text is completely preserved: Μεσσάνιοι καὶ Ναυπάκτιοι ἀνέθεν Διί. For bibliography, see Tod no. 65; Meiggs and Lewis no. 74; and Pritchett, *Essays* 162 n. 29.

The picture which emerges from the epigraphical evidence is that at some early period, the Ozolian Lokrians had a settlement at Naupaktos, which was strengthened by the Eastern Lokrians before the city was taken over by the Athenians for the settlement of the Messenians, who then co-existed with the Naupaktians on peaceful terms. The two nationals apparently wished to retain their separate identity, and the Messenians hoped to return to their homeland; but militarily and politically they acted as a unit. There is no action more political than going to war. Both shared the worship of Athena Polias.

3. RECONSTRUCTION OF THUCYDIDES' SCENARIO

The withdrawal of the Messenians was made ὑπόσπονδοι. We would reconstruct the scenario, which must have consumed many days, without violation of the text. Before leaving Ithome, the Messenians were assured of a safe haven, which was made by the Athenians. Some communication was sent to Athens, just as earlier the Lakedaimonians had appealed to Athens for help, resulting then in the dispatch of Kimon and a large force (1.102.1; Aristophanes *Lysistrata* 1137ff.). There were many ports of departure, and the Messenians must have had their ultimate destination in mind before they set out. The truce provided that they had free passage to that port. The Athenians took Naupaktos, across the straits of the Korinthian Gulf near Antirhion. Their periplous of the Peloponnesos required 4-5 days. Since Naupaktos entered into a sympoliteia with the Messenians after the settlement, and the Lokrians were allowed to coexist with the Messenians, the usual ravages of warfare were not observed. For their part, the Lokrians now had added protection against the Aitolian tribes, a few kilometers removed. The Messenian families made the long trek from Ithome to the coast, presumably at

72 THUCYDIDES' PENTEKONTAETIA AND OTHER ESSAYS

Rhion, or to some other port agreed upon, and were transported across the Gulf in Athenian ships. The epigraphical evidence cited above establishes that the occupation of Naupaktos was by the Messenians (and Lokrians) alone. It is important to note that the Athenians did not remain. We are told in Pausanias 4.25 that after the Messenians occupied Naupaktos, they soon marched against Oiniadai. The Athenians had withdrawn from the scene, and the Messenians and Lokrians later made joint dedications. The polis of Naupaktos functioned with Messenian and Lokrian inhabitants. The two nationals joined side by side in assisting the Athenian cause.

Naupaktos was taken as a separate operation. The Lokrians were forced to accede; but they remained and with the Messenians formed a polis. The Messenians did not flee helter-skelter from Ithome, but were organized and knew their destination and port of exit before they withdrew for the long trek by land. One envisages considerable negotiations, especially before the Messenians left their fortress on Mount Ithome where walls still remain today.

4. THE ADVERB νεωστί

The thrust of Badian's argument (166–168) is that the Lokrian occupation of Naupaktos was recent. "This probability approaches certainty if we devote some attention to the adverb νεωστί, which has perhaps been unduly neglected in this debate. ... The little adverb, properly interpreted, provides one more instance of Thucydides' persistent apologia for Athens that characterizes his first book."

We repeat the phrase in question: Ναύπακτον ... ἣν ἔτυχον ἡρηκότες νεωστὶ Λοκρῶν τῶν Ὀζολῶν ἐχόντων. Citing the use of ἄρτι and νεωστὶ, the position is taken that the adverb precedes the verb and hence modifies ἐχόντων. I see the problem differently, namely, the position of the adverb outside the genitive absolute construction. Moreover, I think that the adverb normally attaches itself to the nearest verb, in this case ἡρηκότες.

I. THUCYDIDES' PENTEKONTAETIA 73

If νεωστί modified ἐχόντων, I believe he would have placed it within the genitive absolute. See 3.3.1, τοῦ πολέμου ἄρτι καθισταμένου; 4.34.2, τῆς ὕλης νεωστὶ κεκαυμένης; 4.108.5, τῶν Ἀθηναίων … νεωστὶ πεπληγμένων; 7.1.4, τοῦ Ἀρχωνίδου νεωστὶ τεθνηκότος.[11]

The best treatment of the genitive absolute known to me is that of E. H. Spieker, "On the so-called genitive absolute and its use especially in the Attic Orators," *AJP* 6 (1885) 310-343, with a note by Gildersleeve. Earlier, J. D. Goodell, *TAPA* 15 (1884) 15, had counted, without references, examples of the construction in Sophokles, citing one example in Greek, οὗ δῆτα ποικίλως αὐδωμένου. Spieker gives the Greek of few passages (the common τούτων οὕτως ἐχόντων, οἴνου δὲ μηκέτ᾽ ὄντος, ἡμῶν ταύτην τὴν γνώμην ἐχόντων) of the hundreds for which he gives references; but the construction is regularly a unit. Clearly, rhythm, hiatus, intonation, may be factors. "The Greek wrote as he deemed best for the purpose of rhythm, etc." (pp. 325-326). I possess W. R. M. Lamb's *Clio Enthroned. A Study of Prose-form in Thucydides* (Cambridge 1914), and have read with profit his contentions against Cornford's doctrine that simplifies history by making money the *primum mobile* and regards the *History* as real, but only as real, as an Aischylean drama; but his study of prose rhythm, or intonation, is a long argument, which I do not underrate, but one which I have never pursued. Nor have I imitated Demosthenes, who, on the word of Lucian, *Adversus Indoctum* 4 (102), copied out the *History* eight times. But in the passage in 1.103.3, I believe that we can spare Thucydides the allegations made against him by interpreting νεωστί with

---

[11]Spieker (p. 327) notes that generally the noun, as the important element, is put first.

74 THUCYDIDES' PENTEKONTAETIA AND OTHER ESSAYS

ἡρηκότες and take the genitive absolute as a separate period in accord with Thucydidean usage.[12]

When Hornblower (1 p. 160) writes, "E. Badian, 'Athens, the Locrians and Naupactus', *CQ* 40 (1990), 364ff. (partly drawing on W. Oldfather, *RE* articles on Lokris and Naupaktos) acutely notes that the Greek should mean that the *Lokrian* seizure of the place was recent," he does not inform his reader of the post-1914 archaeological evidence, or weigh the import of the epigraphical evidence.

5. TOLMIDES' CAMPAIGN

Lewis (*CAH* V² [1992] 117-118, 500) and some of his predecessors (Unz, *CQ* 80 [1986] 75 and 84; Badian, *CQ* 84 [1990] 368) postulate that Naupaktos was not taken until the expedition of Tolmides, obviously made to damage Sparta, which Thucydides recounts (1.108.5) as taking place after Oinophyta. Indeed, this theory is a mainstay of those who discredit the chronology of Thucydides. The only source which connects Naupaktos with Tolmides is Diodoros. Aischines implies that the expedition was by land!

For Tolmides' circumnavigation of the Peloponnesos, we have the following testimonia:

1. Thucydides 1.108.5 (Loeb):

> And the Athenians, under the command of Tolmides son of Tolmaeus, sailed round the Peloponnesus, burned the dock-yard of the Lacedae-monians, took Chalcis, a city of the Corinthians, and making a descent upon the territory of the Sicyonians defeated them in battle.

---

[12]This is by no means to suggest that adverbs are always within the noun-verb complex of the genitive absolute or next to the verb. Emphasis is a major factor. Cf. Demosthenes 9 *Phil.* III 15: ἄρτι τῆς εἰρήνης γεγονυίας.

I. THUCYDIDES' PENTEKONTAETIA

2. Aischines 2.75 and scholion (tr. of Fornara, no. 84):

Aeschin. 2.75: I bade you emulate ... (the actions at Plataea, Salamis, Marathon, Artemisium) and the generalship of Tolmides, who marched without fear with one thousand picked Athenian troops through the center of the Peloponnesus though it was hostile territory.

Scholion: Tolmides. He sailed around the Peloponnesus with the Athenians and won brilliant fame and seized Boiai and Cythera when Kallias was Archon at Athens (456/5). Tolmides also set fire to the dockyards of the Lacedaemonians.

3. Diodoros 11.84 (Loeb);

While Callias was archon in Athens, in Elis the Eighty-first Olympiad was celebrated, that in which Polymnastus of Cyrenê won the "stadion," and in Rome the consuls were Servius Sulpicius and Publius Volumnius Amentinus. During the year Tolmides, who was commander of the naval forces and vied with both the valour and fame of Myronides, was eager to accomplish a memorable deed. Consequently, since in those times no one had ever yet laid waste Laconia, he urged the Athenian people to ravage the territory of the Spartans, and he promised that by taking one thousand hoplites aboard the triremes he would with them lay waste Laconia and dim the fame of the Spartans. When the Athenians acceded to his request, he then, wishing to take with him secretly a larger number of hoplites, had recourse to the following cunning subterfuge. ...

When all the other preparations for his expedition had been made, Tolmides set out to sea with fifty triremes and four thousand hoplites, and putting in at Methonê in Laconia, he took the place; and when the Lacedaemonians came to defend it, he withdrew, and cruising along the coast to Gytheium, which was a seaport of the Lacedaemonians, he seized it, burned the city and also the dockyards of the Lacedaemonians, and ravaged its territory. From here he set out to sea and sailed to Zacynthos which belonged to Cephallenia; he took the island and won

76 THUCYDIDES' PENTEKONTAETIA AND OTHER ESSAYS

over all the cities on Cephallenia, and then sailed across to the opposite mainland and put in at Naupactus. This city he likewise seized at the first assault and in it he settled the prominent Messenians whom the Lacedaemonians had allowed to go free under a truce. At this time, it may be explained, the Lacedaemonians had finally overcome both the Helots and Messenians, with whom they had been at war over a long period, and the Messenians they had allowed to depart from Ithomê under a truce, as we have said, but of the Helots they had punished those who were responsible for the revolt and had enslaved the rest.

4. Plutarch *Perikles* 18.2 (Loeb):

But he [Perikles] was admired and celebrated even amongst foreigners for his circumnavigation of the Peloponnesus, when he put to sea from Pegae in the Megarid with a hundred triremes. he not only ravaged a great strip of seashore, as Tolmides had done before him, but also advanced far into the interior with the hoplites from his ships, and drove all his enemies inside their walls in terror at his approach.

5. Pausanias 1.27.5 (Loeb):

On the pedestal [of the temple of Athena] are also statues of Theaenetus, who was seer to Tolmides, and of Tolmides himself, who when in command of the Athenian fleet inflicted severe damage upon the enemy, especially upon the Peloponnesians who dwell along the coast, burnt the dock-yards at Gythium and captured Boeae, belonging to the "provincials," and the island of Cythera. He made a descent on Sicyonia, and, attacked by the citizens as he was laying waste the country, he put them to flight and chased them to the city.

6. Polyainos 3.3: Repetition of the stratagem from Diodoros 11.84.

There are differences in the accounts. Aischines gives the number of troops as 1,000, the ἐπίλεκτοι; Diodoros as 4,000.

I. THUCYDIDES' PENTEKONTAETIA 77

Diodoros also gives the number of triremes (50). The Aischines scholion and Pausanias report the capture of Boiai and the island of Kythera. Only Thucydides mentions Chalkis,[13] whereas Diodoros alone mentions Methone, Zakynthos, Kephallenia, and Naupaktos.[14]

Thucydides puts the settlement of the Messenians at Naupaktos and the end of the Third Messenian war earlier (1.103.1-2) and omits Naupaktos in his account of Tolmides' periplous, whereas Diodoros alone assigns Naupaktos to Tolmides. Recent scholars, including D. Lewis, have voted for Diodoros, whose general value as an historian of the period will be appraised below. One who looks at a map will recognize one glaring error in Diodoros: the capture of Methone is put before that of Gytheion, whereas Methone is located at the southwestern tip of Peloponnesos. Moreover, Methone in 431, in contrast to Zakynthos and Kephallenia, was Spartan. E. Meyer put the matter succinctly (*RE* s.v. Methone [1980] 1383.56-66):

> Nach Diodor. XI 84, 6 soll Tolmides bei seiner Fahrt um die Peloponnes auch M. kurze Zeit erobert, beim Anrücken der Spartaner aber wieder aufgegeben haben. Das Ganze ist aber ungeschichtlich und aus Thuk. II 25, dem Unternehmen des J. 431,

[13]Thucydides mentions the two most prominent achievements of Tolmides' campaign, the burning of the dock yard and the seizure of Chalkis. Chalkis, one of the five Aitolian cities in the Homeric catalogue (*Il.* 2.640), was in the hands of the Korinthians and later served as an Athenian naval station in the operations of Phormio. The seizure of it could not have been an easy operation. The kastro, variously called Γαυρολίμνη, Βασιλική, or Ἑβραιόκαστρο (Jews' Fortress, a common title of remains), is on a terrace about one-half hour climb from the coast. I have visited the port, but have not made the climb. Nor did Leake (*NG* 1.110 ff.). Photographs in Woodhouse, *Aetolia* facing page 110, and Hope Simpson-Lazenby, pl. 9b.

[14]For the subsequent friendship of Athens with Zakynthos and Kephallenia, see Thucydides 2.7.3; 2.9.4; 2.66; and 3.30.2.

78 THUCYDIDES' PENTEKONTAETIA AND OTHER ESSAYS

herausgesponnen (s. Busolt Griech. Gesch. II 1², 326). Im J. 431 versuchten die Athener den befestigten Ort zu erobern, doch mißlang das Unternehmen infolge des Eingreifens des Brasidas (Thuk. II 25 = Diod. XII 43, 2f.).

If the flatfooted Diodoros incorrectly inserted Methone from Thucydides 2.25, it is easy to believe that he added Naupaktos from 1.103.1-2.

Thucydides has the Messenian settlement as part of an operation under a truce. The Messenians did not give up their strong position at Ithome until they had assurance of a safe haven. The scenario in Diodoros is that after Tolmides has ravaged Lakonian territory, he has the Messenians depart from Ithome under truce; and we infer that by some coincidence they would arrive at Rhion after Tolmides had taken Naupaktos. Diodoros' chronology is a muddle.[15] In 11.63-64, he puts the outbreak of the revolt and Kimon's expedition in 469/8, and says the war lasted ten years; but in 11.84.7-8 he puts the end of the war in 456/5.

6. ATHENIAN ALLIANCE WITH NAUPAKTOS

We deal briefly with the problem of the alliance of the Athenians with Naupaktos, which P. Deane makes the thrust of chapter 2 of his book *Thucydides' Dates* 465-431 B.C. (Ontario 1972). In the sentence following the account of settlement of the Messenians at Naupaktos, Thucydides writes (1.103.4): προσεχώρησαν δὲ καὶ Μεγαρῆς ᾿Αθηναίοις ἐς ξυμμαχίαν, "And the Megarians also entered into an alliance with the Athenians." The words δὲ καί "and also" imply that the Athenians concluded the settlement of the Messenians with an alliance. Deane, on the other hand, writes (p. 32):

[15]In writing about Tolmides and Naupaktos, Badian (p. 238) refers to "the Atthidographer on whom Diodorus' information is ultimately based," and on p. 168, objects to Gomme "in refusing to accept what Diodorus offers, however reasonable it seems to be and however well it fits together."

I. THUCYDIDES' PENTEKONTAETIA 79

> Naupaktos was an Athenian possession, lately acquired from the Lokrian settlers, and the Athenians established the Messenian refugees there. There was no Messenian state with which the Athenians entered into alliance, as was done in the cases of Argos, Thessaly, and Megara. These Messenians and later the Messenians at Pylos are listed among the Athenian allies: at 2.9.4 as Messenioi hoi en Naupakto and at 7.57.8 in the roster just before the battle in the Great Harbour at Syracuse as hoi Messenioi nyn kaloumenoi ek Naupaktou kai ek Pylou tote hyp' Athenaion echomenes. In both cases the formula Thucydides uses in describing them indicates where they live but that they are what might be described as "displaced persons," men without a state. They are allies, but no formal xymmachia could be made between two states. ... The settlement of the Messenians is an anticipation and not in sequential order.

A community that makes dedications at Delphi and Olympia in the name of Μεσσάνιοι καὶ Ναυπάκτιοι is a polis, or "state" to use Deane's term. Dedications made by ᾿Αθηναῖοι o r Κορίνθιοι were not made by "displaced persons." The people who entered into a sympoliteia operated as a state. The Messenians and Lokrians were left to govern themselves; the Athenians left behind no military governors. The Messenians οἱ ἐν Ναυπάκτῳ are listed as formal allies in 2.9.4. The phrase αὐτοὺς (the Messenians) οἱ ᾿Αθηναῖοι δεξάμενοι prepares the way for the next sentence προσεχώρησαν δὲ καὶ Μεγαρῆς ... The Athenians received the Messenians as an independent state, and they were joined also by the Megarians. Thucydides did not elaborate on the terms of the settlement; but he makes it clear that Naupaktos was received into the alliance as a state after Argos and Thessaly (1.102.4). In short, the Athenians made four alliances: Argos, Thessaly, Naupaktos, and Megara.

80 THUCYDIDES' PENTEKONTAETIA AND OTHER ESSAYS

7. THE OZOLIAN HOSTAGES OF 1.108.3

In 1.108.3, we are told that after Oinophyta, when the Athenians became masters of Boiotia and Phokis, they took as hostages a hundred of the wealthiest persons from Opuntian Lokris. Badian regards this action as in anticipation of the seizure of Naupaktos, which he attributes, following Diodoros, to Tolmides. Hornblower summarizes as follows:

> Why are the Opuntians singled out for this harsh treatment? Badian, 'Athens, the Locrians ...' (103. 3n.), 368, conjectures that the Athenians were already planning the *periplous* of Tolmides and the settlement of the Messenians at Naupaktos; the Athenians planned to require the Opuntian (East) Lokrians to take back their colonists the Ozolian (West) Lokrians, under the terms of the colonization decree ML 20, and were now demanding 'the most solid guarantees on the part of the Opuntians'.

I would presume with others that the hostages were representatives of the famous "hundred families," or houses, of Opuntian Lokris (Polybios 12.5.7), which formed in old times the ruling-body in the province; cf. Walbank, *HCP* 2.334, and Oldfather, *RE* s.v. Lokris (1926) 1244–1245. The Athenians wanted assurance that the Opuntians, who were "naturally hostile to Phokis" (Gomme), would not act against the Phokians, "naturally friendly to Athens as an enemy of Sparta." Grote, in chapter 45, explained the matter: "Phocis and Lokris were both successively added to the list of their dependent allies, — the former being in the main friendly to Athens and not disinclined to the change, while the latter were so decidedly hostile that one hundred of their chiefs were detained and sent to Athens as hostages." For any who, relying on Diodoros, wish to attribute the Messenian settlement to Tolmides and regard the seizure of Opuntian hos-

I. THUCYDIDES' PENTEKONTAETIA   81

tages as a preliminary act, it may be observed that Diodoros (11.83.2) dates the latter *after* Tolmides' campaign. Utter confusion reigns in this pick-and-choose method of rewriting history. The seizure of the hostages had nothing to do with Naupaktos, far removed.

S. Bommeljé, "Aeolis in Aetolia," *Historia* 37 (1988) 297–316, our leading authority on Aitolia, concluded his article on Thucydides 3.102.5 with the statement, "The history of the Corinthian Gulf, however, has yet to be written."

SECTION 5

NAXOS, THASOS, AND THEMISTOKLES' FLIGHT

In 1.98.4, Thucydides writes:

Ναξίοις δὲ ἀποστᾶσι μετὰ ταῦτα ἐπολέμησαν καὶ πολιορκίᾳ παρεστήσαντο. πρώτη τε αὕτη πόλις ξυμμαχὶς παρὰ τὸ καθεστηκὸς ἐδουλώθη, ἔπειτα δὲ καὶ τῶν ἄλλων ὡς ἑκάστη ξυνέβη.

After this they waged war upon the Naxians, who had revolted, and reduced them by siege. And this was the first allied city to be enslaved in violation of the established rule; but afterwards the others also were enslaved as it happened in each case. (Loeb)

He follows this with a digression on the causes of revolt (1.99). He resumes the narrative with the statement (1.99.1):

Ἐγένετο δὲ μετὰ ταῦτα καὶ ἡ ἐπ᾽ Εὐρυμέδοντι ποταμῷ ἐν Παμφυλίᾳ πεζομαχία καὶ ναυμαχία Ἀθηναίων καὶ τῶν ξυμμάχων πρὸς Μήδους.

After this occurred at the river Eurymedon in Pamphylia the land-battle and sea-fight of the Athenians and their allies against the Persians. (Loeb)

82 THUCYDIDES' PENTEKONTAETIA AND OTHER ESSAYS

In *JHS* 107 (1987) 5–6, Badian argues that the siege of Naxos required two seasons,[1] although Thucydides does not so specify, as he does in some other multi-campaigns. Badian writes in part as follows:

> I would suggest that Thucydides has been misunderstood at this point, where he returns from a digression and tries to reconnect his narrative. The μετὰ ταῦτα καί is his way of doing it: it takes up the μετὰ ταῦτα of 98.4 and is intended to let us know (after the digression) that, in addition to the revolt of Naxos, something else *also* happened after the same events (the capture of Scyrus and Carystus), viz. the battle of the Eurymedon. If this is correct, we must posit rough contemporaneity between Naxos and the Eurymedon, and not succession. But there is more to be said. It is commonly assumed that the Naxos affair was over in a single season. There is no warrant for this in the text, and it is historically unlikely. In the only other cases of wars against major allied states in this period (Thasos and Samos), we know how difficult victory was, and how long the fighting: three seasons in the one case, two in the other. At a time when Athenian power and skill was much less overwhelming, Naxos is not likely to have been significantly easier. ... Thucydides needs it merely as the first of the revolts against Athens. The siege and capture take up four words, leading to the reflections in the digression. The negative conclusion, that the war as such was quick and easy, is totally unjustified: we are not told how long it took, any more than we know how long (e.g.) the siege of Eion took. But at least two seasons, with a winter intervening, must surely be allowed, in the light of the other major rebellions. If Themistocles encountered the Athenian fleet at Naxos early in 465, as seems likely, we may put the siege either in 466–65 or in 465–64, if we allow two seasons for it. In fact, three, as in the case of Thasos, would not be absurd, given the size and importance of Naxos.

[1] Cf. Badian, *From Plataea to Potidaea* (1993) 77.

I. THUCYDIDES' PENTEKONTAETIA 83

The use of καί is commonplace. Although we have nothing like the classifications of adverbial καί for Thucydides such as E. Powell has made for Herodotos, Denniston (p. 307) writes of the word following demonstratives as follows: "The particle here denotes that the words *following* it add something, and something important, to the content of the demonstrative" (italics supplied).[2] It is only *after* (μετά) the completion of the siege of Naxos (πολιορκία παρεστήσαντο) that the battle of Eurymedon took place. There is no suggestion of "contemporaneity."

In Hiller's map of Naxos (*IG* XII.5.2 p. xxiii), the largest island of the Cyclades, measuring about 19 miles in length and 15 in breadth at its widest point, he marks the town of Naxos at the site of the temple on the west coast. There are other ancient sites on the island, near the village of Sangri, at Epano Kastro, near Philoti, etc. I have visited Naxos, but my goal was the quarry with the famous colossal archaic statue at the northern end of the island. Kontoleon, in the *Princeton Encyclopedia*, says that the polis lay on a hill commanding the harbor, and that the acropolis is below the modern town, Kastro.[3] L. Talcott and Alison Frantz, *This is Greece* (New York 1941) 47, publish a photograph by Carl Blegen of the modern town at the water's edge. R. V. Schoder, *Ancient Greece from the Air* (London 1974) p. 150, publishes an aerial photograph of the city, marking the excavation site. In *PAE* 1979 (1981) pl. 155, Lamprinoudakis publishes a high-altitude photograph of the modern town and the partly submerged harbor. There has been a change in sea-level here as in most

---

[2] I was taught that this use of καί gave a thin underlining to what followed, which is in accord with Denniston. I can thank the gods for having given me no one but Gildersleeve or Shorey PhDs as teachers from high school through college and well into graduate school.

[3] The island had several names in antiquity: Στρογγύλη from its shape, Διονυσίας from its excellent wine, μικρὰ Σικελία from the fertility of its soil (Diodoros 5.50–52; Pliny 4.12.22), and Δία (Ovid). For a recent description of Naxos, see W. Ekschmitt, *Die Kykladen* (Mainz 1993) 263–273.

84 THUCYDIDES' PENTEKONTAETIA AND OTHER ESSAYS

places in Greece. D. Müller, *Topographischer Bildkommentar* (1987) 984–986, offers four photographs of the city and island. D. Leekley and R. Noyes, *Archaeological Excavation in the Greek Islands* (1975) 48, report that at least 19 sites have been identified on the island, many Cycladic and Mycenaean. My cursory search has turned up no reports of fortification walls at the town of Naxos, where the excavations of Kontoleon and Lamprinoudakis have unearthed the agora and tetragonal stoa. Scranton, Winter, and Lawrence give no report on any walls at Naxos, although one of the four-storied towers in the countryside is famous. Neither in Müller's account nor that of Kaletsch in S. Lauffer's *Griechenland: Lexikon* (1989) 461–465, is there any mention of walls. The town was famous in Venetian times, when much of the materiel must have been used for building purposes; but traces of walls may remain in the submerged part, if they existed.

By contrast, the ancient walls of Thasos and Samos were extensive and in part well preserved. In fig. 4 of G. Daux, *Guide de Thasos* (1967), the author publishes a sketch of the circuit wall with its many towers and gates. The walls date from about 412 B.C., but were built on earlier foundations. The mighty fortifications round the city of Samos were originally more than 6.4 kilometers in length and are regarded as of the sixth century: so G. Shipley, *A History of Samos* (Oxford 1987) 77. They are preserved today on high ground.

Herodotos (6.96) writes of the Persians under Datis and Artaphernes in 490 B.C. (Loeb):

> When they approached Naxos from the Icarian sea and came to land (for it was Naxos which the Persians purposed first to attack), the Naxians, mindful of what had before happened, fled away to the mountains, not abiding their coming. The Persians enslaved all of them that they caught, and burnt even their temples and their city; which done, they set sail for the other islands.

I. THUCYDIDES' PENTEKONTAETIA

Later, Naxos sent only four ships to Salamis (8.46.3). By contrast, Thasos offered no resistance (6.44) and later received and feasted Xerxes' army (7.118). In the second period of the quota-lists, Naxos paid much less than half of that of its smaller neighbor Paros, but this is partly explained by the settlement of Athenian klerouchs on the island: *ATL* 3.286–287. Thereafter, Naxos does not bulk large in the literature, although a famous battle was fought off its shores in the fourth century.

We have no archaeological grounds for assuming a siege of two or more years for Naxos in comparing its low position at the water's edge with the formidable fortifications of Thasos and Samos.

The determination of the date of the Athenian seizure of Naxos involves another passage in Thucydides, one not in the Pentekontaetia, which has defied convincing resolution in spite of many attempts: so Gomme (*HCT* 1.402); Rhodes (*Historia* 19 [1970] 399–400);[4] Hornblower (1 p. 222). Hornblower provides recent bibliography:

> The problem has been endlessly discussed: see Frost, *Plutarch's Themistocles: A Historical Commentary* (Princeton, 1980), 206–8, retaining 'Naxos', as does Milton (see introductory n. to 128 above). Forrest, 'Pausanias and Themistokles Again' (above, 131.1 n.) adopts a suggestion of Lewis, most fully developed in *Towards a Historian's Text*, 66ff., 160ff. (see also *Historia*, 2 (1953/4), 418 n. 1), that the text of Th. was altered from Θάσον to Νάξον by a scholar in antiquity who 'knew' from Ephorus that Themistokles was received by Xerxes, not Artaxerxes, i.e. in the early 460s, and went past Naxos, not Thasos, On this view 'Thasos' is right. But I in-

[4]Rhodes (p. 394) writes, "The very 'fact' that Themistocles passed any island to which the Athenians were laying siege may be not a fact but merely the embellishment of the less interesting truth that 'Themistocles crossed the Aegean in my ship and urged me to steer clear of the Athenians at all costs.' It may be unwise to assume even that one or other of the rival versions must be true." This sentiment is repeated in *CAH* V[2].66.

86   THUCYDIDES' PENTEKONTAETIA AND OTHER ESSAYS

cline to agree with Rhodes that neither the Thasos nor the Naxos tradition should be used for the reconstruction of chronology, both being equally worthless.

We extract the critical features of Themistokles' flight in Thucydides 1.137 (Loeb):

> And when, not long afterwards, the Athenians and Lacedaemonians came and made urgent demands for him, Admetus would not give him up, but, since he wished to go to the King, gave him an escort overland to Pydna on the other sea, the capital of Alexander. There he found a merchant vessel putting off for Ionia, and going on board was driven by a storm to the station of the Athenian fleet which was blockading Naxos. ... The captain did as he was bidden, and after riding out the gale for a day and a night just outside the Athenian station, duly arrived at Ephesus. ... Then proceeding into the interior with one of the Persians who dwelt on the coast, he sent on a letter to King Artaxerxes son of Xerxes, who had lately come to the throne.

Plutarch also relates at length the flight of Themistokles at the conclusion of which he writes (*Themistokles* 27.1, Loeb):

> Now Thucydides and Charon of Lampsacus relate that Xerxes was dead, and that it was his son Artaxerxes with whom Themistocles had his interview; but Ephorus and Dinon and Clitarchus and Heracleides and yet more besides have it that it was Xerxes to whom he came. With the chronological data Thucydides seems to me more in accord, although these are by no means securely established.

There are two critical passages in the preceding text:

> And Thucydides says that he made his way across the country to the sea, and set sail from Pydna, no one of the passengers knowing

I. THUCYDIDES' PENTEKONTAETIA   87

who he was until, when the vessel had been carried by a storm to Naxos, to which the Athenians at that time were laying siege, he was terrified, and disclosed himself to the master and the captain of the ship, and partly by entreaties, partly by threats, actually declaring that he would denounce and vilify them to the Athenians as having taken him on board at the start in no ignorance but under bribes, — in this way compelled them to sail by and make the coast of Asia. ... After landing at Cymé, and learning that many people on the coast were watching to seize him, and especially Ergoteles and Pythodorus, — for the chase was a lucrative one to such as were fond of getting gain from any and every source, since two hundred talents had been publicly set upon his head by the King, — he fled to Aegae, a little Aeolic citadel. Here no one knew him except his host Nicogenes, the wealthiest man in Aeolia, and well acquainted with the magnates of the interior. With him he remained in hiding for a few days.

We now have one important piece of evidence about the chronology which was not known to Gomme and *ATL* 3, when they prepared their chronological tables. Whereas there was a Babylonian cuneiform legal text, noted by M. E. White in *JHS* 84 (1964) 142 n. 13, which seemed to place Xerxes' death in December 465 B.C., this text has been misread according to M. W. Stolper, *JHS* 108 (1988) 196–198. On the other hand, Stolper publishes a Babylonian astronomical text, containing reports of lunar eclipses, from which it is deduced that Xerxes died between August 4–8 465 B.C. According to his chronological table (*HCT* 1.394–396), the former text seems to have been known to Gomme. After arriving in Asia Minor, Themistokles sent a letter to Artaxerxes who had lately come to the throne (νεωστὶ βασιλεύοντα). Themistokles' arrival in Asia Minor is to be dated after August 465.

In the quotations from Plutarch, we note that Plutarch puts Themistokles' disembarkation port in Asia at Kyme, not at Ephesos as Thucydides has it, although he had clearly read the

88   THUCYDIDES' PENTEKONTAETIA AND OTHER ESSAYS

historian. Moreover, the oldest manuscript of Plutarch, the Seitenstettensis of saec. XI-XII, reads Θάσον rather than Νάξον of the Loeb. Wilamowitz, in *Aristoteles und Athen* 1 (1893) 150, reviewing the career of Themistokles, postulated that Θάσον represented the authentic reading in Thucydides. Plutarch is very deliberate in stating Θουκυδίδης ... φησιν. The reading of Thasos was adopted for Plutarch in the old Teubner of Lindskoz and in the Budé (1961), and was supported for Plutarch by Flacelière in *REA* 55 (1953) 5–8, who believed that there were rival versions. We believe that Thasos was the reading in Thucydides.

In *CR* 76 (1962) 15–16,[5] F. J. Frost maintained that the correct reading in Thucydides was for Naxos, arguing that the route of the merchant ship from Pydna was due southeast through the Sporades and across the open sea to the southern tip of Chios, in the course of which it was blown to Naxos. The distance from the southern tip of the Sporades at Skopelos to the southern tip of Chios is about 125 nautical miles. From the southern tip of Skyros to that of Chios is 70 nautical miles of open sea. Skyros was occupied by the Athenians: Thucydides 1.98.2. From the southern tip of Chios to the town of Naxos measures a little more than 70 nautical miles. There is a chain of islands (Andros Tenos, Mykonos) intervening, one of which would be more likely for a ship in distress. Naxos lies almost due south of Chios. If the gale blew from the northeast, the ship would have been carried towards Tenos or Mykonos. To reach Kyme/Ephesos from Naxos, Themistokles' ship would have had to reverse direction against adverse winds. Indeed, I wonder whether a merchant ship of the

---

[5]See the same author's *Plutarch's Themistokles* (Princeton 1980) 206–208. Earlier, R. J. Lenardon, *Historia* 8 (1959) 40–44, had strongly defended the reading of Νάξον, arguing on the basis of the occurrence of the word in other sources recounting the episode. He is mistaken, however, in saying that the context of Plutarch's passage requires Naxos. The context requires only that the island in question be under siege by the Athenians.

I. THUCYDIDES' PENTEKONTAETIA 89

period would have withstood a gale which blew it 70 miles off course.[6]

Of paramount consideration to my mind is the likely route for a merchant ship in the first half of the fifth century from Pydna to Kyme/Ephesos. I believe that, as Gomme has suggested in general terms (*JHS* 53 [1933] 16), merchant ships regularly crept along the coast. As he notes, there was a radical difference between warships and merchantmen. Rather than endangering his ship by sailing across the open sea, I believe that the captain would have followed the route of Xerxes' fleet, possibly using Xerxes' canal, which Herodotos (7.24) states was wide enough to float two triremes rowed abreast,[7] hugging the coast until north of Thasos, he was blown south to Thasos, then under siege, whence he sailed along the coast southeast to Lesbos and to Kyme/Ephesos. Thucydides says the merchant ship rode out the storm for a day and night ὑπὲρ τοῦ στρατοπέδου; so its position at the time the gale struck must have been near the island in question. Such a position accords well with one hugging the coast past Thasos, but not with the Sporades-Chios route. I do not know what is meant by Frost's reference to the "iron" coast of Thrake. There is a harbor at Eion on the Strymon and a large port at Neapolis/Kavalla. Between the two were the ports of Galepsos and Oisyme. To the east is a long stretch of low coast-

[6]Most of the modern literature is about warships. In the index to J. S. Morrison and R. T. Williams, *Greek Oared Ships* (Cambridge 1968), there are only two references to merchantmen. In the Tsopelas' map of Greece for tourists, his table gives the distances between the ports of Skopelos and Chios as 137 nautical miles and of Chios and Naxos as 88 nautical miles. I question that any ship would have been blown so far off course within 24 hours, or that a captain would have endangered his ship by taking such a route.

[7]For Xerxes' canal, see Thucydides 4.109.2; *The Liar School of Herodotos* (1993) 292. The statement that the captain rode out the gale for a day and a half without landing proves that the ship was not in dire distress and had some control over its course.

line, probably formed by the alluvium from the Nestos, with an airfield today. Alexandroupoli is on the coast, and between Kavalla and Alexandroupoli was the ancient coastal city of Abdera. The end maps in D. Lazarides, Ἀμφίπολις καί Ἄργιλος (Athens Center of Ekistics No. 13. 1972) mark heavy settlements in the region of the Strymonic Gulf and on the Thrakian coast opposite Thasos, which indicate considerable ancient traffic.

The Etesian, or "Yearly winds" as the ancients called them, blow from the northern quadrant. Our best guide to the winds of the Aegean today is the British Admiralty's three-volume geographical handbook on *Greece* (1935/45 ?), which charts winds for all ports. In 2 (1944) 224, the authors write:

> Most winds of gale force occur during winter, when winds strong enough to cause a rough sea in the Aegean blow between northeast and north-west, or between south-east and south-west. In summer, gales are rare and come almost entirely from northerly quarters. In this connexion it is interesting that the ancient Greeks did not go to sea in the winter and that they selected their harbours with a view to the north wind only: hence many of them face south, and are as exposed in the winter as the open sea.

Loomis, *Historia* 39 (1990) 489–490 n. 18, has an interesting passage on the Etesian winds, which collects ancient testimonia. When W. Leaf explored the Troad for his book *Strabo on the Troad* (Cambridge 1923), he wrote at length about the harbors of Sestos and Abydos, the passage of the Hellespont, and the strait of the Dardanelles forty statute miles in length. He observed that "the strong N.E. winds, the Etesians, blow for about nine months in the year.... The Etesian winds, though blowing strongly through the middle of the day, are generally light in the morning and evening." He noted that in his day the lower part of the strait was lively with tug boats for sailing vessels.

I. THUCYDIDES' PENTEKONTAETIA 91

The first and primary consideration in our judgment is to determine the route across the Aegean from Pydna to Kyme/Ephesos. I believe that merchantmen skirted the coast, and that when the gale arose Themistokles' ship was off Kavalla and was blown to Thasos. Next, we turn to the manuscript tradition. Following Wilamowitz, I suggest that Plutarch's copy of Thucydides, whom he cites 127 times,[8] represents a better tradition than that of our codices. We acknowledge that preserved codices of other authors in antiquity who mention the episode suggest that they had copies of Thucydides which read Naxos: Nepos 2 *Themistokles* 8.6; Polyainos 1.30.8; Pseudo-Themistokles *Epistle* 20. Different copies of Thucydides circulated in antiquity, and we are reminded of the one in minuscules and contractions used by Libanius in the fourth century (A. W. Spratt, *Book* III p. xi). Naxos was in the pre-archetype of our received codices. We do not believe that the port of Torone was Kolophon (5.2.2), nor have we hesitated to suggest that Therme should be read for Beroia in 1.61.4 to avoid having Kallias take his hoplites on a march of over 125 kilometers within three days when he had transports available at Pydna to cross the narrow part of the upper Thermaic Gulf. The first prerequisite for any student of Thucydides is a knowledge of the text with which he is working. The "Anhang" commentaries of the various volumes of the Classen-Steup edition are filled with discussions of places in which we cannot pronounce with certainty which of several alternatives Thucydides may have written. Many passages remain where the general meaning is fairly clear, but we can apply only provisional remedies. J. de Romilly's maxim, non auctoritate sed

---

[8] See W C. Helmbold and E. O'Neil, *Plutarch's Quotations* (1959) 71–72. C. Pelling's first paper in P. A. Stadter (ed.), *Plutarch and the Historical Tradition* (London 1992), shows that not only was Plutarch thoroughly familiar with Thucydides' work, but also Plutarch assumes that his reader will be no less so.

92   THUCYDIDES' PENTEKONTAETIA AND OTHER ESSAYS

judicio,[9] was based, not on corruptions in numerals and toponyms,[10] but on the general condition of the MSS., as exemplified in Hude's critical apparatus. We believe that an early hypothetical scribe of our archetype altered Kyme to Ephesos possibly because the ultimate destination is given as Ionia, and Kyme to him was Aiolian.[11] *ATL* 3.201, in debating the early membership of the League, postulated that Themistokles' merchant ship, the ultimate destination of which was Ionia, stopped at both cities. We do not dispute this, but believe that the ship first stopped at Kyme.

The next domino in the Naxos/Thasos chronology is the date of Pausanias' death. Studies of the problem include M. E. White, "Some Agiad Dates: Pausanias and his Sons," *JHS* 84 (1964) 140–152; P. J. Rhodes, "Thucydides on Pausanias and Themistokles," *Historia* 19 (1970) 387–400. See also Milton, *Historia* 28 (1979) 264–265.[12] The account of Pausanias' fate is given in 1.128.3–1.134.4, followed by the account of Themistokles' flight in 1.135.3–1.138.6. Pausanias died, having taken refuge in a sanctuary of Athena of the Brazen House at Sparta and having been starved out there. The Spartan authorities proceeded to use what they thought they had discovered to discredit the Athenian Themistokles, now ostracized and living in Argos. Forewarned, Themistokles fled to Kerkyra and then overland to Pydna. M. E.

[9]See *Essays* 168–169.

[10]For a selection of corrupt toponyms at the beginning of Book 8 of Strabo, see *Topography* 5.171.

[11]For the purpose of tribute payment, Kyme was Ionian. It is often surmised that Kyme was introduced into the record by Ephoros because he was born there, and Ephoros' corruption resulted in the reading of Thasos. See, for example, Cawkwell, *Auckland Classical Essays Presented to E. M. Blaiklock* (1970) 56 n. 18.

[12]For Pausanias at Byzantion, see Loomis, *Historia* 39 (1990) 486–492.

I. THUCYDIDES' PENTEKONTAETIA

White, p. 143, who charted the career of Pausanias and his sons,[13] states, "The lower limit, then, for Pausanias' death should be placed c. 467/6." In the *CAH²* V (1992) 101 (cf. p. 46), D. Lewis claims that Pausanias was starved out "c. 466." The exact date of Themistokles' ostracism is not known: "some time in the late 470s-early 460s," Hornblower, p. 220. For a sound paper on Pausanias, see Lazenby, *Hermes* 103 (1975) 235–251. In n. 46, he endorses the position that Themistokles' ship sailed past Thasos.

Battle of the Eurymedon. Thucydides puts the battle of the Eurymedon between the revolts of Naxos and Thasos. This has been regarded by many scholars (Jacoby [*CQ* 41 (1947) 3 n.1],[14] Wade-Gery, *ATL*, Cawkwell, Forrest, et al.) as confirmed by an episode recounted by Plutarch (*Kimon* 8.8) that at the Dionysia in the spring of 468 when Sophokles won his first dramatic victory, Kimon and his fellow generals were acclaimed when they entered the theater and were persuaded by the archon to be the judges. This acclaim and the honor of judging at the Dionysia were, it is suggested, the people's tribute to the victorious generals for the Eurymedon campaign the year before. See M. E. White, *JHS* 84 (1964) 147. There is, however, dissenting opinion about the connection; see A. Blamire, *Plutarch. Life of Kimon* (= *BICS* Suppl. 56) 1989..22 for bibliography, especially Milton, *His-*

---

[13]White's argument was that Pausanias must be allowed time to sire three sons, the eldest of whom Pleistoanax, being called νέος in 1.107.2, was, she concluded, under twenty at the battle of Tanagra.

[14]D. Lewis, *CAH* V² 45 n. 39, writes, "The suggestion about Cimon's judging of the tragedies was first made by Jacoby." Actually, the suggestion permeated the early literature, going back at least to the eminent grammarian, K. W. Krüger's *Historisch–philogische Studien* I (1837) 52; W. Pierson, *Philologus* 28 (1869) 333. Cf. Morris, *AJP* 7 (1886) 333, who explained the matter clearly. The early debate was whether the recognition was over the return of Theseus' bones or Eurymedon. Rhodes (*CAH* V² 67) finds a political basis for the award of the prize to Sophokles.

94 THUCYDIDES' PENTEKONTAETIA AND OTHER ESSAYS

toria 28 [1979] 269). The suggestion that generals were singled out to restore order seems weak. V. Ehrenberg (*Gnomon* 45 [1973] 671) supports the connection, "It is simply not good enough to say that 'the appointment as judges needs no other explanation than the authority of their office.' We know of no similar case." Diodoros (11.61.1) puts the battle under the archon for 470/69 B.C.

SECTION 6

DRABESKOS

Following his determination, based in part on a misunderstanding of the Greek participle, that Ithome is out of chronological order, Badian (pp. 80ff.) proceeds to Drabeskos, which, we are told (p. 80), "should no longer be misinterpreted to fit in with a view of his [Thucydides'] technique (i.e. chronological order) that is now known to be mistaken." Badian's interpretation of Drabeskos is rejected by both Hornblower (p. 155) and David Lewis (*CAH* V² 13) without detailed argument. Believing that the technique of chronological order may be defended for Drabeskos, we attempt to review the opinions of historians and archaeologists familiar with the region, which, although sometimes not conclusive, will point up the problems. There has been considerable archaeological activity in Eastern Makedonia, reported largely in Greek publications which may have escaped us. For all students of Makedonia, the new annual publication summarizing excavations, beginning with volume 1 (1987), *To Archaiologiko Ergo ste Makedonia kai Thrake* (*AEMTh*), is indispensible. I have seen five volumes.

After Kimon had vanquished a Thasian force at sea and blocked up the city by land as well as by sea, Thucydides reports what seems to have been part and parcel of the same scheme, the establishment of a powerful colony on Thrakian ground, resulting in a defeat near Drabeskos, a place evidently convenient for

I. THUCYDIDES' PENTEKONTAETIA

the mining district. The testimonia about Drabeskos include the following:

1. Thucydides 1.100.3 (Loeb):

About the same time they sent to the river Strymon ten thousand colonists, consisting of Athenians and their allies, with a view to colonising the place, then called Nine Ways, but now Amphipolis; and though these colonists gained possession of Nine Ways, which was inhabited by Edoni, yet when they advanced into the interior of Thrace they were destroyed at Drabescus in Edonia by the united forces of the Thracians, to whom the settlement of the place was a menace.

2. Thucydides 4.102.1–4 (Loeb):

During the same winter, Brasidas, with his allies in Thrace, made an expedition against Amphipolis, the Athenian colony on the river Strymon. This place, where the city now stands, Aristagoras the Milesian had tried to colonize before, when fleeing from the Persian king, but he had been beaten back by the Edonians. Thirty-two years afterwards the Athenians also made another attempt, sending out ten thousand settlers of their own citizens and any others who wished to go; but these were destroyed by the Thracians at Drabescus. Again, twenty-nine years later, the Athenians, sending out Hagnon son of Nicias as leader of the colony, drove out the Edonians and settled the place, which was previously called Ennea-Hodoi or Nine-Ways. Their base of operations was Eion, a commercial seaport which they already held, at the mouth of the river, twenty-five stadia distant from the present city of Amphipolis, to which Hagnon gave that name.

By giving a time-span of thirty-two years before and twenty-nine years later, Thucydides regards the entire Drabeskos episode as falling into one year.

96 THUCYDIDES' PENTEKONTAETIA AND OTHER ESSAYS

3. Herodotos 9.75 (tr. E. Powell):

> And in after time it befell Sophanes himself, when he was captain of the Athenians together with Leagrus the son of Glaucon, to be slain at Datum by the hand of the Edoni, fighting bravely for the gold-mines.

I interpret the Herodotos reference to be to the Drabeskos expedition, since Pausanias names the same two generals. Herodotos has given one of the objectives, or goals, of the expedition. This accords with the statement of Thucydides in 1.100.2 that the revolt of Thasos was caused by a quarrel about the emporia and mine on the coast opposite Thasos (περὶ τῶν ἐν τῇ ἀντιπέρας Θράκῃ ἐμπορίων καὶ τοῦ μετάλλου).[1]

4. Pausanias 1.29.4–5 (tr. Frazer):

> The first buried here were the men who in Thrace, after conquering the country as far as Drabescus, were surprised and massacred by the Edonians; it is said, too, that thunderbolts fell upon them. Amongst their generals were Leagrus, who had the chief command, and Sophanes of Decelia, who slew the Argive Eurybates. This Eurybates had won a victory in the pentathlum at Nemea, and he was fighting for the

---

[1]Plutarch *Kimon* 14.2–3, states that Kimon later acquired for Athens the gold mines on the mainland opposite Thasos and also annexed the territory which the Thasians had controlled. "From there, as it was thought in Athens, he could easily have invaded Makedon and appropriated a large part of it, and, because he would not do so, was accused of taking bribes from King Alexander." Having control of the mining area of Mount Pangaion, the Athenian charge was that he should have pushed westward into Makedon. Rather than endorsing the statement (Badian, p. 85), "That charge could hardly have been made if the Athenians had just suffered, in that same area, much the worst disaster in their history to date," I would interpret the passage to mean that the Athenians continued to persevere in deep interest in the area, including the gold mines and timber.

I. THUCYDIDES' PENTEKONTAETIA   97

Aeginetans when he fell. This was the third army which the Athenians
sent outside of Greece.

I expressed my disagreement with some translations of πρῶτοι as
an adverb in discussing the Demosion Sema in *War* 4.112–113, 178–
179. The casualty-list for what is taken by many scholars to be
that for the year of Drabeskos, although the toponym is not
preserved, has been most recently published (1994) as *IG* I³ 1144
(= I² 928), from which I extract two sentences:

> Fragmenta quinque quae ad monumentum ex pluribus stelis non
> contiguis compositum pertinere videntur. ... Nonnulli hic enu-
> merati Thaso, Eione, ad Hellespontum perierunt; quo loco plurimi
> ceciderint titulus non monstrat, sed prope certum est eos Drabesci
> a. 464 periisse; cf. Bradeen, loc. cit., quamquam dubitationes ali-
> quas profert Meiggs et de Eurymedonte cogitat Milton.[2]

Since Leagros is mentioned by Pausanias, his Drabeskos monument is securely tied to the Herodotos passage.

    5. Diodoros 11.70. Under the archonship of Archedemides
       (464/3 B.C.), Diodoros writes (Loeb tr.):

> For, speaking generally, the Athenians, now that they were making great
> advances in power, no longer treated their allies fairly, as they had
> formerly done, but were ruling them harshly and arrogantly.
> Consequently most of the allies, unable longer to endure their severity,
> were discussing rebellion with each other, and some of them, scorning
> the authority of the General Congress, were acting as independent states.
>
>   While these events were taking place, the Athenians, who were now
> masters of the sea, dispatched ten thousand colonists to Amphipolis,

---

[2]For Meiggs' position, see *The Athenian Empire* (Oxford 1971) 416. This is
endorsed by B. Isaac, *The Greek Settlement in Thrace* (Leiden 1986) 26–27, as
convincing. The reference to Milton is *Historia* 28 (1979) 267–269.

98 THUCYDIDES' PENTEKONTAETIA AND OTHER ESSAYS

recruiting a part of them from their own citizens and a part from the allies. They portioned out the territory in allotments, and for a time held the upper hand over the Thracians, but at a later time, as a result of their further advance into Thrace, all who entered the country of the Thracians were slain by a people known as the Edones.

Diodoros clearly puts the entire operation under one archonship. Diodoros, or his source, is following Thucydides. There is no conflict. Thucydides says that only after the colonists held sway over Ennea Hodoi (Ἐννέα ὁδούς ... ἐκράτησαν) did they advance into the mesogeia. Whether we place Ennea Hodoi at Hill 133 or Amphipolis, the entire region of the lower Strymon is vast. The Makedonian city was of huge dimensions. The distribution of land was a regular first step; see Thucydides 3.50.2, Diodoros 11.88.3, Pausanias 1.27.5, etc. After the colonists had wrested from the Edonians the lower Strymon district about the later Amphipolis, their further progress into the interior was opposed by the Thrakian tribes to whom the occupation of the district was a constant menace of war. Whether we place "together" (ξυμπάντων or ξύμπαντες) with the Athenians or the Thrakians, not all the widely separated Thrakian tribes can be meant; but it is natural to suppose that all those that were imperiled joined the Edonians. It seems remarkable that this passage (or any other in Diodoros) would be made the lynch-pin in inventing a scenario that the Ennea Hodoi-Drabeskos episode must have lasted several years.

> 6. Isokrates 8 *Peace* 86. We give the Loeb Greek text and translation of G. Norlin, who was President of the University of Colorado at a time when University Presidents were first-class scholars and has given us what I regard as the best text of Isokrates, certainly one of the better Loebs:
> καίτοι πλείοσι καὶ μείζοσι περιέπεσον ἐπὶ τῆς ἀρχῆς ταύτης τῶν ἐν ἅπαντι τῷ χρόνῳ τῇ πόλει

I. THUCYDIDES' PENTEKONTAETIA — 99

γεγενημένων. εἰς Αἴγυπτον μέν γε διακόσιαι πλεύσασαι τριήρεις αὐτοῖς τοῖς πληρώμασι διεφθάρησαν, περὶ δὲ Κύπρον πεντήκοντα καὶ ἑκατόν· ἐν δὲ τῷ Δεκελεικῷ πολέμῳ μυρίους ὁ- πλίτας αὐτῶν καὶ τῶν συμμάχων ἀπώλεσαν, ἐν Σικελίᾳ δὲ τέτταρας μυριάδας καὶ τριήρεις τετ- ταράκοντα καὶ διακοσίας, τὸ δὲ τελευταῖον ἐν Ἑλλησπόντῳ διακοσίας.

And yet they were involved in more and greater disasters in the time of the empire than have ever befallen Athens in all the rest of her history. Two hundred ships which set sail for Egypt perished with their crews, and a hundred and fifty off the island of Cyprus; in the Decelean War they lost ten thousand heavy armed troops of their own and of their allies, and in Sicily forty thousand men and two hundred and forty ships, and, finally, in the Hellespont two hundred ships.

Where some editors, including the Budé, read ἐν Δάτῳ and historians have almost unanimously followed by referring the passage to Drabeskos, Norlin reads ἐν δὲ τῷ Δεκελεικῷ πολέ- μῳ. The reading was discussed at length in *War* 5.210. The manuscript Urbinas III and its derivative Ambrosianus 144 are reported as reading ἐν Δάτῳ. The vulgate tradition, including Vaticanus 65, the earliest manuscript, which was the basis of ear- lier editions before Bekker's discovery of Urbinas III, reads ἐν δὲ τῷ Πόντῳ. The reading of Norlin's text is found in an Egyptian papyrus of the first century A.C. He regards it as preferable be- cause of the loss of 10,000 "hoplites," whereas Thucydides says "colonists" for Drabeskos. Laistner, *CQ* 15 (1921) 81–82, favored the papyrus reading because the sequence would be in chrono- logical order. The true reading is immaterial to our investigation since Daton is attested in Herodotos 9.75. Indeed, if a learned scribe knew his Herodotos, it is easy to conjecture that he altered the text. But we refrain from speculation. When we have used Isokrates in the past, we have sometimes been shot down. I do not

100 THUCYDIDES' PENTEKONTAETIA AND OTHER ESSAYS

share the present enthusiasm for Isokrates, particularly by the Peace-at-any-Price cult, which masquerades under the name of Peace and Non-violence. While recognizing Isokrates' influence upon the oratorical art, his moral lessons, patriotic common-places, and self-satisfied reflections on the wonderful work of his life are sheer weariness. The intriguing feature about the three variations in the Isokrates readings is that they cannot be explained on palaeographical grounds. Some quasi-historians have been at work. I offer this observation as a reminder to any who may wish to combat my alteration of Naxos/Ephesos to Thasos/Kyme in the text of Thucydides 1.137, or to defend the reading of Κολοφωνίων instead of Κωφόν in 5.2.2 (*Essays* p. 1), or of Στράτος for the Akarnanian site called Lykoniko (*Essays* p. 217).

7. Scholiast to Aischines 2 *Embassy* 31 [Blass, 34 Dindorf] (tr. C. W. Fornara, *Archaic Times to the End of the Peloponnesian War* [Baltimore 1977] no. 62):

Aeschin. 2.31: As to the original possession of the territory and of the so-called Ennea Hodoi (Nine Ways) ....

Scholion: Ennea Hodoi. The Athenians met with misfortune nine times at the so-called Nine Ways, which is a place in Thrace now named Chersonesus. They suffered misfortune because of the curses of Phyllis, who loved Demophon and expected him to return in order to fulfill his promises to her. After going to the place nine times, since he did not come, she prayed for the Athenians to suffer misfortune that number of times at the place. The disasters occurred as follows: first, when Lysistratos, Lykourgos, and Kratinos campaigned against Eion on the (river) Strymon, (the Athenians) were destroyed by the Thracians after they seized Eion, in the archonship of Phaidon (476/5) at Athens. Second, the klerouchs with Leagros, in the archonship of Lysikrates. ... When Hagnon,

I. THUCYDIDES' PENTEKONTAETIA   101

the Athenian, colonized Ennea Hodoi, he named it Amphipolis, in
the archonship of Euthymenes (437/6) at Athens.

The scholiast reads Lysikrates, the name of the Athenian archon
of 453/2, which seems to most of us an impossibly late date for
Ennea Hodoi/Drabeskos. it is generally assumed that the error is
palaeographical, which makes Lysistratos (467/6), Lysanias
(466/5), and Lysitheos (465/4) candidates. Following the lead of
Lang, Badian, however, is an exception (pp. 85–86):

> It is clear that the only date for Drabescus that we have is the
> one (453/2) given by the scholiast. Now, a scholiast may, of course,
> get an archon's name wrong: in this particular note, the last of the
> five is in fact wrong — but it is a scribe's error, for we have gibber-
> ish (Καλαμινος for Καλλιμήδους) and not another name. Until
> we have a better date to set against it, we should surely accept the
> date he gives us, which gives the colony a perfectly plausible life of
> about twelve years, instead of proposing emendations that, what-
> ever their paleographic plausibility, do not make historical sense.

I fail to follow the logic, since militarily the emendation makes excellent sense. The only test that we have is that of the "scribe"
who clearly made an error in one or more proper names. But errors in proper names are too well known to detain us. In one
passage in Pausanias (10.10), we have half-a-dozen proven errors
in proper names, and the same is true in Dionysios *De Thuc.* 5.
Leagros is a correction for Leagoras of the scribe,[3] and, if correct,
securely ties the scholion to Herodotos 9.75 and to Pausanias
(1.29.5), who specifically names the general in connection with

[3]D. MacDowell gives a good discussion of Leagros in *RM* 102 (1959) 376–378.
Davies places his birth about 525. Unless we emend, the scholiast has omitted
the notorious disaster from his list, although he refers to it as a klerouchy. On
the confusion between 'klerouchs' and 'colonists' in later writers, see *ATL*
3.285.

102 THUCYDIDES' PENTEKONTAETIA AND OTHER ESSAYS

the monument for Drabeskos; see Davies, *APF* pp. 90–91. The general value of scholia in Aischines is not discussed, but we do not believe that our scholiast, whatever his date, had any evidence, independent of all our preserved sources, pointing to a four- or twelve-year campaign.

Since the chronology of Ephoros was not annalistic,[4] those who put credence in Diodoros usually favor the reading of Lysitheos, the archon preceding Diodoros' Archedemides, i.e. the spring or early summer of 464 B.C. In any case, all of our literary sources may be interpreted as putting the entire operation in one year.

TOPOGRAPHY

We are given three topographical check-points in connection with Thucydides' Drabeskos campaign:[5]

1. Ennea Hodoi
2. Drabeskos
   A. Mesogeia
3. Daton (Thrakian district) and Datos (Thasian town)

1. Ennea Hodoi.[6] It is not with pride of discovery, but for lack of any contradictory evidence, that we believe that Ennea Hodoi is to be located on the broad flat-top hill with an elevation of 133 m., three kilometers to the north of Amphipolis, sherded by E. Vanderpool and myself in 1960 and offered as a candidate by us in *Topography* 1.42–43 with pls. 45–50 and in an Appendix by Vanderpool on pp. 46–48. For the Edonian inscribed sherd, see J. and L. Robert, *REG* 80 (1967) 507. All the sherds we saw on the

---

[4]See Meiggs, *The Athenian Empire* (Oxford 1972) 452–453.

[5]The site of Eion has been surveyed by a British team; see *War* 5.211 n. 311.

[6]For the explanation of the name, as given by Hyginus 59, see *Topography* 3.321. Perdrizet (*BCH* 46 [1922] 40–42) believes it is a Greek corruption of a Thrakian name.

I. THUCYDIDES' PENTEKONTAETIA

surface were earlier than the foundation of Amphipolis. Subsequently, trenches were dug by Lazarides on Hill 133, as conveniently summarized in *BCH* 89 (1965) 824–828 with figs. 6–10, and 90 (1966) 881–885 with figs. 13–22.[7] Fragments of a Roman relief were found; but the sherds date from prehistoric to early classical. A short stretch of an early wall of small stones with clay foundation was exposed at a depth of about 1 meter.[8]

The other side of the coin is that Lazarides informed us that no pre–437 B.C. sherds had been found in his extensive excavations within Amphipolis.[9] The excavations are continuing, but

[7] For the date of the numerous graves, see Lazarides in *Princeton Encyclopedia* pp. 53–54. For a later summary in English, see *AAA* 8 (1975) 65–75.

[8] B. Isaac, *The Greek Settlements in Thrace until the Macedonian Conquest* (Leiden 1986) provides good bibliography, but writes without autopsy. On pp. 5 and 7, he states that an early inscription (= *SEG* 27.249) with Parian lettering was found near Hill 133. Actually, it was found in the fortification wall of Amphipolis.

[9] We have followed excavation reports throughout the lifetime of Lazarides, and subsequently those of his daughter, and visited the site several times; but there has been no report of artifacts within the walls dateable to the first half of the fifth century, although the excavators have found within the walls on the museum site a grave with a gold wreath which they suggest might be that of Brasidas or Hagnon: *ADelt*. 31 (1976 [1984])*Chr*. 304–307. Thucydides (5.11.1) says that Brasidas was buried ἐν τῇ πόλει πρὸ τῆς νῦν ἀγορᾶς οὔσης. On the left bank of the Strymon and outside the northern wall, a sanctuary has been found with early pottery: *PAE* 1975. 64–65. Our studies of the battle of Amphipolis were published in *Topography* 1.30–48, and *Topography* 3.298–346. As discussed in *Topography* 8.142 n. 51, there was one stretch of polygonal wall running for 143.30 m. (*Topography* 1 pls. 33b, 34a, b, and c), which I have taken as part of the southern wall of 424 B.C. The most recent study of the battle is that of Barbara Mitchell, "Kleon's Amphipolitan Campaign," *Historia* 40 (1991) 170–182. In *Mnem*. 26 (1973) 376–368, I attempted to refute the charges of Woodhead, *Mnem*. 13 (1960) 289–307, that Thucydides had twisted and

104 THUCYDIDES' PENTEKONTAETIA AND OTHER ESSAYS

pending further discoveries, Hill 133 is a logical candidate for Ennea Hodoi. It is marked on various maps in Lazarides' *Amphipolis kai Argilos* (Athens 1972) with a question mark.

In reply to those who wish to conjure up a scenario of Athenian occupation for many years, we would observe that it would seem highly probable that 10,000 colonists in a foreign and hostile land would have constructed a formidable circuit wall of polygonal masonry as a place of refuge. Moreover, they would have left considerable archaeological remains, whatever the site.

Harpokration glosses Ἐννέα ὁδοί as τόπος ἐν Θρᾴκη περὶ τὴν Ἀμφίπολιν. Thucydides tells us that Ennea Hodoi was later called Amphipolis. It is important to note that Herodotos, Thucydides, Strabo, and others used the name of a polis to designate the entire chora of a city. For confusion over this usage, see *Essays* 205–206. Add Owen on Euripides *Ion* 294; Wade-Gery in *HSCP* Suppl. 1 (1940) 155; Jebb on Sophokles *Phil.* 4. See, in particular, Strabo 8.3.31.356. This usage extends well into Roman times, where we have Thasos for the chora of Thasos on

---

suppressed the facts of the Amphipolis campaign, preferring Diodoros, although the latter article has been translated into the *Wege* series and continues to be cited by Thucydidean detractors without reviewing the topography and the epigraphical evidence. Our site for Trailos has now been confirmed by excavations; see, for example, *JHS Arch. Reports* 1992–93. 59. We add that in the latest issue of *Mnemosyne* to reach us (48 [1995] fasc. 2), the inside cover contains the announcement that in a future issue, an article will be published by I. G. Spence with the title, "Thucydides, Woodhead, and Kleon." Since our article, "The Woodheadean Interpretation of Kleon's Amphipolitan Campaign," was published in *Mnem.*, we look forward to new light on the subject.

I. THUCYDIDES' PENTEKONTAETIA   105

the Thracian mainland, including some segment of the Via Egnatia: J. P. Adams, *Ancient Macedonia* 4 (1986) 33. Ennea Hodoi was in the chora of Amphipolis.[10]

2. Drabeskos. The reader may wish to consult the contour map of Papazoglou in *BCH* 106 (1982) 90, which will give a topographical picture of the region. Paul Collart, who says in his Introduction that he spent more than ten years in the region and assembled the literature through 1936, in his two-volume study, *Philippes. Ville de Macédoine* (Paris 1937) 67 n. 1, writes of Drabeskos as follows:

> Cf. P. Perdrizet, *loc. laud.*, p. 14 à 17. Le nom de Drabeskos s'est conservé dans celui de Sdravik, jusqu' à nos jours. Cette identification, proposée déjà par E.-M. Cousinéry (*Voyage dans la Macédoine*, t. II, p. 51) et acceptée par Th. Desdevises-du-Dézert (*Géographie ancienne de la Macédoine*, p. 396), puis, plus récemment, par S. Casson (*Macedonia, Thrace and Illyria*, p. 45), par G. Glotz (*Histoire grecque*, t. II, p. 135) et par G. Bakalakis ('Εφ. ἀρχ., 1936, p. 40, note 1 du tirage à part), est établie, en outre, par les témoignages de Strabon (*Geogr.*, VII, 331, fragm. 33: εἰσὶ δὲ περὶ τὸν Στρυμονικὸν κόλπον πόλεις καὶ ἕτεραι, οἷον Μύρκινος, Ἄργιλος, Δραβῆσκος, Δάτον ...) et d'Appien (*Bell. civ.*, IV, 105, § 440: ... ἐκ δὲ τῆς δύσεως πεδίον μέχρι Μυρκίνου τε καὶ Δραβήσκου καὶ ποταμοῦ Στρυμόνος, τριακοσίων που καὶ πεντήκοντα σταδίων, εὔφορον πάνυ καὶ καλόν ...), qui placent Drabeskos à l'extrémité occidentale de la plaine de Philippes, dans le voisinage de Myrkinos et du Strymon. Les auteurs qui se sont cependant prononcés contre elle (W. M. Leake, *Travels in Northern Greece*, t. III, p. 183; G. Perrot, *Rev. arch.*, 1860[II], p. 73; Heuzey-Daumet, *Mission archéologique de Macédoine*, p. 140 à 142;

[10]D. Müller, *Topographischer Bildkommentar zu den Historien Herodots* (Tübingen 1987) 76–77, regards Hill 133 as one of three candidates for Myrkinos, which I think is impossible.

106 THUCYDIDES' PENTEKONTAETIA AND OTHER ESSAYS

Philippson, dans Pauly-Wissowa, *RE*, s.v. *Drabeskos*, col. 1613; R. Kiepert, *FOA*, XVI, p. 5) ont considéré comme un argument décisif la présence, sur la *Table de Peutinger*, d'une localité nommée Daravescos et située à douze milles au nord de Philippes, sur la route d'Héraklée de Sintique. Mais l'autorité de ce document, d'époque tardive, ne saurait être mise en balance avec celle des témoignages citees plus haut, d'autant moins que, pour la région de Philippes, il est impossible d'accepter sans modifications les itinéraires portés sur la *Table*. Comme, néanmoins, l'on a tout lieu de croire que cette station de Daravescos doit être identifiée avec Drama (cf. *infra*, p. 507), il faut admettre qu'elle n'est pas la Drabeskos dont parle Thucydide; car on ne peut, sur ce point, suivre K. J. Beloch (*Greichische Geschichte*, 2ᵉ éd., t. II 1, p. 148, note 2), qui tente de tout concilier en faisant passer par Sdravik la route d'Héraklée de Sintique à Philippes.

Beloch had written as follows:

Drabeskos (*Daravescos*) lag nach der Peutingerschen Tafel an der Straße von Philippoi nach Herakleia Sintike, 12 Milien vor ersterer Stadt und 8 vom Strymon; die eine dieser Zahlen muß verderbt sein, und zwar die erstere, oder es ist zwischen *Philippis* und *Daravescos* eine Station ausgefallen; denn Drabeskos lag nach Appian *Bürgerkr.* IV 105 nicht weit von Myrkinos und dem Strymon. Vgl. Perdrizet, *Klio* X, 1910, S. 14 f.

Again, on p. 507 n. 2, Collart wrote:

En raison de l'analogie des deux noms et de la distance portée sur la Table entre Daravescos et Philippes, l'identification de Daravescos avec Drama n'est guère discutable (cf. C. Müller, ad Ptol., III, 12, 127, p. 510). En revanche, la localisation à Drama de Drabeskos, où les Athéniens subirent, en 465 avant J.-C., un désastre retentissant, se heurte à d'insurmontables objections (cf. *supra*, p. 67 et note 1). K. J. Beloch, qui l'a reconnu, propose de

I. THUCYDIDES' PENTEKONTAETIA

modifier les données de la Table de Peutinger de telle sorte que Daravescos puisse être placée à proximité du Strymon et de Myrkinos (*Griechische Geschichte*, 2e éd., t. II 1, p. 148, note 2). Cette hypothèse n'est pas compatible avec les résultats de notre enquête sur le réseau routier de la région de Philippes, et l'on admettra, avec P. Perdrizet (*Klio*, X, 1910, p. 17), qui'il y eut, dans cette région, deux localités distinctes aux noms analogues, l'une, Drabeskos, à Sdravik, au ve siècle avant J.-C., l'autre, Daravescos, à Drama, à l'époque romaine.

The most recent commentator on the site in a non-Thucydidean context is R. Baladié in the 1989 Budé of Strabo VII (p. 281):

Drabeskos *Drabescus* fr. 33: Ville de Macédoine de la basse vallée du Strymon qui, probablement, n'était plus qu'une komé d'Amphipolis à lépoque de Strabon. Voisine de Myrkinos (cf. Appien. *De bell. ciu.*, IV, 105), on a proposé de la reconnaître (Samsaris, p. 142) à des vestiges antiques qui se trouvent au lieu-dit Phragala, dans la plaine à 2 km au sud du village moderne de Drabeskos, sur la rive gauche et près du confluent de l'Angitis avec le Strymon, au N.-O. du district minier du Pangée.

The reference Baladié gives is D. K. Samsaris, Ἱστορικὴ γεωγραφία τῆς Ἀνατολικῆς Μακεδονίας κατα τὴν ἀρχαιότητα, Thessaloniki 1976, who on pages 142–143 writes:

Στὴν τοποθεσία αὐτὴ βρέθηκαν τελευταῖα, διάφορα ἀρχαιολογικὰ εὑρήματα (κιονόκρανα, ἐπιγραφὲς ρωμ. ἐποχῆς, νομίσματα κἄ.) καὶ πιθανῶς ἀπὸ δῶ προέρχονται καὶ οἱ ἀρχαιότητες (ἕνας βωμὸς καὶ ἕνα ἐπίγραμμα τοῦ 4ου–3ου π.Χ. αἰ.) πού ἐντόπισε τὸ 1899 ὁ P. Perdrizet, (Scaptésylé, 16) μέσα καὶ κοντὰ στὸ χωριό.

108 THUCYDIDES' PENTEKONTAETIA AND OTHER ESSAYS

Samsaris made a survey of the region. Subsequently, in *ADelt.* 42 (1987 [1992]) 450–451, under the heading Μαυρόλοφος — Δραβήσκος, is published a report that during ploughing at Φραγκάλα were found late tombs and a wall of stone, brick, and concrete and by it a marble base. Part of an archaic bronze necklace was turned over by the landowner, which is taken to have come from a field one kilometer to the west, where there are tombs of poros stone not yet published by the Archaeological Service:

Στο όργωμα του χωραφιού αριθ. 2018 Κοινότητας Μαυρολόφου, ιδιοκτησίας Ανεστάκη Σταύρου του Μανούση κατοίκου Δραβήσκου, βρέθηκαν τον Οκτώβριο του 1987 υπολείμματα τοίχου. Το χωράφι είναι 500 μ. περίπου δυτικά από το Μαυρόλοφο και βρίσκεται στη θέση Φραγκάλα, που εκτείνεται και στην περιοχή της κοινότητας Δραβήσκου και όπου παλιότερα είχαν βρεθεί ρωμαϊκές και βυζαντινές αρχαιότητες.

Ο τοίχος είναι χτισμένος με πέτρες, πήλινες πλίνθους και ασβσετοκονίαμα ως συνδετικό υλικό. Στο σημείο του τοίχου βρέθηκε και μαρμάρινη βάση κίονα με εγκοπές σε δύο πλευρές, μάλλον για θωράκιο που μετατοπίστηκε στο όργωμα από την αρχική της θέση.

Από τον Ανεστάκη παραδόθηκε χάλκινη αμφικωνική ψήφος περιδεραίου, αρχαϊκής εποχής, που δήλωσε ότι προέρχεται από το χωράφι του αριθ. 1283 Κοινότητας Δραβήσκου (αριθ. ευρ. Μ. Καβάλας Μ 1601). Το χωράφι βρίσκεται στη θέση Μαλαθράδες 1,5 χλμ. περίπου δυτικά από το Δραβήσκο και σύμφωνα με πληροφορίες του κ. Ανεστάκη είχαν βρεθεί τάφοι σε παλιότερες ισοπεδώσεις, χωρίς δυστυχώς να ειδοποιηθεί η Αρχαιολογική Υπηρεσία. Αυτό που διαπιστώθηκε τώ-

I. THUCYDIDES' PENTEKONTAETIA

ρα ήταν αρκετές πλάκες από πωρόλιθο, που πιθανώς να ανήκουν σε κατεστραμμένους τάφους.

In 1995, we visited Maurolophos and located Phrangela 500 meters west of the town. The name is applied to a spring in a depression, north of a bridge which carries a new road to Serres, now under construction. We sherded the fields in the immediate area, but found only medieval pottery and tiles. The site may have been a Frankish one. However, on a large archaeological map of the province in the Kavalla Museum, "Drabeskos" is marked as a site with classical remains, as is Myrkinos near the junction of the Angites and Strymon. Drabeskos is two kilometers north of Maurolophos. This area of rolling hills is immense, and it is difficult to conceive of land more favorable for action by cavalry. Our inspection was restricted to Maurolophos. The only site which is clearly Edonion is Hill 133. As J. Camp surveyed the landscape with his experienced topographical eye, he spotted a hill, called Philokoryphe, which looked promising as a site, but it proved to be a prehistoric one with much surreptitious digging, apparently unpublished. It is located on the western side of the Angites, near Myrkinos.

Since Thucydides says that Drabeskos was in Edonia (or Hedonia), the location of that Thrakian tribe is part of our problem. Here we are dependent upon Hammond. In *HM* 2 Maps 2 (p. 66) and 3 (p. 67), pp. 72–73; and 1 (p. 427), Hammond places the Edones in a district including the junction of the Strymon and Angites extending northwest to Lake Prasias,[11] where mines are reported, although on Map 4 (p. 128) he marks Drabeskos at what appears to be Drama without discussing that site.

The next part of our problem is the routes of the Peutinger Table and the Via Egnatia. We have seen above that Collart and

---

[11]The problem of the identification of Lakes Prasias and Kerkinitis is discussed by E. N. Borza, *The Ancient History Bulletin* 3 (1989) 60.

Perdrizet rejected the designation Draveskos on the Peutinger Table as evidence for a classical site of that name. Scholars who have studied the via Egnatia in the field are agreed that the segment from Amphipolis to Philippi did not go to modern Drama. See the maps of D. Lazaridis, *Amphipolis kai Argilos* (1972) pl. 8; J. P. Adams in *Ancient Makedonia* 4 (1986) 22; and, in particular, Papazoglou, *BCH* 106 (1982) 90. Cf. Adams in *AM* 5 (1993) 29–39. It ran north of Mount Pangaion from Amphipolis– Zdravik (mod. Drabeskos)–Kalambaki–Philippi. The Peutinger Table, by contrast, takes one north of Amphipolis along the right bank of the Strymon to Heraklea Stantica, then east to Scotusa (not to be confused with the well-known Skotoussa near Pharsalos), Sarxa, Strymon, Darvescos, Philippi. See Karte 163 in K. Miller, *Itineraria Romana* (1916). This latter route is studied by D. K. Samsaris in *Ancient Makedonia* 4 (1986) 541–548.[12] The "Strymon" of the Table is far removed from that river, being a northern tributary of the Angites.

D. K. Samsaris has traced the route of the Peutinger Table from Herakleia Sintika to Philippi. In *RE* s.v. Strymon (1931) 393, Oberhummer collects the testimonia for that river, concluding, "Eine Station S. verzeichnet Tab. Peut. VIII zwischen Sarxa und Drabeskos, also abseits vom Strom und jedenfalls an falscher Stelle, s. K. Miller Itin. Rom. 522. 585, 599. Die Itinerare kennen sie nicht." Since the Table is wrong about the two sites preceding "Draveskos" (Sarxa for Serrai and Strymon for Angites), and we lack any epigraphical evidence, the assumption that the scribe

[12]For bibliography on the Via Egnatia, see F. W. Walbank, *Historia Einzelschr.* 40 (1983) 131–147. As reported in *Topography* 6.123–125, our search for two impressive Roman bridges with six and two arches which carried the Via Egnatia between Philippi and Amphipolis near modern Symbole proved that since the time of Collart (1937) one of the bridges (pl. 198) which spanned the Angites has been covered over and the other could not be located. The roads and rivers have been redirected.

also made an error in "Draveskos" would allow us to reconcile all the evidence known to me.[13] He applied not only the name Strymon, but a town near the Strymon, to a region to the northwest. The former name of the modern Drabeskos, two kilometers removed from Samsaris' site of Phragala, was Sdravik = 'ς Δραβήκι, with the addition of the preposition as Stamboul, Stalimene (Lemnos), etc. See Hesseling, *REG* 3 (1890) 189ff.[14]

Taking our cue from Collart, an alternative is to assume that in late Roman times the natives revived the name of "Draveskos," as they did with that of Krenides (Dio 47.35). According to Nicolet, the Peutinger Table does not reflect the map of Agrippa, but roads of the fourth or fifth century A.C.

Finally, we note that no archaeological evidence is adduced by Badian, who holds that the early fifth century B.C. Drabeskos was at Drama.[15]

A. Μεσόγεια. Concerning the phrase προελθόντες δὲ τῆς Θρᾴκης ἐς μεσόγειαν διεφθάρησαν ἐν Δραβησκῷ, Badian writes (p. 83):

> The aorist προελθόντες makes it clear that the colonists *had* advanced into the *mesogeia* before they were annihilated. In other words, we must deduce that Drabescus was in what he called the Thracian *mesogeia*. Would a march taking them about ten kilometers (a total of about twelve and a half kilometers from the coast)

[13]There are other errors in the Table. In *Essays* 184, we noted that Kaledon and the Evenos river were misplaced. Cf. Gisinger, *RE* s.v. Peutingeriana (1938) 1407–1410.

[14]Zahrnt in S. Lauffer's *Griechenland* (Munich 1989) 201–202, writes, "In byzantinischen Urkunden taucht er als Dorf unter dem Namen Astrabikion auf."

[15]E. N. Borza, *The Ancient History Bulletin* 3 (1989) 64, writes, "Wherever one wishes to put Roman Dravescus, the location of Drabeskos in the lower Strymon valley must be regarded as virtually certain."

112 THUCYDIDES' PENTEKONTAETIA AND OTHER ESSAYS

take them into the *mesogeia*? I think this is very unlikely. There are few, if any, demes in the much smaller *mesogeia* of Attica that are so close (by road) to the coast, even in the east, where they come closest. Thucydides himself regards Stratus as being in the *mesogeia* of Acarnania (2.102.1: just possibly also Coronta, which is indeed much closer — but probably not, since it is implied that the Athenians took it on their return from Stratus to the sea). He appears to regard an area not too far from Aegitium as being in the *mesogeia* of Aetolia (3.95). These places are a considerable distance from the coast. (His other uses of the word are unfortunately not illuminating.) Enlarge the picture to the scale of Thrace, and the use of the term for a place so close to the coast seems inconceivable.

Any student who consults the examples in *TGL* could put the matter aright. There are many instances in Strabo, Xenophon, and Polybios (23). In 13.59.1.611, Strabo writes, ἐν δὲ τῇ μεσογαίᾳ τῶν Ἁλικαρνάσεων, "in the interior of the Halicarnassians." Polybios states, (πύλη) ἐπὶ τὸ μεσόγαιον φέρουσα (13.4.6), (κόλπος) προβαίνων εἰς τὴν μεσόγαιαν (4.13.6). Herodotos (18 examples) uses the phrase, τὴν μεσόγαιαν τάμνων τῆς ὁδοῦ (7.124, 9.89.4), ἐς τὴν μεσόγαιαν τῆς ὁδοῦ τραφθέντες (4.12). The most familiar example is that of Herodotos at Marathon (6.113.1), which by all reconstructions applies to the plain bordering the coast: ἐδίωκαν ἐς τὴν μεσόγαιαν. The word means no more than inland in contrast with coastal. Cf. E. Powell for Herodotos and A. Mauersberger ("Binnenland") for Polybios. In 2.102.1, Thucydides says that the Athenians landed at Astakos and then invaded the mesogeia of Akarnania, going to Stratos, Koronta, and other places. As the crow flies, Koronta is about 15 kilometers from the site of Astakos, but the distance is immaterial. Unfamiliar with common Greek topographical usage in which the destination or most important place is named first, Badian confuses the issue by suggesting that

I. THUCYDIDES' PENTEKONTAETIA 113

Koronta was taken only on the return march.[16] Koronta lies on the Astakos-Stratos road, and the Athenians hardly by-passed it on their way to Stratos. In short, Drabeskos was not on the coast, but inland. The phrase affords no clue to the distance.

The only scenario that I can reconstruct from Badian's theory that Drabeskos was at Drama and that the colonists were repulsed only after twelve years of occupation is that after landing at the mouth of the Strymon, the colonists proceeded to penetrate into the broad and fertile valley of the Angites until they reached Drama,[17] where the Edones belatedly rallied the Thrakian tribes and slaughtered them. That the Thrakians would have stood by peacefully for twelve years while they abandoned their rich agricultural land to foreigners is not a theory that I would wish to entertain. Moreover, the attractiveness of such a lengthy occupation would have permitted strong defensive operations on the part of the colonists and their followers. The episode reads like one which brought precipitous action on the part of the Thrakians, and a site for Drabeskos near the mouth of the

[16]In Plato *Phaedo* 111A, the distinction is made between those who dwell on the sea and those in the mesogaia. A glance at a map of Akarnania will show that Koronta was not on the sea. In *IG* II².1244–1248, we have a number of decrees of the Athenian Mesogeia, a club which met in the city trittys of Akamantis and had lost all contact with the Mesogeia district; see W. S. Ferguson, *Hellenistic Athens* (1911) 232. For the inland demes of Attika, including Aphidna and Eitea which were certainly not far from the coast, see End-map 2 in J. S. Traill, *The Political Organization of Attica* (Princeton 1975).

[17]According to the British Admiralty's *Handbook of Macedonia* 327–328, on Bulgarian maps at the time of the First World War, it was 28 1/4 miles by cart road from Chai Aghizi, at the mouth of the Strymon on the right bank, to Angista Station, and then 16 miles to Drama (alt. 344 ft.). By today's paved road, it is 61 1/2 kilometers from Amphipolis to Drama. The *Handbook* reported that Drama was an important center for trade in tobacco, and that there was much malaria. From Kavalla to Drama is 36 kilometers.

114 THUCYDIDES' PENTEKONTAETIA AND OTHER ESSAYS

Angites accords well with such action. For the fate of the captives, see *War* 5.209–211.

3. Daton (Thrakian district) and Datos (Thasian colony). Writing without reference to the Thucydidean site of Drabeskos, Hammond, in his detailed study of the mining districts and the Thrakian tribes, regards Daton as a district on the eastern side of the Strymon near the junction with the Angites. This identification accords fairly well with a site for Drabeskos near Phragela (or Phrangela), near the confluence of the two rivers, agreeing with Herodotos' statement that Leagros was slain at Daton by the Edones and Pausanias' report of Leagros being slain by the Edones as the colonists advanced on Drabeskos. Hammond, rejecting the testimony of Appian, writes in part as follows (*HM* 2.72):

> I take it that Datum was on the eastern side of the Strymonic lakes, in 'the country beyond the Strymon' (fr. 34), and near the Odomanti (fr. 36). Now the phrases 'up to Paeonia' and 'Paeonian land' give us a chronological clue, because Strabo cannot be referring to the Paeonia of the middle Axius valley but must be referring (as in fr. 34) to the 'Paeonia this side of the Strymon', that is to 'the Paeonian land' by Lake Prasias, near which Herodotus said there was a silver mine (5.17.2; 7.124; 8.115.3). This interpretation fits the fact that all three fragments were concerned with the Strymon basin. Once again it seems that Strabo's source was Hecataeus, because this was a sixth-century use of 'Paeonia'. Some fragments of Hecataeus survive which reveal his knowledge of the Strymon basin: F 152 Galepsus, a city of Thrace and Paeonians (belonging to the Paeonian period of power) and F 155 Aegialus of Thrace alongside the Strymon. ... The equation Crenides = Datum = Philippi was due to Appian (*BC* 4.105), but it runs counter to Strabo and to Herodotus who attributes Datum to the Edoni, and Appian is inferior to either as an authority for the situation *c.* 500 B.C.

I. THUCYDIDES' PENTEKONTAETIA   115

However, the most recent commentator on Daton, R. Baladié in the Budé Strabo VII (1989), p. 279, writing without reference to Hammond, favors the plain of Philippi:[18]

Datos (ou Daton). Daténiens *Datum, Dateni* fr. 33, 36: Paraît avoir désigné la riche plaine de Philippes, puis la colonie thasienne fondée en son centre sur l'emplacement de la cité qui s'est appelée ensuite Crénides et enfin Philippes. Datos est attesté comme ville: 1) sur la liste des théarodoques d'Épidaure, *IG* IV², 94, l. 32 (entre 365 et 311); 2) dans une inscription du musée de Kavala (Δάτου χώρα); 3) dans [Skylax] 67: Δάτον πόλις Ἑλληνὶς ἦν ὤκισε Καλλίστρατος Ἀθηναῖος; 4) dans Éphore et Théopompe cités par Harpocration; 5) dans Appien, *Bell Ciu.* IV, 105. Comme nous savons par un témoignage exactement daté (*IG* II² 12 [sic = 127]) que la colonie thasienne portait le nom de Crénides quand Philippe II s'en fut emparé, il convient, semble-t-il, de rectifier le témoignage d'Appien qui veut que le nom de Crénides ait précédé et non suivi celui de Daton. Ce dernier, qui semble (cf. Detschev, p. 120) d'origine thrace, devait être le nom de la plaine avant de devenir momentanément le nom de la ville; il a continué à désigner le riche terroir de Philippes quand la ville, qui en était le centre et qui l'exploitait, a changé du nom.[19]

---

[18] See also D. Müller, *Topographischer Bildkommentar zu den Historien Herodots* (Tübingen 1987) 45–47, who provides extensive bibliography.

[19] The inscription containing the phrase Δάτου χώρα, dated to 335 B.C., was published in 1982 by Vatin, the text of which is reproduced in *SEG* 34.664. The phrase occurs in the bottom line of a column. The remainder of the line is lost. The inscription gives the text of a letter sent by ambassadors of Philippi to Alexander reporting a decision concerning the territory of the city. The inscription has evoked an enormous bibliography, of which the following is known to me: L. Missitzis, *The Ancient World* 2 (1985) 3–14; Bokotopoulou, *Ancient Macedonia* 4 (1986) 87–114; Hatzopoulos, *REG* 100 (1987) 436–439; Hammond, *CQ* 82 (1988) 382–391; Badian, *ZPE* 79 (1989) 64–68; Hatzopoulos,

116 THUCYDIDES' PENTEKONTAETIA AND OTHER ESSAYS

Unfortunately, the thearodokoi list presents a puzzle. After naming Argilos (line 17), Amphipolis (18), Berga (19, some 25 miles above Amphipolis), and other cities, the column ends with Thasos (31) and Datos (32). Whatever the order, at the time Datos was a city.[20] Hiller comments on Datos: "Adiecta est colonia: 32 Δάτος a. 356 Philippis conditis hausta. Philippson *Realenc.* IV² 2229; Fredrich IG XII 8, p. 81."

I would reconcile Hammond's study of the tribes and the fifth-century location of the district of Daton near the conflu-

---

REG 102 (1989) pp. 428 and 435; Borza, *The Ancient History Bulletin* 3 (1989) 60–66; Hammond, *ZPE* 82 (1990) 165–175; Hatzopoulos, *REG* 104 (1991) p. 505; Badian, *ZPE* 95 (1993) 131–139. In *REG* 106 (1993) pp. 516–517, Hatzopoulos pronounces the debate between Hammond and Badian as "une polémique stérile." Nonetheless, Hammond responded in *ZPE* 100 (1994) 385–387, and Badian, in turn, in *ZPE* 100 (1994) 388–390. To this last paper, the editors append a notice: "Notiz der Redaktion: Damit schliessen wir die Debate." Vatin read col. B line 10 as: τὴν δὲ γῆν τὴν ἐν Δυ[....]ι μηθένα πῶλειν. Missitzis examined the stone and reported the reading as: τὴν δὲ [ὕλ]ην τὴν ἐν Δυ[σώρ]ωι ..., associating Dysoron with the name of the mountain in Herodotos 5.17, rising above Lake Prasias, from the mines of which Alexander drew a daily revenue of a talent of silver. Mount Dysoron is studied by D. Müller, *Topographischer Bildkommentar zu den Historien Herodots* (Tübingen 1987) 168–169 with two photographs and map on p. 127. However, Missitzis (p. 13), who gives an English translation, notes that there are other candidates for both names. Incidentally, A. W. Lawrence on the Herodotean passage writes, "Old silver workings have been noticed in a number of localities in Thrace and eastern Macedonia (Jirecek, Arch.-epigr. Mitt. aus Ost.-Ungarn, 1886, pp. 77, 83, 84)." Hammond (*CQ* 82 [1988] 384 n. 6) writes, "Missitzis, p. 12, restored 'on Dysoron' and judged the restoration 'pretty safe'; but it is geographically very improbable, since Herodotus located that mountain to the west of the Strymon basin." Borza, accepting the reading of Dysoron and applying it to the traditional location west of the Strymon (see Müller), argues that the chora of Datos was the territory on the east bank of the lower Strymon.

[20]In line 9, Perdikkas is named. Hiller says he reigned from 369–359.

I. THUCYDIDES' PENTEKONTAETIA 117

ence of the Strymon and Angites by assuming that about 360 B.C. a town of Datos was founded at what in 356 became the site of Philippi. According to Harpokration, Skylax 67, Zenob. 4.34; Isokrates 8 *Peace* 24; Diodoros 16.3.7; and Schäfer, I[2] 137, the exile Kallistratos of Athens (*PA* 8157) founded Datos as a Thasian colony at this time.[21] This interpretation obviates any assumption that the Athenian colonists under Leagros would have exposed their supply line by advancing from Ennea Hodoi about sixty kilometers to the region of Drama and Philippi or that the Thrakians would have permitted this.[22] Moreover, it seems quite possible that Kallistratos gave a name to his city which had nothing to do with the Thrakian tribe. Hesychios glosses Datos as ὁ τρυγητός, ἢ πόλεως ὄνομα, ἐπὶ λίαν εὐδαιμόνων. Pape-Benseler (p. 275) gives the etymology of Datos:

> Gabel d.h. Gabenvertheilern (von δαίω, δάζω, δαστός, ἄδαστος u. ἄδατος, nach Et. M. s. δατῶ, u. so auch nach Hesych. = τρυγητός), od. *Suchenheim, denn δατέν steht = ζητεῖν, Hesych., u. Δατός also = ζητητός, wie ζητίρων = ζητητόρων, Hesych., vgl. mit Lob. par. 13, (ist doch δατοῖς = δόλοις bei Suid. d.h. durch künstlich Gesuchtes oder Ausgedachtes) thracische Stadt am strymonischen Meerbusen mit Goldaruben.

The word is used as a proper name for persons who were clearly not Thrakians; see *RE*.[23]

---

[21]Zenobios (*Prov. Graec. Cent.* 3.71) and Eustathius (*ad Dionys. Perieg.* 517) both state that Datos was a colony of Thasos.

[22]The importance of the lower part of the Strymon as a source for Athenian timber is underscored by R. Meiggs, *Trees and Timber in the Ancient Mediterranean World* (Oxford 1982) 127. See also for the importance of Makedonia, E. N. Borza, *PAPhS* 131 (1987) 32–52. Amyntas sold much ship-timber to Athens for the reconstitution of her fleet between 377 and 373: Xenophon *Hell.* 6.1.11.

[23]The name Κρηνίδες, Bornstädt, Springtown, is self explanatory.

118 THUCYDIDES' PENTEKONTAETIA AND OTHER ESSAYS

IG II² 127 (= Tod, *GHI* no. 157) records an alliance of the Athenians with Ketriporis the Thrakian and with Lyppeios the Paionian and with Grabos the Illyrian, securely dated in 356/6 B.C. It is studied by Griffith and refers to the Krenidians. In *HM* 2.246–247, he writes, "The dated text of the Athenian treaty of alliance with the three kings shows, almost for certain, that already at this date (July 26) the three kings were in alliance with each other, and that Philip already was in possession of Crenides." Diodoros, after saying that in 360 B.C. the Thasians founded Krenides as a populous city (16.3.7), reports in 16.8.6–7 that Philip took Krenides in 358/7 and changed its name to Philippi; see Griffith 246 n. 3, who notes the error in Diodoros' chronology. Tod writes:

> Crenides (l. 45), a Thasian colony planted in 360–59 by the Athenian exile Callistratus, appealed in 356 to Philip II of Macedon for help against a Thracian attack, directed perhaps by Cersebleptes rather than by Cetriporis (Collart, *op. cit.* 152ff.). He promptly responded, fortified the place, settled a number of additional inhabitants there and renamed it after himself Philippi (cf. Collart, *op. cit.* 39ff., 133ff.; J. Schmidt, *R.-E.* xix.2206ff.).[24]

For the short period of its survival, our sources apply either the name Krenides or the name Datos to the Thasian colony. After that, apparently the remnants of the Thasian colony were transplanted to another site retaining the name Datos. The position after Thasos in the theorodokoi list suggests that a close tie with Thasos was continued. That the new site was near the coast is suggested by the facts that [Skylax] 67, which was written between 338 and 335, says it was near Neapolis (Νεάπολις, κατὰ Δάτον πόλις ῾Ελληνίς, ἣν ᾤκισε Καλλίστρατος) and Strabo

---

[24]For the harbor-dues of Kallistratos, see Ps.-Aristotle, *Oec.* 2.22.1350a.

I. THUCYDIDES' PENTEKONTAETIA 119

refers to it as having ναυπήγια.[25] Indeed, Lolling suggested that Datos was the same as Neapolis or near Neapolis; see Geyer, *RE* s.v. Makedonia (1974) 656. It cannot be Neapolis because the Athenians in 355 passed a decree receiving an embassy from that city and in 354 Charon apparently made Neapolis the base for the Athenian fleet: Tod, *GHI* no. 159.[26]

In his recent publication, *Philip of Macedon* (Baltimore 1994), Hammond writes (p. 209 n. 18):

> Theophrastus, *CP* 5.14.5, described the change after Philip took possession of the plain round Philippi which was then forested and waterlogged. 'When the water had been drained off, the land mostly dried out, and the whole territory was brought into cultivation.' The inscription which has been cited above (p. 37) gave an example of such reclaimed land. See *HM* 1.149 and 2.658f., citing similar changes in post-war Albania.[27]

The inscription is the one published by Vatin. On p. 35, Hammond also observed that at the time (356) Philip also made Oisyme a colony of Thasos. In the inscription published by Vatin, dated to 335 B.C., we believe that the chora of Datos was some

[25]Leake (*NG* 3.223–224) wrote, "The 'good things' which made Datus the subject of a proverb could not have been complete if it had not been a sea-port."

[26]At the present time, Datos is the name of a village between Kavalla and Philippi. SSW of Kavalla, Lazarides (fig. 25) marks two coastal sites at Anticara and Nea Perama. The latter is labelled "Oesyme Ematheia." Since Skylax (67) mentions Datos and Strabo (7 frg. 33) refers to dockyards (ναυπήγια), one wonders whether the former may be a candidate for Datos; cf. Collart, p. 44. Excavations at Oisyme in 1987 by E. Yiource and Ch. Koukoule-Chrysanthake carried out on top of the fortified citadel revealed a sanctuary, probably of Athena Poliouchos, and part of an archaic temple: *AEMTh* 1 (1987) 363–387, 535. The excavators report that the finds disclose a close relationship with Thasos.

[27]Cf. Hammond, *CQ* 82 (1988) 384.

120 THUCYDIDES' PENTEKONTAETIA AND OTHER ESSAYS

region between Philippi and the coast. Because of the etymology and its association with Thasos, we suggest that the post-360 town Datos had nothing to do with the early fifth-century Thrakian district of Daton including Drabeskos on the lower Strymon, miles removed from Philippi. Collart (p. 44 n. 3) writes,

> On a plus de chances, croyons-nous, de retrouver le souvenir de Daton dans le nom du village de *Bereketli* (ce qui signifie, en turc, *fertile*, ou, littéralement, *pourvu de bénédiction*; cf. Heuzey-Daumet, *op. laud.*, p. 34), situé à la lisière du marais non loin de la route de Cavalla à Philippes, que dans celui du gros bourg de *Doxato*, à mi-chemin entre Philippes et Drama (cf. J. N. Svoronos, *L'hellénisme primitif de la Macédoine*, p. 70, dont l'hypothèse paraît bien aventureuse).[28]

It is well to be reminded, as one who will consult many toponyms in the *RE* can confirm, that many ancient Greek cities were given more than one name,[29] and, more importantly, that many Greek towns in modern times have been relocated while retaining the old name. In our chapter on Akarnania in *Essays* (p. 191 n. 12), we noted that many of the villages of that province have been transplanted since the time of the travelers without changing the name.[30] In antiquity, "Old" Pleuron and "New" Pleuron is a well

---

[28]J. Murray's *Handbook for Travellers in Greece*[6] (London 1896) 872, states that at Bereketlou, Octavian and Antony obtained the great victory in B.C. 42 which terminated the existence of the Roman Republic.

[29]See, for example, Pausanias 8.39.2, 9.20.2, 9.40.5, 10.36.5; Strabo 9.2.10.404, 9.2.24.408, 9.5.14.435, 9.5.19.440, 10.2.6.451. Cf. *Topography* 8.151–152.

[30]Dio, writing of 42 B.C. (47.35), says that Brutus, after encamping near Philippi, did not try to take the direct road, but went around by a longer road to Krenides, where he overpowered a garrison. The terms Philippi and Krenides are here applied to different places. The villagers in Roman times revived an old name which had nothing to do with the town of 360–356 B.C. Today, there is a town Krenides on the road between Philippi and Drama.

I. THUCYDIDES' PENTEKONTAETIA

attested example. Pydna is another example, the site being moved by Archelaos.

Hammond (*HM* 1.428 n. 1) has observed that the name Edones applied to a cluster of tribes. I would assume that Herodotos' Daton (ἐν Δάτῳ) was a Thrakian district located near the confluence of the Angites and Strymon with the town Drabeskos within its territory. Our authorities are agreed that Datos/Krenides was founded in 360 as a Thasian colony. A. J. Graham, *Colony and Mother City in Ancient Greece* (Manchester 1964) 88, states of the Thasian colony "Daton/Crenides," "According to the most recent study, the bronze coins of the first three years of the colony's existence were struck in Thasos," referring to G. Le Rider, *BCH* 80 (1956) 16ff. The coins do not bear the names of Datos or Krenides, but are inscribed ΘΑΣΙΟΝ ΗΠΕΙΡΟ, Thasians of the mainland. When Philip took the city in 356, renaming it Philippi, part of the population was transplanted to a new city Datos, which was on or near the coast, but not at Kavalla. The name of the fourth-century Thasian colony is to be distinguished from an early fifth-century district of a Thrakian tribe. The name Daton cannot be used to support the position that there was a battle near Drama.

We conclude this section on Drabeskos by stating that we believe that the record in Thucydides stands in chronological order and that the events occurred in the source of one archon year; that the Thrakians would not have given the colonists time enough to dig in by a lengthy occupation, that the Thrakian district Daton and the town Drabeskos were near the junction of the Angites and Strymon rivers, and certainly not at Drama. We would emend the name of the archon in the Aischines scholion and reject Diodoros' account as a muddle, and certainly not traceable to any *Atthis*.

122 THUCYDIDES' PENTEKONTAETIA AND OTHER ESSAYS

SECTION 7

THUCYDIDES 1.107–108: THE ATHENIAN LONG WALLS

The next domino involves the attribution to Thucydides of "ring composition."[1] Our concern is only with the application of the theory to the Pentekontaetia, as exemplified in J. R. Ellis, "Thucydides I.105–108: The Long Walls and Their Significance," *Ventures into Greek History*, ed. I. Worthington (= Hammond Festschrift, Oxford 1994) 3–14. We extract what we think represents the core of the argument (pp. 11–13):

> Ring composition is the instrument he uses to highlight the significance of the decision to build the Long Walls, sandwiching the critical reference between two appropriate analogies.
>
> But does the real world come as conveniently structured as a text? As historians will not need reminding, the matter can not simply be left there, because the chronological relationship between the start and completion of these walls has always been a cause of scholarly headache. The battles in the Megarid date in Diodorus to 458/7; so does Tanagra. And in our text these two bracket the beginning of the wall building. Oenophyta, two months later, dates to the next year, early 457/6, and the end of the wall building apparently follows shortly afterwards (108.2–2). Yet the process of constructing these walls, some thirteen kilometres in length, seems in that case to have been speedy beyond belief — especially when we remember that a surviving fragment of Cratinus (at Plut. *Pericles* 13.7) pokes fun at how *long* the project took. And Plutarch elsewhere (*Cimon* 13.8) implies that the Long Walls were begun before Eurymedon, probably several years earlier. There is a

[1]We draw a sharp distinction between "thesis-proof-thesis," common in all forms of logical presentation, and "ring structures" which are charted to show that such composition caused the author to misplace the facts or to create falsehoods.

I. THUCYDIDES' PENTEKONTAETIA

serious problem here, highlighted by the fact that the chronology of this whole narrative of the Pentekontaetia has come increasingly under attack. But how easily this one element of the dating problem might be resolved if we were to conclude that, in order to locate it where its *significance* would be graphically exposed by its new context, Thucydides transplanted the beginning of the wall building from its proper place in, say, the early or mid-460s down to 458/7![2]

Testimonia about the long walls include the following:

1. **Thucydides 1.107.1** (after a battle in the Megarid): ἤρξαντο δὲ κατὰ τοὺς χρόνους τούτους καὶ τὰ μακρὰ τείχη ᾿Αθηναῖοι ἐς θάλασσαν οἰκοδομεῖν.

2. **Thucydides 1.108.3** (after Tanagra): τά τε τείχη ἑαυτῶν τὰ μακρὰ ἀπετέλεσαν.

3. **Thucydides 2.13.7** (Loeb tr.):

> For the length of the Phalerian wall was thirty-five stadia to the circuit-wall of the city, and the portion of the circuit-wall itself which was guarded was forty-three stadia (a portion being left unguarded, that between the Long Wall and the Phalerian); and the Long Walls to the Peiraeus were forty stadia in extent, of which only the outside one was guarded; and the whole circuit of the Peiraeus including Munichia was sixty stadia, half of it being under guard.

By this text the length of the two long walls was seventy-five stadia.

---

[2]Diodoros (11.79) puts the Megarid and Tanagra battles under the archon year 458/7, and Oinophyta in 457/6 (11.82), but his Oinophyta is not that of Thucydides. Busolt (3.1.319) posits that Diodoros mistook two accounts of the battle of Oinophyta for the same battle; see also Kirsten, *RE* s.v. (1937) 2257.

124 THUCYDIDES' PENTEKONTAETIA AND OTHER ESSAYS

4. Plutarch *Kimon* 13.7 (Loeb):

And it is said that, though the building of the long walls, called 'legs,' was completed afterwards, yet their first foundations, where the work was obstructed by swamps and marshes, were stayed up securely by Cimon, who dumped vast quantities of rubble and heavy stones into the swamps, meeting the expenses himself.

5. Plutarch *Perikles* 13.5 (Loeb):

For the long wall, concerning which Socrates says he himself heard Pericles introduce a measure, Callicrates was the contractor. Cratinus pokes fun at this work for its slow progress, and in these words: —
> 'Since ever so long now
> In word has Pericles pushed the thing; in fact he does not budge it.'

6. Plutarch *Mor.* 351A (Loeb):

Yet Cratinus pokes fun even at Pericles for his slowness in accomplishing his undertakings, and remarks somewhat as follows about his Middle Wall:
> Pericles in his talk makes the wall to advance,
> By his acts he does nothing to budge it.

The Kratinos fragment is no. 300. The Loeb editor states that the two references are to the same passage in Kratinos, the former being metrically correct. Both Kock and Edmonds publish the two under the same number. The last six words are identical. Plutarch uses τὸ μακρὸν τεῖχος in the *Perikles* passage, περὶ τοῦ διὰ μέσου τείχους in the other.

I. THUCYDIDES' PENTEKONTAETIA 125

7. Plato *Gorgias* 455E (Jowett tr.):

Gor. I like your way of leading us on, Socrates, and I will endeavour to reveal to you the whole nature of rhetoric. You must have heard, I think, that the docks and the walls of the Athenians and the plan of the harbour were devised in accordance with the counsels, partly of Themistocles, and partly of Pericles, and not at the suggestion of the builders.

Soc. Such is the tradition, Gorgias, about Themistocles; and I myself heard the speech of Pericles when he advised us about the middle wall.

8. **Scholiast to Plato *Gorgias*** (tr. C W. Fornara, *Archaic Times to the End of the Peloponnesian War* [Baltimore 1977] no. 79):

He calls "the middle wall" that which even until now exists in Hellas. For he built the middle wall as well (as the others) at Mounychia, part heading to the Piraeus and part to Phaleron, so that if the one section were thrown down, the other would largely serve.

9. **Andokides 3 *Peace* 7:** καὶ τὸ τεῖχος τὸ μακρὸν τὸ νότιον ἐτειχίσθη. The reference is to activities during the Thirty Years' Peace, and is taken to refer to the Middle Wall. Meiggs, *The Athenian Empire* (Oxford 1972) 188, suggests that there is a possible reflection of the building of the Middle Wall in *IG* I² 343 line 90 (= *IG* I³ 439 line 77, 444/3 B.C.).

10. **Harpokration:**

ΔΙᾺ ΜΈΣΟΥ ΤΕΊΧΟΥΣ ᾿Αντιφῶν πρὸς Νικοκλέα. τριῶν ὄντων τειχῶν ἐν τῇ ᾿Αττικῇ, ὡς καὶ

126 THUCYDIDES' PENTEKONTAETIA AND OTHER ESSAYS

Ἀριστοφάνης φησὶν ἐν Τριφάλητι, τοῦ τε βορείου καὶ τοῦ νοτίου καὶ τοῦ Φαληρικοῦ, διὰ μέσου τῶν παρ' ἑκάτερα ἐλέγετο τὸ νότιον, οὗ μνημονεύει καὶ Πλάτων ἐν Γοργίᾳ.

THE MIDDLE WALL. Antiphon *Against Nikoles*. There were three walls in Attika, as Aristophanes says in the *Triphales*, the north wall, southern wall, and the wall to Phaleron. The southern wall was said to be in the middle of the ones on each side ...

Plutarch makes a distinction between τὰ μακρὰ τείχη, or the "Legs" (ἃ σκέλη καλοῦσι),[3] and the θεμελίωσις anchored by Kimon (ἐρεισθῆναι διὰ Κίμωνος) in filling up the swamps. Thucydides, in using the term "Long Walls," is referring to construction above ground which seems natural.

The passages in the *Mor.*, *Gorgias* with the scholion, Andokides, and Harpokration, all refer to the Middle Wall built under Perikles. In the lengthy inscription detailing the repair of the walls in 307/6 B.C. (*IG* II² 463), W. Judeich takes the reference in line 120 to be the north wall and the middle wall. On p. 156 (*Topographie von Athen²*), he offers a diagram of the three walls. More recently, R. E. Wycherley, *The Stones of Athens* (Princeton 1978) 16, also offers a plan of the three walls, writing, "After several years, on Perikles' suggestion, as Plato tells us (*Gorgias* 455e), a third wall was added, running parallel to the original wall to Peiraeus at a distance of about 167m. The line of the two parallel walls has been well-established by remains found here and there."[4] The terms τὸ διὰ μέσου and νότιον τείχος are sometimes used for the same wall (Judeich p. 157). The Phaleron, or southernmost wall of the three, was not rebuilt after the destruction (Lysias 13 *Agoratos* 8; Xenophon *Hell.* 2.2.11, 15) in

[3]In *Lysistr.* 1172, Aristophanes refers to the Megarian walls as τὰ Μεγαρικὰ σκέλη.

[4]J. S. Boersma, *Athenian Building Policy from 561/0 to 405/4* (Groningen 1970) 65–67, dates Perikles' Middle Long Wall to c. 445–443.

I. THUCYDIDES' PENTEKONTAETIA

404 B.C. The middle wall, or Periklean wall, then became the southern wall. Since Kratinos's jibe at Perikles in the *Mor.* passage specifically refers to the Middle Wall, it follows that the same jeer in the *Perikles* passage is directed at the same wall, as the commentators on Kratinos, as well as Judeich, have taken it.

Ellis' suggestion ("the early or mid-460s down to 458/7") is a bizarre idea, offered without any documentation. Pausanias (4.27.5) and Diodoros (15.66) attribute the building of Messene, which may have included more than the walls, to Epameinondas. Diodoros (15.67.1) gives the figure of eighty-five days.[5] Plutarch (*Agesilaos* 31.1) puts the number of Epameinondas' force as 40,000 hoplites with many light-armed. Diodoros (15.62) gives the number of 70,000 men. A force estimated at eight thousand men built the so-called Demosthenes wall on Pylos in eight days, which, after it was turned over to the Messenians, the Spartans were not able to take for fifteen years, when the Messenians were starved out; see *Essays* 161. After the Athenians began their siege at Syrakuse, walls were built by both sides. The hoplite was experienced in wall-building. Not only did the Athenians build the long walls at Athens, but Thucydides tells us that earlier (1.103.4), "They built for the Megarians the long walls which run from the city to Nisaea, and held it with a garrison of their own troops." This wall was the first line of defense against a Peloponnesian attack. According to Thucydides (4.66), the walls were eight stadia in length, but according to Strabo (9.1.4.391) eighteen stadia. Frazer (on Pausanias 1.44.3) says that in his day Megara was a mile and a half from the ancient harbor. Long walls, each of 12 stadia, were built between Korinth and Lechaion (Strabo 8.6.2.380). Long walls to harbors were also built, under Athenian influence, at Patras in 419 (Thucydides 5.52.2) and at

---

[5]Cf. Plutarch *Agesilaos* 32.8. The construction of the walls of Messene, with its circuit of five and a half miles, among the finest specimens of Greek fortifications in existence, was a far greater project than that of the Athenian long walls.

128   THUCYDIDES' PENTEKONTAETIA AND OTHER ESSAYS

Argos in 417 (Thucydides 5.82.5). For a study of this type of fortification, see A. W. Lawrence, GAF 155–158.[6]

Oddly, Ellis ignores a passage in the Pentekontaetia which relates to the building of the Themistokles circuit wall. Thucydides writes in part (1.90.3, Loeb): "… the whole population of the city, men, women, and children should take part in the wall-building, sparing neither private nor public edifice that would in any way help to further the work, but demolishing them all." Remains at the Dipylon and elsewhere show the stone socle; the greater part of the wall was apparently of unbaked brick. I. T. Hill, The Ancient City of Athens (London 1953) 32, writes, "With such a method of construction, it would certainly have been possible to complete it in the short space of a month or so."[7] The defenses of Athens remained for centuries essentially the Themistoklean wall.

The essential element for wall-building is the number of workers on the job. In his zeal to convict Thucydides, Ellis has failed to address the problem. That armies built walls is quite clear, for example, at Poteidaia where the Athenians built a wall on the north side of Poteidaia and garrisoned it. Later, after the arrival of Phormio, he built a wall south of Poteidaia.

It is a mistake to regard the building of the three walls as a single project. Thucydides rightly separated the two outer walls from the Periklean middle wall mentioned by other authors, and placed them in their proper chronological sequence. Ellis' claim

---

[6]R. E. Wycherley, The Stones of Athens (Princeton 1978) 15, provides bibliography on the Athenian long walls. Sections of the walls or the gates are constantly being discovered; see, for example, JHS Arch. Reports 1984/5 p. 10, 1985/6 p. 9, 1988/9 p. 11, 1990/1 p. 6, 1992/3 p. 10.

[7]Actually, Themistokles' delaying tactics were protracted, and the period may have been longer. Thucydides says, ἐν ὀλίγῳ χρόνῳ. Diodoros (11.40) puts the rebuilding under the archonship of Timosthenes (478/7 B.C.). Shear, "The Persian Destruction of Athens," Hesperia 62 (1993) 383–482, esp. 416–417, in a brilliant rebuttal to Francis and Vickers, who seem to be wrong about much that they touch, presents the archaeological evidence.

I. THUCYDIDES' PENTEKONTAETIA 129

that ring composition resulted in an anachronism, here as elsewhere, results from a lack of understanding of ancient and modern literature. On the one hand, reference is made (p. 11) to Thucydides' "subtlety" in constructing his text; on the other hand, we are told (p. 6) that Thucydides is not "at his creative best," and that the chronology of the Pentekontaetia is at fault. The sentence in 1.107.1 about the start of the long walls is not in its chronological position, but is sandwiched (Diagram 4) between four statements about Myronides' victory over the Korinthians extracted from 1.106 and four statements about the Lakedaimonians extracted from the campaign of Tanagra (1.107.2–4). Ellis writes (p. 13) of the long walls, "Its *significance* would be graphically exposed by its new context." Confusing Perikles' wall with the two long walls, Ellis adduces no evidence to support his claim that the latter were begun in the early 460s and required a decade to build. Nor does he offer any explanation as to why it is more "significant" to place the long walls between Megara and Tanagra than in what he regards as their correct position. We would regard the completion of the walls as more "significant" than the beginning. That the pattern of Thucydides' process of thought was controlled by the pattern of lines adduced by Ellis is utterly bizarre.

According to Plutarch *Kimon* 13.6, Kimon cleared the marshes and actual construction does not begin until some years later. The actual building operations above ground began after Megara (1.107.1), were still in process at the time of Tanagra (1.107.4), and the project was completed after Oinophyta (1.108.3).

A complete history of the long walls has been given by David H. Conwell, *The Athenian Long Walls: Chronology, Topography and Remains*, in an impressive 1992 Pennsylvania dissertation (700 pages) with bibliography and charts, and description of known sections.

130 THUCYDIDES' PENTEKONTAETIA AND OTHER ESSAYS

The literature that has gathered about the Pentekontaetia is immense. We have concerned ourselves only with crux passages which have been cited against Gomme's treatment. Some, like the hounds in Xenophon's *Kynegetikos* (3.5), μανικῶς περιφερό- μενοι ὑλακτοῦσι περὶ τὰ ἴχνη. Thucydides has been better served by Gomme than by any other scholar of the guild of which I am a humble member. He knew the language well and could never have generated a Frankenstein of a Greek participle or of the historical present; he excelled as an authoritative asker of questions. Some answers prove to be not "either-or" but "both-and." But Gomme supplied the ancient testimonia on any given problem and canvassed the archaeological literature. He did not dismiss every tough problem as due to human frailty, nor did he accept Meritt's *Athenian Financial Documents* as the basis for his chronology. Polybios wrote that an essential thing in history was to see the sites, and it was on αὐτοπάθεια that he laid the main emphasis. The modern historian has a great deal of work to do before the cartographer can set up his drawing-board. Gomme was no γωνιοβόμβυξ (Ath. 5.222a), but, realizing that the best test we have is to examine the topography, he of- fered sketch-maps based on his own autopsy. He belonged to the "muddy boots" school of history, and might have endorsed the quotation given in our Introduction, "What historians need is not more documents but stronger boots." Thucydides wrote of campaigns and battles for an audience that saw military service. He recognized, as all antiquity recognized, that war is the rule and peace the exception. Ares holds the scales, the grim χρυσαμοιβὸς σωμάτων, as Aischylos (*Agam.* 437) calls him. The balance of power was the balance of fear — τὸ ἀντίπαλον δέος (3.11.1). Fortunately, Thucydides will never lack students, even if they are not as well equipped as his critics pretend to be. In his 87-page introduction to *HCT* 1, Gomme presents the problem of

I. THUCYDIDES' PENTEKONTAETIA   131

the background which any serious student of Thucydides must possess.[8]

[8]As an example of treating a Thucydidean problem in isolation, I cite S. Hornblower's discussion (*Greek Historiography* [Oxford 1994] 26–28) of Thucydidean examples of "stades," in which he writes, "The conclusion, as before, has to be that Thucydidean accuracy is capricious and unreliable." This statement ignores the fact that distance in stades, as given by Herodotos, Artemidoros, Strabo, Pliny, Arrian, and others, rarely agree and are generally inaccurate. See, for example, *Topography* 4.238–242, and *Essays* 176 n. 46, with references to students of geography. For measurements of the Peloponnesos, see Strabo 8.2.1.335. In 8.8.5.389, Strabo complained that Polybios measured by a route some general marched, not in a straight line. Baladié on 8.2.3 (p. 58) discusses the various measurements given for the Korinthian Gulf (Thucydides 2.86). Herodotos and Thucydides had no maps worthy of the name (see *Liar School* pp. 122–123), and corruptions in transcribing numerals were not uncommon (see the critical apparatus on Strabo 8.8.5). As Gomme noted, Thucydides often underestimated. It would be interesting for the modern critic to repeat the process without a map. Pausanias (10.38.4) says Amphissa lay 120 stades from Delphi, Aischines (3.123) 60 stades. Both, as Frazer noted, are wide of the mark. C. Müller (*GGM* 1 p. 37) states, "Graecos fretis angustis heptastadii latitudinem saepius attribuere supra monui"; cf. his pp. 21 and 55. on p. 18, he comments on the common confusion of the numeral δ and δύο. His commentaries on the various *Periploi* are replete with catalogues of differences in measurements, some attributable to alleged errors in the transmission of numerals.

II

THUCYDIDES 1.61.3–5

I N HIS CHAPTER VI, Badian publishes an essay which had not previously appeared, concerning the relationship of Athens with Makedon at the outbreak of the Peloponnesian War. I concern myself with that part which has to do with the topographical passage of 1.61.3–5, for which there is a large bibliography. The passage in question reads (de Romilly's text):

ἀπανίστανται ἐκ τῆς Μακεδονίας, 4 καὶ ἀφικόμενοι ἐς Βέροιαν κἀκεῖθεν ἐπὶ Στρέψαν καὶ πειράσαντες πρῶτον τοῦ χωρίου καὶ οὐχ ἑλόντες ἐπορεύοντο κατὰ γῆν πρὸς τὴν Ποτείδαιαν τρισχιλίοις μὲν ὁπλίταις ἑαυτῶν, χωρὶς δὲ τῶν ξυμμάχων πολλοῖς, ἱππεῦσι δὲ ἑξακοσίοις Μακεδόνων τοῖς μετὰ Φιλίππου καὶ Παυσανίου· ἅμα δὲ νῆες παρέπλεον ἑβ-δομήκοντα. 5 Κατ᾽ ὀλίγον δὲ προϊόντες τριταῖοι ἀφίκοντο ἐς Γίγωνον καὶ ἐστρατοπεδεύσαντο.

The phrase ἐπὶ Στρέψαν is a widely accepted emendation for ἐπιστρέψαντες of the codices.

Pertinent bibliography includes the following:

1. Pluygers in Cobet, *Mnemos.* 6 (1857) 288.
2. Müller-Strübing, *Jahrbuch für classische Philologie* 1883. 600–605, endorsing Classen's conjecture of Θέρμην.
3. Gomme, *HCT* 1 (1948) 214–218; 3 (1956) 726–727, 735.
4. C. F. Edson, "Notes on the Thracian Phoros," *CP* 42 (1947) 100–104.
5. Wade-Gery, *JHS* 69 (1949) 84–85.
6. S. Pelekides, "Γύρω ἀπὸ τὰ Ποτειδεατικά," Πανεπι-στήμιον Θεσσαλονίκης: Ἐπετήρις τῆς Φιλ. Σχολῆς 6 (1950) 1–47.
7. Gomme, *CR* 65 (1951) 137–138.

8. A. G. Woodhead, "The Site of Brea: Thucydides 1.61.4," *CQ* 46 (1952) 57–62.
9. C. Edson, "Strepsa (Thucydides 1.61.4)," *CP* 50 (1955) 169–190.
10. J. A. Alexander, "Thucydides and the Expedition of Callias," *AJP* 83 (1962) 265–287.
11. H. B. Mattingly, "Athenian Imperialism and the Foundation of Brea," *CQ* 60 (1966) 172–192.
12. N. G. L. Hammond, *A History of Macedonia* 1 (1972), for historical geography, esp. 183, and 2 (1979) 123.
13. J. A. Vartsos, "The Foundation of Brea," *Ancient Macedonia* 2 (1977) 13–16.
14. M. Zahrnt, "Die Entwicklung des makedonischen Reiches bis zu den Perserkriegen," *Chiron* 14 (1984) 325–368.
15. E. Kirsten, "Makedoniens Flüsse und Küsten im Altertum," *Byzantina* 13 (1985) 219–235.
16. D. Müller, *Topographischer Bildkommentar zu den Historien Herodots* (Tübingen 1987).
17. M. B. Hatzopoulos, "Strepsa: A Reconsideration or New Evidence on the Road System of Lower Macedonia," in Hatzopoulos/Loukopoulou, *Two Studies in Ancient Macedonian Topography* (Athens 1987) 21–60.
18. M. Tiberios, "Ὄστρακα από το Καραμπουρνάκι," *To Archaiologiko Ergo ste Makedonia kai Thrake* 1 (1987) 247–260.
19. P. Chrysostomos, *AEMTh* 3 (1989) 106–107.
20. E. N. Borza, *In the Shadow of Olympus* (Princeton 1990) 294–295.
21. E. Badian, *From Plataea to Potidaea* (Baltimore 1993) Chapter 6, esp. pp. 174–179.
22. A. Panayotou and P. Chrysostomos, "Inscriptions de la Bottiée et d' Almopie en Macédoine," *BCH* 117 (1993) 359–400.

II. THUCYDIDES 1.61.3-5

23. P. B. Phaklaris, "Aegae: Determining the Site of the First Capital of the Macedonians," *AJA* 98 (1994) 609–616.

In the following pages, these works will be referred to by author and page only.

We take up the problem of the Athenians' route for Kallias and his hoplites from Pydna to Poteidaia under the following headings:

1. Land Route: Pydna to Poteidaia
2. Sea Route: Pydna—Chalkidiki
3. Towns:
   A. Strepsa
   B. Therme
   C. Gigonos
   D. Beroia
   E. Pydna
4. Text:
   A. Ἀπανίστανται ἐκ τῆς Μακεδονίας
   B. Καὶ ἀφικόμενοι ἐς Βέροιαν
   C. Κατὰ γῆν
   D. Ἐπιστρέψαντες
   E. Κατ' ὀλίγον προϊόντες

1. LAND ROUTE: PYDNA TO POTEIDAIA

It has always been accepted until 1987, so far as I am aware, that the only land route from Pydna to Therme and Poteidaia in the fifth century was through Beroia and the site of Pella. Gomme (*CR* 65 [1951] 137) referred to it as the "lowest practicable crossing of the Haliacmon (a wide and deep river)". So also Edson, *CP* 50 (1955) 169–184. Edson writes (p. 177):

136 THUCYDIDES' PENTEKONTAETIA AND OTHER ESSAYS

The distance along the ancient road from Pydna to Beroea has been estimated at about 40 to 45 kilometers, or around 27 *m.p.* The Peutinger Table gives the distance between Beroea and Pella as 30 *m.p.* The distance between Pydna and Pella along the road passing by Beroea will have been about 57 *m.p.*, 84 kilometers, or 52 English miles. After his defeat of Perseus, Aemilius Paulus with the entire Roman army took two days to move from Pydna to a distance of one *m.p.* from Pella. The Roman army averaged about 28 *m.p.*, 42 kilometers, or 26 English miles on its two day advance from Pydna to Pella. This is of course very good marching.

The distance from Pella to Thessaloniki is 35–40 kilometers. W. E. Thompson, *Hermes* 96 (1969) 223 n. 3, says it is 129 km. from Pydna to Thessaloniki and claims that the march was one of five days at 25 km. per diem.

Herodotos (7.123) refers to Pella (Powell tr.), "of which the seaboard (τὸ παρὰ θάλασσαν) is possessed by the cities of Ichnae and Pella." In 2.99.4, Thucydides writes, the Bottiaeans "acquired a narrow strip of Paeonia extending along the river Axius from the interior to Pella and the sea" (Loeb). According to Plutarch (*Demetr.* 43), Demetrios compared Pella to Peiraieus, Chalkis, and Korinth as a great place for building warships. The literature is large; but Oberhummer in *RE* s.v. Pella (1937) 345, published three maps (after Struck) showing the encroachment of the alluviation with three rivers flowing into the gulf, resulting later in the formation of Lake Loudias. Similar maps are published by Hammond in *HM* 1.145 and 150, and by D. Müller in *Topographischer Bildkommentar* (1987) 127. In the fifth century on Oberhummer's first map, the only road is marked as crossing the upper Haliakmon east of Beroia, then northwards to strike a road leading eastwards to Pella and Therme.[1] Gomme referred to

---

[1]Smith's old *Dictionary* gives convenient testimonia on Pella. Leake (*NG* 3.262–263) described the site based on Livy's detailed account (44.46.5–7). Livy (26.25.5–8, 15–17) describes Philip's expedition to Thrace and return to Dion

II. THUCYDIDES 1.61.3–5

the road from Pydna to the head of the gulf as "at least 120 kilometers by road through recently hostile country." Livy (44.43.8) refers to the difficulty of crossing the Axios near Pella in 168 B.C. (propter difficultates transitus). The Axios was the principal river in Makedonia. Euripides (*Ba.* 568) refers to the ὠρυρόας Ἀξιός. Strabo (7.327 frg. 21) calls it muddy (θολερός). Leake (*NG* 3.258–259) wrote that on November 16, 1806 the Axios was rapid and deep; near the mouth it was two miles in breadth. He crossed on a bridge 1800 feet long. In the time of Herodotos (7.127), the Ludias or Loudias joined the Haliakmon; and Leake (3.437) thought that it was a discharge of the marshes of Pella. Leake (3.293) mentions the gorges of the Haliakmon near Beroia. Doubtless there were fords in classical times, and at least in Roman times ferries and bridges. We have one description of a crossing of the Acheloos in 219 B.C. in Polybios 4.64.6, "Philip ordered his peltasts to cross the river first in close order with the shields of each company locked together" (Walbank). Because of forts on either side of the river, we can pinpoint the position.

In the *RE* s.v. Ludias (1927) 1711, one is referred to Roedias, treated by Philipp (1914) 960–961, who discusses it as a river in Makedonia. The name is taken from Pliny 4.34, and Philipp says it is the same as the Δοιδίας, Λυδίης, or Λυδίας of other ancient writers. A lake Loudias is mentioned in Strabo 7 frg. 20 (ἐν λίμνῃ τῇ καλουμένῃ Λουδίᾳ). In the same fragment, Strabo says that the Loudias is navigable inland to Pella, a distance of 120 stades (= 22.2 kilometers). Today it is 27 kilometers as the crow flies, a difference which the Strabo editor Baladié attributes to the alluviation of the three rivers since antiquity. Under the lemma Lydias in the *RE* (1927) 2204–2205, Oberhummer gives a detailed treatment of the river without reference to the Philipp's article. He states that the river was navigable for warships from Pella to the coast in the fourth century B.C.

---

and Pella in 211 B.C. In 44.42.1–46.11, Livy describes Aemilius' advance to Pydna and the surrender of Beroia, Saloniki, and Pella.

138 THUCYDIDES' PENTEKONTAETIA AND OTHER ESSAYS

M. Zahrnt, *Chiron* 14 (1984) 325–368, publishes sketch-maps on p. 331 and facing p. 346, showing that any road from Pydna to Beroia would have passed through or close to Palatitsa and Vergina. E. Kirsten, "Makedoniens Flüsse und Küsten im Altertum," *Byzantina* 13 (1985) 219–235, offers some modifications from his predecessors, including Struck. Just where the fifth-century B.C. road would have crossed the various rivers or their tributaries, all of them strong, is not clear to me. I know of no one who has actually traced an ancient road on a modern map from Greek Pydna to Palatitsa and Beroia; see Hammond's map in *HM* 1.124. Advocates of this route for Kallias' army write about it as if all was easy going without any obstacles. By the modern road map, there is a way from Pydna north to Μεθώνη (10 kilometers), 5 kilometers to the junction of a road which leads west to Μελίκη (13 kilometers), 6 kilometers to Παλατίτσια, 3 kilometers to Βεργίνα, 7 kilometers to 'Αγ. Βαρβάρα crossing the Haliakmon, and 5 kilometers to Beroia, a total of 44 kilometers. The ancient route would have been more direct. K. Miller's Map 183 on p. 575 shows the route of the Peutinger Table, as he conceived it to be in 1916. He marks the distance from Beroia to Pydna as 17 miles as the crow flies. It is important to note that such a route would have taken the Athenians through the Makedonian palace at Palatitsia-Vergina, the burial place of Makedonian kings.[2]

H. B. Hatzopoulos, in *Two Studies in Ancient Macedonian Topography* (Athens 1987) 17–60, has offered a restudy of one of the roads of the Haliakmon and Axios region on the basis of several recently discovered late Roman milestones, none found in situ. None have a toponym. Examining the various Roman Itineraries of the late imperial period,[3] he posits a late main

---

[2]See Hammond, *HM* 2.13.

[3]Claude Nicolet, *Space, Geography and Politics in the Early Roman Empire* (Anne Arbor 1991) 103, states that the Peutinger parchment is "dated certainly

II. THUCYDIDES 1.61.3–5

Roman road along the southern and eastern shores of "Lake Loudiake," from Beroia to Thessaloniki. I am not able to control his exact route, especially since he uses modern toponyms not found on standard maps. I assume that his Lake Loudiake is the same as Lake Loudias of Strabo 7 frg. 20, marked on Hammond's *HM* 1 Map 14. Hatzopoulos' work may well be a valuable contribution to the study of late Roman roads. But Hatzopoulos advances the position that his late Roman road applies to the fifth century B.C., a difference of many hundreds of years.

The reader may wish to consult a recent sketch-map of the region of the Thermaic Gulf, that published by M Zahrnt in *Chiron* 14 (1984) facing p. 346. See also the end-map in Hatzopoulos and the map of Chrysostomos in *BCH* 117 (1993) 361. Leake, Philippson, Oberhummer, Casson, Danoff, Hammond, D. Müller, Edson, Zahrnt, all of whom I have consulted, are in agreement that the waters of the sea extended at least to Pella at the time of Xerxes' invasion and in the fifth century B.C. Our concern is not with late Roman roads on the eastern coast of Makedonia in the region of the Haliakmon and Axios, but with the extent of the waters of the Thermaic Gulf into the mainland in the fifth century B.C. Badian (pp. 174–179 with notes) has now endorsed the position of Hatzopoulos that the late Roman road applies to the time of Thucydides. The Peutinger and other Itineraries take one from Thessaloniki to Pella and then to Beroia. Hatzopoulos' position is that the road from Pella to Beroia went east, not west, of his "Lake Loudiake." He offers no clue about the configuration or history of this lake, which all other scholars I have consulted (except Badian) believe was open sea in the fifth century B.C. The positions of the stations after Beroia are much disputed. Neither scholar offers any refutation of the numerous scholars named about the waters of the Thermaic Gulf in the fifth century, although Badian has an arti-

---

from the fourth or fifth century A.D." He disputes the claim that the prototype was Agrippa's map.

cle in the same volume as Zahrnt. Both seem to assume that the coastline from Pydna to Thessaloniki was solid earth broken only by the various rivers. We noted that in 1806 Leake reported that the mouth of the Axios was two miles in breadth. The British Admiralty's *Handbook of Macedonia* (London 1920) 106, has an illuminating statement on the estuaries of the rivers: "Eleftherochori (10 kilometers north of Pydna). From the Skala of this place a traveller to Salonica would certainly take a boat, as the land route involves for the greater part of the year a great detour to get round the marshes at the mouths of the Vistritza (Haliakmon) and Vardar (Axios) rivers. The track proceeds across ridges and valleys." The Romans built bridges, as attested by Collart in the region of Philippi.

The above summary of the bibliography was written before our visit to the region in May 1995 with John Camp, when we had the opportunity to discuss the course of the roads with three experienced archaeologists, who generously gave us of their time, Manthos Besios at Pydna, Ms. Angelike Kottaridou at Palatitsia-Vergina, and P. Chrysostomos at Pella. Besios believes that the ancient route from Pydna went to Methone, Kyseli (= ancient Aloros), Vergina, to Beroia. The difficulty was in crossing the Haliakmon. Ms. Kottaridou said that she was publishing an article on a shorter path, only a monopati, from Pydna to Beroia, not touching Vergina, which she has explored. P. Chrysostomos, director of excavations at Pella, kindly gave us a reprint of an article in *AEMTh* 3 (1989) 103–117, in which he rejects the position of Hatzopoulos, writing on p. 107: "Οι απόψεις αυτές είχαν ακαδημαϊκό χαρακτήρα και είχαν διαμορφωθεί, χωρίς τη γνώση του χώρου και χωρίς τοπογραφική και ανασκαφική έρευνα της περιοχής. Η άποψή μας, που θα τεκμηριωθεί σε άλλη μελέτη, λύνει τα τοπογραφικά και τα ιστορικά προβλήματα της Βοττιαίας, που δεν είχαν βρει ικανοποιητική ερμηνεία." He explained that, although there are no road-beds, by studying the position of tombs and settlements, any road from Beroia to Pella and Therme in Makedonian times

II. THUCYDIDES 1.61.3-5

went west and northwest of the so-called Lake Loudiake. Actually what Hatzopoulos calls Lake Loudiake does not exist today. It was drained in 1928–1935. He focuses on the route used by Aemilius Paulus in 168. No fifth-century route could have run east of this. In *BCH* 117 (1993) 393, Chrysostomos publishes a milestone with the toponym of Pella. The topography has been greatly altered. The region today is dotted with rice-paddies. We inspected a Roman bridge which once spanned the Loudias, astride the National Highway, a few kilometers east of the village of Kleidi and west of the present bed of the Loudias. By using the technique of taking mortar samples developed recently by W. J. Cherf, it might be possible to date this and other Roman bridges in the region.

The weight of the evidence seems to be firmly in support of the position that the road of the fifth century B.C. circled from Pydna to Beroia and Pella west of the estuaries of the various powerful rivers; and, in turning to the text of Thucydides below, we shall regard such a route as the only feasible one for those who wish to advocate a land route for Kallias' army. Indeed, we are skeptical about the late Roman route, based on the interpretation of milestones found near Beroia, giving no provenances and not found in situ; but perhaps a geological coastal team may adjudicate the problem.[4]

2. SEA ROUTE: PYDNA–CHALKIDIKI

[4]The thrust of Hatzopoulos' presentation is that he has proved that there was in the third century A.C. a road leading northeast out of Beroia to modern Stavros and Alexandria, by today's road 26 kilometers, but this does not disprove the position that in the fifth century B.C. the only feasible route was one leading northwest out of Beroia around the waters of the upper Thermaic Gulf, where there were four strong rivers having mouths within a space of 15 miles; see, for example, the contour sketch-maps in E. N. Borza, *In the Shadow of Olympus* (Princeton 1990) esp. p. 39.

142   THUCYDIDES' PENTEKONTAETIA AND OTHER ESSAYS

From Pydna to Cape Τοῦζλα, the westernmost point of the Chalkidiki, is about 20 kilometers. To sites in the Gulf of Thessaloniki at Sedes or Kalamaria is another 15 kilometers or so. The port of Pydna, as viewed twenty-five years ago, appears to the right in *Topography* 2 pl. 135. Today the whole area is developed with a hotel and tavernas. Gomme states that there must have been troop transports at Pydna.[5] At the beginning of our paragraph, Thucydides states that the Athenians sent 2,000 hoplites and 40 ships to Pydna under Kallias. B. Jordan, *The Athenian Navy in the Classical Period* (Berkeley 1975) 187–210, has collected testimonia for the numbers of hoplites aboard triremes in sea-battles; but, in any case, it seems unlikely that 50 hoplites would have been aboard each trireme in the long trip from the Peiraieus to Pydna. In 1.59.2, we learn that there were already 30 ships at Poteidaia, and in 1.61.4, we have the fleet of 70 ships united before the army reached Gigonos. Since the army was brought to Pydna by ship, it would have been folly not to use the same ships to transport it across the Thermaic Gulf rather than to take it by land on a journey of 120 kilometers or more across several strong rivers and through country formerly hostile. Only one sailing was required;[6] they certainly did not come by shuttle from Peiraieus. The operation could have been completed in one day. It was only after landing that they were joined by allies.

Long ago, Grote, in a note to chap. 47, believing from Stephanos Byz. that there was a second town by the name of Beroia, wrote:

[5]For transports, see Thucydides 1.116, 4.116.2, 6.25, 6.31.3, 6.43, 6.44.1, 7.7.3, 8.25, 8.30.2, 8.62.2; Xenophon *Hell.* 1.1.36. Common words for a troop-transport are ὁπλιταγωγός and στρατιῶτις (*IG* I³ 21.10). Dover (*HCT* 4.309) states that large numbers of soldiers were not carried on triremes.

[6]Gomme, *HCT* 1.20, states that a trireme would normally cover from 35 to 45 miles in a day.

II. THUCYDIDES 1.61.3-5

The Athenians, raising the siege of Pydna, crossed the gulf *on shipboard* to Beroea, and after vainly trying to surprise that town, marched along *by land* to Gigônus. Whoever inspects the map will see that the Athenians would naturally employ their large fleet to transport the army by the short transit across the gulf from Pydna (see Livy, xliv, 10), and thus avoid the fatiguing land-march round the head of the gulf.

The Livy reference is to Gaius Marcius in 169 B.C. (Loeb tr.):

Recalling the soldiers to the ships and abandoning the siege of Thessalonica, they made thence for Aenea. This city is fifteen miles away, set opposite Pydna in fertile land. After devastating its territory they followed the shore and arrived at Antigonea.

3. TOWNS

A. Strepsa. Although Gomme (*HCT* 1.217), Edson (*CP* 42 [1947] 100–104), J. A. Alexander (*AJP* 83 [1962] 268), and presumably Woodhead (*CQ* 46 [1952] 57–58) wished to place Strepsa south of Therme, the prevailing view has been that of *ATL* 1.551, 3.220 n. 122 and 314–316; and Hammond *HM* Map 14, pp. 140–141, that the site was northwest of Therme. However, in his *The Macedonian State* (Oxford 1989) 81 n. 27, Hammond writes:

Earlier views of the position of Strepsa (e.g. in *HM* I. 183) are outmoded by the arguments of M. B. Hatzopoulos in *Meletemata* 3 (1987) 22–60 and by the subsequent discovery of an inscription which placed Strepsa within Chalcidian territory, an inscription now published in *Meletemata* 5 (1988) 17, line 17.

Announcement of the text was made by H. Pleket in *SEG* 37 (1987) 535. The inscription, found at Porta, the site of Kassandreia, and published by M. B. Hatzopoulos, *Une Donation du roi Lysimaque* (Meletemata 5; Athens 1988) 17–54, is now con-

144 THUCYDIDES' PENTEKONTAETIA AND OTHER ESSAYS

veniently republished in *SEG* 38 no. 619. The text mentions the territories of Sermylia, Olynthos, and Strepsa. Hatzopoulos (p. 40) places Strepsa at modern Basilika: cf. *REG* 102 (1989) p. 433 nos. 453 and 456.[7] In visiting Olynthos, I have gone NNE to Πολύγυρος, then to Thessaloniki by way of Γαλάτιστα and Βασιλικά. Basilika is 12 kilometers southeast of Σέδας, with an additional 11 kilometers to Thessaloniki. The coastal road from Poteidaia is shorter. In *Meletemata* 11 (1992) 28, Hatzopoulos restated his position about Strepsa.

In visiting Basilika in 1995, we relied on the bibliography given by Hatzopoulos in our reference in note 7. The literature cited refers to prehistoric finds, a fourth-century inscription (*Makedonia* 2 [1953] 621), two of a late date (one dated in *SEG* 29.648 to 198–199 A.C., the other in *SEG* 29.563 no. 8, regarded as probably "protobulgarian"), and a report of sherds southeast of the village. Our inquiry of the natives in the village elicited no report of any antiquities or excavations within the region. However, later, in Catling's *JHS Reports* for 1986/7, 34, we found the following report of excavations as taken from Greek newspapers:

> **Ayia Paraskevi** (18 km. SE of Thessaloniki). Greek Press reports refer to continuing excavation at the cemetery (*AR 1984–85*, 42–3) and the settlement at **Vasilika** to which it belongs, at the 200 m. contour on a level-topped hill, where occupation from the 6th—4th cent. B.C. has been identified. 450 tombs have now been dug in the cemetery, mostly unlooted. Male burials face W, and are furnished with military equipment and gold mouthpieces. Women face E, with gold rings, pendants, necklaces of glass and gilded beads and sea shells. Children's graves have equivalent offerings according to sex. Vases include imported Attic bf, Cor, Island and Ionian fabrics. Other vases come from local workshops. The settlement might be identifiable with ancient **Anthemous**, granted to

---

[7]For the ancient remains at Basilika, see Hatzopoulos (1987) p. 59 n. 156.

II. THUCYDIDES 1.61.3-5

Hippias before his flight to Persia, later given by Philip II to Olynthos as a sop. The settlement seems to have been abandoned at the founding of Thassaloniki (*Makedonia* 25.7.86).

Nea, 24.7.86 illustrates three gold mouthpieces with relief ornament, Cor vases, an Attic bf column krater (Dionysiac), a horse-head amphora and an Attic rf column krater (lyre-player).

Catling's earlier report in *JHS Reports* for 1984/5, 42–43, summarizes a detailed account of the excavation of a Makedonian tomb at Ayia Paraskevi "μέσα στὸν κάμπο τῶν Βασιλικῶν," published by K. Sismanidis in *AAA* 15 (1982) 267–284. The excavator says that the tomb was covered by a mound 6.50 m. high and lay 4.00 m. below ground surface. L. Rey, in *BCH* 41/43 (1917/19) 128, published a photograph of a "toumba" carrying a church of Ayia Paraskevi a kilometer and 200 meters to the west of the village. See also his photograph in *BCH* 40 (1916) 263. The mound was earlier noted by Wace, *BSA* 20 (1913/14) 128, who also reported what he regarded as another "prehistoric" mound to the east of Basilika. Sismanidis gives no bibliography, but it seems probable that the two mounds are the same.

Both Hammond and Hatzopoulos regard the site at Basilika as Strepsa rather than Anthemous. The important point remains that Strepsa must be in the Chalkidike.

B. **Therme.** For the site of Therme, D. Müller in *Topographischer Bildkommentar* (1987) 224–225 gives three candidates in the literature,[8] and in S. Lauffer's *Griechenland* (1989) 677, votes in favor of Sedes,[9] which is four kilometers from the coast

---

[8] For the site, see also M. Vickers, *Studies in Honor of Charles Edson* (Thessaloniki 1981) 327–333.

[9] Sedes is only one kilometer south of modern Therme. We found no road sign for Sedes, but visited the hill which has many sherds in the scarp. M. B. Hatzopoulos in *Meletemata* 11 (1992. "Recherches sur les marches orientales des Temenides") 29, summarizes reports of excavations in the region, includ-

on the modern Thessaloniki-Basilika road and eleven kilometers south of Thessaloniki. Charles Edson, *CP* 47 (1947) 100–104, strongly rejects the site of Sedes and argues for the old city of Salonika. See also Edson, *IG* X.2.1 (1972) p. 274. I find most appealing the position of Michelis Tiberios, Ὄστρακα ἀπό το Καραμπουρνάκι, *AEMTh* 1 (1987) 247–260, who advances four reasons for the site at Cape Mikro Karabournaki: 1. Therme, according to Herodotos, must be a port. We visited the site and saw two harbors on either side of the point of the cape. There is a military base above the cape. 2. Pliny (*NH* 3.10.36) distinguishes between Thessaloniki and Therme. 3. Pottery found in the excavations reveals sherds from Mycenaean and all later periods; see Tiberios 255–260. The site was discovered by the French in the First World War and published by L. Rey, *BCH* 41–43 (1917–1919) 96–100 with pl. 16 and an aerial photograph. See also *Albania* 2 (1927) 48–57; 3 (1928) 60–66; 4 (1932) 67–76. 4. At the site was discovered a bronze hydria with the inscription Ἀθεναῖοι· ἄθλ{ο}α ἐπὶ τοῖς ἐν τοῖ πολέμοι. The hydria is one of three bronze vases of the fifth century B.C. with identical inscriptions marking them as prizes given by the Athenians at games for those who died in the Persian wars, and published by E. Vanderpool in *ADelt*. 24 (1969) Meletai 1–5.

C. Gigonos. The conjectural site of Gigonos is placed by D. Müller (*Bildkommentar* 172–173 with photograph) on the coast four kilometers northwest of the village of N. Ἡράκλεια. As the crow flies, this is about thirty kilometers from Poteidaia. Hammond, *HM* 1.188, places it at Cape Epanomi a few kilometers to the north, but mentions no remains, and is followed by Hatzopoulos on his map in *Meletemata* 3, who likewise mentions no remains.

---

ing, "En juin 1988 dans le village Thermi fut découverte toute une nécropole du Vᵉ siècle av. J.-C. d' époque archaïque."

II. THUCYDIDES 1.61.3-5   147

I know of no survey team in the region, offering identifications on the basis of the evidence of pottery. We have in Herodotos 7.123.3 and Stephanos many toponyms for the region. Archaeologically speaking, Makedonia is a very active field with many congresses and festschrifts, but I have found nothing more recent in the literature known to me.

D. Beroia. The ancient city on the eastern slopes of Mount Bermion is described by Petsas in *The Princeton Encyclopedia of Classical Sites* (1976) 150–151. He writes: "It is situated on the crossing of the E-W road via the S of the three passes over Bermion and the N-S road across the W side of the marsh which elsewhere covers a good part of the lower Macedonian plain." See also Müller/Günther in S. Lauffer's *Griechenland Lexikon* (1989) 703–704. Oberhummer, *RE* s.v. Beroia 2 (1897) 306, following Grote and citing the scholia to Demosthenes 1.9 and 18.69 (248), mentioned the possibility of a second Beroia on the western coast of the Chalkidiki. If so, it would have turned up in the quota-lists. The scholiast says that Poteidaia was in his day called Beroia.

E. Pydna. The seashore city of Pydna is immediately south of the modern town of Makryialos. See Petsas in *The Princeton Encyclopedia of Classical Sites* (1976) 745, and D. Müller in S. Lauffer, *Griechenland Lexikon* (1989) 575–577. There has been much recent archaeological activity here, as reported almost an-nually in the *JHS Arch. Reports*. A sketch-map was published in *Topography* 2 p. 147. For many years, Manthos Besios has been excavating in the region; see, for example, *AEMTh* 1 (1987) 209–218. He kindly escorted us to two sites, currently being excavated. One is a cemetery of ancient Pydna, just outside what he deduces was the ancient mud-brick wall of the city.

148 THUCYDIDES' PENTEKONTAETIA AND OTHER ESSAYS

4. TEXT

A. The phrase ἀπανίστανται ἐκ τῆς Μακεδονίας. Gomme (*HCT* 1.218) writes, "Widmann notes ... that ἀπανίστασθαι in Thucydides always means 'leave by sea', except in 1.2.2; but this may be accidental." The word is used in 7.48.2 and 7.49.1 to relinquish the siege of Syracuse and in 1.139.1 and 1.140.3 to withdraw from Poteidaia. In *CR* 65 (1951) 137, Gomme asserts, "I cannot see that ἀπ. ἐκ τῆς M. can mean anything but '(gave up the siege and) withdrew out of Macedonia'." M. B. Hatzopoulos (p. 54) writes, "ἀπανίστανται is a historical present stressing the beginning of an action." He cites no parallel, and I find none.[10] The historical present was repeatedly studied by Gildersleeve in the *AJP* and the usage summarized in *SCG* 199–200. It is a lively representation of the *past*. In his last statement on the construction, in his famous review of Stahl, reissued as a monograph, Gildersleeve wrote (*AJP* 29 [1908] 393), "That the historical present is used by preference for the turning points of a narrative is another old story."[11] Thucydides uses the construction often in

---

[10]The historical present in 4.46.5 is not an exception. The verb πείθουσι has a conative meaning in the present system, "to urge": "They tried to influence." Here the historical present equals an imperfect of attempt, but the attempt is entirely in the past. Inceptive and conative meanings do not apply to verbs of movement; cf. ἀφικνοῦνται in 4.8.2.

[11]For J. M. Stahl, see his *Kritisch-historische Syntax des griechischen Verbums* (Heidelberg 1907) 90ff. Schweitzer (2.273) recommends the dissertation of A. Svensson, *Zum Gebrauch der erzählenden Tempora im Griechischen* (Lund 1930), who concludes (p. 119): "Der Unterschied zwischen Aorist und Präs. hist. als erzählenden Tempora ist wohl folgender: Der Aorist (das Tempus, welches die Handlung »tamquam uno conspectu complectitur«) steigert die Schnelligkeit, das Präs. hist. die Lebhaftigkeit und die dramatische Spannung der Darstellung." Some authors confuse the historical present with the so-called annalistic present (*SCG* 201),—Δαρείου καὶ Παρυσάτιδος γίγνονται παῖδες δύο (Xenophon's *Anab.* 1.1) and the Parian Marble,—as, for example,

II. THUCYDIDES 1.61.3–5   149

the narrative sections. In 1.59.1 we have ἀφικνοῦνται for completed action, ἀποστέλλουσιν ... πέμπει in 1.91.3, ἐκδιδράσκουσιν in 1.126.10 and 6.7.2, ἀποκτείνουσιν in 6.57.3, ἀπολαμβάνουσι, καταδιώκουσιν, and ἀπολλύουσι in 7.51.2, etc. The construction is frequent in the eighth book, which is all narrative: 8.10.3 (ter), 8.25.3 (bis), 8.25.4, 8.55.3 (ter). Examples are collected in C. Tosatto, *De praesentis historici usu Herodoteo et Thucydideo et Xenophonteo* (Patavii 1921). The use of the historical present in Thucydides is studied by J. L. Rose in *Language* 18 (1942) Suppl. 1 pp. 27–30. Just as one does not say he left the U.S.A. and went to Washington or he left France and went to Paris, we do not believe that Thucydides wrote that Kallias withdrew from Makedonia and went to Vergina and Beroia.

Although the Chalkidike was at times taken by the Makedonians, it was not regarded by Thucydides as part of Makedonia; cf. 1.59, 2.29.6, 2.99.4. Hammond (*HM* 1.192) writes, "The Greek cities of the peninsulas of Chalcidice were remote from Macedonia."

B. Καὶ ἀφικόμενοι ἐς Βέροιαν. Since Kallias had at Pydna the ships which had brought 2,000 hoplites with him from Peiraieus, it would seem bizarre if he sent empty transports across the straits to a coastline in visual contact while taking his hoplites by land on a detour of at least 120 kilometers through the Makedonian capital and Beroia. We are told that Kallias was in a hurry (ὡς ... παρεληλυθώς), and the operation could have been completed with one crossing. We, therefore, agree with Classen, Müller-Strübing, and Gomme that what Thucydides wrote was

---

J. Wackernagel, *Vorlesungen über Syntax* (Basel 1920) I pp. 162ff. This present is common with verbs of birth and death. A historical present may be followed by an imperfect, as in 3.72.3 (καταφεύγει ... εἶχον ... κατέλαβον), but the action of the verb is complete in itself, not inceptive. For the vivid effect of the historical present and its frequent use by Thucydides, see Ps.-Longinus *On the Sublime* 25.

150   THUCYDIDES' PENTEKONTAETIA AND OTHER ESSAYS

Θέρμην. Hude daggers the word Βέροιαν. Palaeographically, a malformed theta might be mistaken as a beta. W. Schubart (*JJP* 4 [1950] 83) makes it clear that in a copy of a text of Plato a cursive script was used in the exemplar resulting in the copier writing ειωθες for εἰωθός, οντα for οὖσα, παις for τούς, εγπυοντοπυ for ἐγένοντο ἐν.

We are told in 1.57.6 that the Athenians dispatched 30 ships and 1,000 hoplites under Archestratos. When they reached the Chalkidiki and found the cities in revolt, they took Therme and then crossed over from Therme to besiege Pydna (1.61.2). When Kallias arrived at Pydna with 2,000 hoplites and 40 ships (1.61.4), there was a total of 3,000 Athenian hoplites and 70 ships. In the first armament, there were 66+ hoplites per ship; so these were hardly carried on the triremes and there must have been troop-transports. We have a rare case with respect to Sparta where the hoplites constituted the crew,[12] but this was not the case in the Chalkidiki; for when the two armaments were combined, we are told (1.61.4) that the 70 ships sailed along the coast and hence were fully manned, whereas the 3,000 hoplites marched separately. No one has questioned that Archestratos sailed across from Therme to Pydna with his entire force. Transports were available at Pydna for 3,000 hoplites, and Kallias was in a hurry. Thus, we have four factors for the armament leaving Pydna: 1. Kallias was in a hurry. 2. He withdrew from Makedonia. 3. He had troop transports available. 4. The only port on the western coast of the Chalkidiki in Athenian hands was Therme.

Corruptions similar to that of our proposed substitution of Θερμήν for Βέροιαν are not uncommon. Using the critical apparatus in Hude's 1898 edition, we offer a partial list of names,

---

[12]Dover comments (*HCT* 7.1.3): "Since Gylippos and Pythen had four ships, with a total crew of some 800, and in § 5 infr. we find 700 of these serving as infantry (this number includes the epibatai), it seems that Alkibiades' recommendation (vi.91.4) to send 'men who would row themselves and serve as hoplites immediately on arrival' had been carried out."

II. THUCYDIDES 1.61.3-5   151

comparing Hude's text with variant readings found in one or more of the principal codices of Thucydides in three books (1, 5, and 8). A few of Hude's readings may not be in accord with those of later editors, but they indicate what one scholar who had intimate familiarity with the codices was prepared to accept. Sometimes only one scribe is at fault, but in many cases the alleged erroneous reading is found in all.

PASSAGE	VARIANT READING	HUDE'S TEXT
BOOK 1		
3.2	3 variations	Φθιώτιδι
6.5	Ὀλυμπιακῷ	Ὀλυμπικῷ
30.1	Λευκίμμῃ	Λευκίμνῃ
30.1	Κερκύρας	Κερκυραίας
47.1	Μετ or Μῆ	Μικιάδης
61.4	ἐπιστρέψαντες	ἐπὶ Στρέψαν
65.2	Ἑρμυλίων	Σερμυλιῶν
110.4	Ἀθηναίων	Ἀθηνῶν
112.3	Κιτειον, Κίττιον	Κίτιον
114.1	Βοιωτίας	Εὐβοίας
115.2	Πελοποννησίοις	Μιλησίοις
115.3	Λῖμνον	Λῆμνον
115.5	Μίλυτον	Μίλητον
117.2	Στληπολέμου	Τληπολέμου
128.3	Ἑλληνικόν	Μηδικόν
134.4	Καιάδαν	Κεάδαν
139.1	Αἶναν	Αἴγιναν
139.3	Μελλισίππου	Μελησίππου

152 THUCYDIDES' PENTEKONTAETIA AND OTHER ESSAYS

PASSAGE	VARIANT READING	HUDE'S TEXT
Book 5		
1.1	Φαρνάκους	Φαρνάκου
2.2	Κολοφωνίων	Κωφόν
4.4	Φωκαίας	Φωκέας
5.1	Λωκρούς	Λοκρούς
5.3	Ἰτωνέας	Ἰτωνιᾶς
6.1	Ἠόνος	Ἠιόνος
6.2	Ἀδομάντων	Ὀδομάντων
7.4	στρατοῦ	Στρυμόνος
8.2	Λιμνίων	Λημνίων
10.2	Ἀθηνᾶς	Ἀθηναίας
14.4	Κυνοσουρίαν	Κυνουρίαν
18.5	Σκῶλος	Στῶλος
18.6	Σιγγαίους	Σιγγίους
18.10	Ἀθήναις	Ἀθήνησιν
19.1	omitted	<Πλειστοάναξ, Ἆγις>
19.2	Ἀλκινίδας	Ἀλκινάδας
19.2	Λάμφιλος	Λάφιλος
19.2	Θεογένης	Θεαγένης
19.2	Ἀριστοκίτης	Ἀριστοκράτης
21.1	Ἰσαγόραν	Ἰσχαγόραν
24.1	Μεταγενένης	Μεταγένης
24.1	Ζευξίλας	Ζευξίδας
24.1	Ἄνθιππος	Ἄντιππος
24.1	Ἀμπεδίας	Ἐμπεδίας
33.1	παρασκευῆι	Παρρασική

II. THUCYDIDES 1.61.3–5

PASSAGE	VARIANT READING	HUDE'S TEXT
Book 5		
35.1	Δεικτηιδιῆς	Ἀκτῆ Διῆς
36.1	Ξενάρκης	Ξενάρης
37.3	Λακεδαί	Λακεδαίμονος
40.3	Ἔσωνα	Αἴσωνα
44.2	Κυνοσουρίας	Κυνουρίας
53.1	Πιθέως	Πυθαιῶς
53.2	Κρανεῖος	Καρνεῖος
57.2	Φιλιοῦντα	Φλειοῦντα
64.3	several variations	Ὀρέσθειον
82.1	Δικτυδιεῖς	Διῆς
Book 8		
22.1	Κύβης	Κύμης
26.1	Ἐλεόν	Λέρον
27.1	Δέρου	Λέρου
39.3	νήσωι	Μιλήτῳ
39.3	Καρίας	Ἀσίας
41.2	Μιλήτου	Μήλου
42.4	various	Τευτλοῦσσαν
44.2	Δινήλου	Λίνδου
75.2	Θράσυλος	Θρασύβουλος
76.2	Θράσυλος	Θρασύβουλος
91.2	4 variations	Ἡγησανδρίδας
92.9	Λᾶς	Λακεδαιμονίας
95.1	Προαστείων	Πρασιῶν
96.4	Βοιωτίας	Εὐβοίας

154   THUCYDIDES' PENTEKONTAETIA AND OTHER ESSAYS

PASSAGE	VARIANT READING	HUDE'S TEXT
Book 8		
102.3	Ἴμπρῳ	ἠπείρῳ
106.1	codd. and edd. differ between Μείδιον and Πύδιον for a river	

K. J. Dover, "The Palatine Manuscript of Thucydides," *CQ* 48 (1954) 76–83, in revising the Thucydidean stemma of MSS., offers several pages of variant readings throughout the eight books, including Φθιώτιδι/Φθιωτία, Λευκαδίας/ Ἀρκαδίας, Παλλήνη/ Πελλήνη, Σελινοῦντα/ἐς ἐλινοῦντα, Ἀστύοχος/Ἀστύμαχος, Εὐπομπίδου/Εὐπολπίδου. See also J. E. Powell, "A Byzantine Critic," *CR* 52 (1938) 2–4, who regards codex E as the work of a facile conjecturer, but not a good critic. In *CQ* 32 (1938) 103–108, Powell develops the story of how a refugee scholar copied a MS. of Thucydides, returned to his native town, and made copies for sale. Such a practice must have been common from earliest times.

In advocating that a word had dropped out of the Thucydidean text for Pylos in *Essays* 1.167–169, we collected opinions about the poor condition of our Thucydidean codices, invoking J. de Romilly's principle, *non auctoritate sed judicio.* There are well-known geographical cruxes in our text. In 6.104.2, Gylippos, sailing from Tarentum to Sicily, was caught by a storm κατὰ τὸν Τεριναῖον κόλπον. But the Terinaen Gulf is on the west coast of Italy. Hude and the Loeb editor follow Goeller in deleting the phrase as a gloss on ταύτῃ. Poppo and Clausen-Steup emend Τεριναῖον to Ταραντῖνον, noting that the term Terinaeus sinus is known only from Pliny. Bergk, *Philol.* 32 (1873) 565, would emend ΚΟΛΠΟΝ to ΙΣΘΜΟΝ. Dover suggests that Thucydides had Skylletion in mind, but called it Terina. J. de Romilly gives κατά the meaning of "à la hauteur de." Arnold

II. THUCYDIDES 1.61.3-5

suggests that it is a matter of the direction of the wind. See also
H. Philipp, *RE* s.v. Terina 3 (1934) 726, and Radke, *Der kleine
Pauly* 5.606. The phrase ἐν τῷ Μαλέᾳ πρὸς βορέαν τῆς
πόλεως in 3.4.5 presents a geographical problem to which
Classen-Steup devote parts of three pages (235–237) of fine print
discussing various conjectures, to which may be added those of
Arnold and Thirlwall. Gomme dismisses the problem as un-
solved. Hornblower suggests that Thucydides' geography is at
fault, rightly rejecting J. Wilson, *Historia* 30 (1981) 144–163.
Herbst in *RE* s.v. Mytilene (1935) 1419, notes that both the sanctuary of Apollo Maloeis and the harbor and camp of the
Athenians were to the north of Mytilene. The epithet and the
toponym explain each other; neither was on the southern Cape
of Malea. Presumably, Thucydides is referring to a settlement at
the harbor. In the Peloponnesos, the town Malea was not on the
famous cape of that name, but far removed on the border between Lakonia and Arkadia (Pausanias 8.27.4; Plutarch *Agis* 8);
see Bölte, *RE* s.v. Malea 2 (1928) 865.[13] Thucydides' toponym was
not on Strabo's Malea, seventy stades south of Mytilene; neither
Malea was on a cape. Currently, excavations are being conducted
on Lesbos, which may shed light on the problem.

In 1955, the Oxford Press published the brilliant posthumous
work of John Jackson, *Marginalia Scaenica*. Beazley told me that
he was partly responsible for the publication. Eduard Fraenkel
wrote the Preface. After winning the Craven Fellowship, the author retired to private life and devoted his time to a study of corruptions in ancient texts, including omissions and glosses, especially of the Greek dramatic texts. We lack a comparable study of
the corruptions in the transmission of names, errors which are
numerous. Some errors are palaeographical, the corrupt text

---

[13]W. Dörpfeld, *Ath. Mitt.* 53 (1928) 131–136, noted that five of the manuscripts
of Strabo 607 read some form of the name Malea where the correct reading is
Elaia and would place Thucydides' Malea not on Lesbos, but at Elaia, the port
of Pergamon, across the straits.

156 THUCYDIDES' PENTEKONTAETIA AND OTHER ESSAYS

having the initial and a few other letters in common with the original. Some can be explained. It is recognized that the scribes of the archetype of our codices of Herodotos and Pausanias substituted the name of common Attic demes for similar toponyms; see *Essays* p. 3. In *Topography* 5.171, we noted in passing numerous errors in transcribing toponyms in one book (VIII) of Strabo. There are far more errors in the spelling of toponyms in Strabo and Pausanias than in Thucydides whose text contains many speeches. If one consults the critical apparatus in the Budé edition of Strabo or the Hitzig-Bluemner of Pausanias, one finds many pages in which the fine-print apparatus is larger than the text. Usually, one attempts to explain errors in transmission on the basis of palaeography or of misunderstanding in dictation. But some errors have nothing to do with palaeography. A conspicuous example is Isokrates 8 *Peace* 86, where we have three readings which have no similarity in spelling: ἐν Δάτῳ of two manuscripts, ἐν τῷ Πόντῳ of all others, but ἐν τῷ Δεκελεικῷ πολέμῳ of a first-century papyrus, over one thousand years earlier than any codex. It would seem that some scribes were quasi-historians or quasi-topographers. The true explanation of errors may never be achieved, but we note that not only were commentaries on the text of Thucydides prepared (*P. Oxy.* 853), but that there were manuscript scholia made by scribes with extra information, who may in some way have corrupted the tradition. The scholiasts, for example, at times had vague knowledge about geography. On Aristophanes *Aves* 145, we read ἡ Ἐρυθρὰ θάλασσα παρὰ τὸν ἀνατολικὸν ὠκεανόν; on *Aves* 188: τινές φασι μεταξὺ Πυθοῦς καὶ Ἀττικῆς εἶναι τὴν Βοιωτίαν.

C. Κατὰ γῆν. This prepositional phrase is, I believe, out of position and should be transferred to follow the phrase ἀφικόμενοι ἐς Θέρμην κἀκεῖθεν: ἀφικόμενοι ἐς Θέρμην κἀκεῖθεν κατὰ γῆν ἐπὶ Στρέψαν. We have examples such as 1.90.2 where scribes have transposed a phrase. Instead of ἀναχώρησιν τε καὶ ἀφορμὴν ἱκανὴν εἶναι, all manuscripts except one have ἱκανὴν

II. THUCYDIDES 1.61.3–5   157

εἶναι ἀναχ. τε καὶ ἀφ.[14] On 1.17, Morris writes: "οἱ γὰρ ἐν Σικελίᾳ ἐπὶ πλεῖστον ἐχώρησαν δυνάμεως. These words are evidently out of place where they stand. The Schol. indeed supposes an ellipsis." The sentence is bracketed by Stahl, Classen, Steup, and Hude as a marginal note. Classen thinks that the sentence was made by some observant reader, and was afterwards introduced into the text in the wrong place. Wex is cited as thinking that the words should be placed after τῶν ἐν Σικελίᾳ in 1.18.1. There are cases where the construction is rough and some scholars suspect a dislocation. In 4.27.1, Göller would place the ἅμα clause after ἐπιλάβοι. Dobree regards περὶ τὴν Πελ. as a gloss on περιπέμπειν. Steup condemns all from ἅμα to περιπέμπειν as an adscript; Jowett says the clause is parenthetical. In 5.20.2, Arnold, Steup, Stuart Jones, Hude, and J. de Romilly believe that there has been a transposition of clauses. M. West, *Textual Criticism and Editorial Technique* (Stuttgart 1973) 28, notes that marginalia are often inserted in the wrong place by the next copyist. However, the practice of leaving out a word and then adding it superscript (or in the margin) by Thucydidean scribes is very frequent. I suggest that the scribe of the archetype of our family of codices saw the phrase κατὰ γῆν superscript or in the margin in the manuscript he was copying and inserted it in the wrong position.

In his 1897 edition of Book 2, E. C. Marchant devoted eight pages of his Introduction (xxviii-xxxvi) to what he considered as corrections in the text. On the transposition of words, he wrote (xxxvii), "This last mistake is very common, variations in the order in different MSS. being of most perplexing frequence." Müller-Strübing maintained that the whole of the text has suffered from being edited in antiquity for school use; cf. Marchant on p. xx of his edition of Book 6. A. W. Spratt, in his Introduction to Book 3, notes (p. xi) that the grammarians distinguished between classes of διφθέραι, the one written carefully

---

[14]Cf. 1.107.4; 1.108.5; 1.117.3; 1.126.3 for single words.

158   THUCYDIDES' PENTEKONTAETIA AND OTHER ESSAYS

in large letters so heavy as to be carried by slaves and only to be acquired at great cost. "Of the second kind we find mention in the pages of Libanius, a sophist of the fourth century A.C., who speaks of a MS. of Thucydides possessed by himself, written in small letters, and quite a pleasure to carry: i.e. an edition written, with contractions in minuscules. Both Galen and Libanius speak of σημεῖα used by those who write εἰς τάχος." *Pap. Oxy.* 724 is an interesting contract of the year A.D. 155 in which one apprenticed his slave to a shorthand-writer for two years to be taught to read and write shorthand.

All warmly endorse the maxim that an ounce of text is worth more than a pound of emendations; but for Thucydides, as any student of J. de Romilly's "Notes complementaires" is aware, there are many passages which are certainly corrupt, and many solutions have been proposed. See, for example, 4.73, 4.117, 4.126, 5.22. Steup, who made a study of what he regarded as interpolations in the text, particularly of 5.13–17 (*RM* 25 [1870] 273–305), concluded (p. 303): "die Interpolation rührt aber wahrscheinlich aus einer weit früheren, der voralexandrinischen Zeit her, da sich später eine solche Textverunstaltung nicht mehr leicht allgemeine Geltung würde haben verschaffen können." While more recent editors overrule Steup, it must be admitted that several passages contain corruptions.

D. Ἐπιστρέψαντες. The emendation ἐπὶ Στρέψαν is accepted by virtually all editors of Thucydides since it was first proposed by Pluygers, as reported by Cobet in *Mnemos.* 6 (1857) 288. This town is named by Aischines (2.29) in the order Anthemous, Therma, Strepsa. To get to Strepsa, one passes through Therme. Strepsa was one of the cities which had revolted from Athens. As we have seen above, it is located by Hatzopoulos at Basilika, southeast of Therme.

Two scholars have recently defended the unemended text. Hatzopoulos writes (p. 56):

Ἐπιστρέψαντες may be intended to convey the sharp turn in direction that an army marching from Pydna to the Chalkidike has to make at Beroia. One could translate then: "they moved to leave Macedonia, and after reaching Beroia and making from that point a sharp turn, and first attempting but failing to take that place by storm, they continued their march towards Poteidaia by land ...".

In turn, Badian writes (p. 176):

> Let us take the text as the ancients saw it and as our manuscripts still show it: an eminent topographer has recently shown that it need not be emended. Some slight improvement is needed. As Gomme rightly notes (p. 216 n. 1): "no one writes, 'they went to X and returned, and having first tried to take it and failed, went by land to Y.'" But that is easy to cure: delete καί before πειράσαντες. The Athenians arrived at Beroea and, turning away from there (having first tried to take the place and failed), marched by land to Gigonus, in the direction of Potidaea.

I find no example in *TGL* or in the historical authors to support the use of ἐπιστρέφω for an army continuing on the march and making a sharp turn. There are of course many sharp turns on Greek mountain roads. The conventional meaning was used by Hobbes (and old translators) who supposed them to have "turned back" to Pydna and thence to have gone by land. Bloomfield supposed that they had passed Beroia and, at a short distance from it, turned back, hoping to surprise it off its guard. By Hatzopoulos' late Roman road, Beroia was on the direct road from Dion and Pydna to Therme.

Badian's translation of the juxtaposition of the participles ἐπιστρέψαντες πειράσαντες sounds well in English, but results in very dubious Greek for which he offers no parallel in Thucydides.

160 THUCYDIDES' PENTEKONTAETIA AND OTHER ESSAYS

Since the Athenians had departed from Makedonia, we believe that they landed at Therme and then went by land to Strepsa, which they failed to take.

E. As to the phrase κατ ' ὀλίγον προϊόντες in 1.61.5, Badian (p. 177 with note 15) writes in part as follows:

> I would suggest that, not for the only time, Thucydides has been misunderstood, and the misunderstanding has been taken over by successive generations of scholars. I do not know who first (clearly a long time ago) translated κατ ' ὀλίγον as referring to a slow pace, or what his evidence for this was. There is certainly none to be found in Thucydides. ... But when applied to armies or war, it always means "in parts" or "in detail" (4.10.4; 5.9.2; 6.34.4). This should surely prima facie be the sense here. The Athenian army marched divided into sections. The misunderstanding is certainly as old as Thomas Hobbes, "by moderate journies" (pp. 30–31 in the reprint London 1822). Translators in other languages have been no better. Not to multiply examples, I quote only J. de Romilly in the Budé edition: "par petites étapes." For another flagrant example of conventional mistranslation, see Chapter 5 above.

The "flagrant example" is the genitive absolute in 1.103.3 discussed above.

The context determines the distributive sense. Of the three examples cited, we have in 4.10.4 κατ ' ὀλίγον μαχεῖται, in 5.92.2 τὸ κατ ' ὀλίγον is contrasted with ἅπαντας ("in detachments and not in a body"),[15] and in 6.34.4 βραδεῖά τε καὶ κατ ' ὀλί-

[15]The *TGL* 5.1878, notes that the scholiast on 5.9.2 interprets the phrase in the singular as κατ ' ὀλίγους. The use of the plural phrase is common in the sense supported by Badian: Herodotos 2.93, 8.113, 9.102, etc. The *Thesaurus* draws a sharp distinction between the frequent use of κατ ' ὀλίγους (1876, roughly, "bands of a few") and κατ ' ὀλίγον (1878, roughly, "gradually"). Oddly, in a

II. THUCYDIDES 1.61.3-5   161

γον προσπίπτουσα. LSJ⁹ p. 1215 translate κατ ' ὀλίγον "by little and little," citing Thucydides 1.93.5 (κατ ' ὀλίγον προϊόντες). Krüger well compares Plato *Timaios* 85D: κατ ' ὀλίγον τὸ πρῶτον ἐμπίπτουσα ... ("penetrates the blood gradually at first," Loeb). In 5.82.2, we have ὁ δῆμος κατ ' ὀλίγον ξυνιστάμενος. Classen-Steup compare 1.64.2 a few passages below: κατὰ βραχὺ προϊών. The regimen in our passage is προϊόντες; they advanced "little by little." English says "step by step." I see nothing in our passage that requires that the advance be made in small units, and would follow *TGL*, LSJ⁹, Krüger, et alii.

We conjecture that the text which Thucydides wrote in this corrupt passage was:

ἀπανίστανται ἐκ τῆς Μακεδονίας, 4 καὶ ἀφικόμενοι ἐς Θέρμην κἀκεῖθεν κατὰ γῆν ἐπὶ Στρέψαν
καὶ πειράσαντες πρῶτον τοῦ χωρίου καὶ οὐχ
ἑλόντες ἐπορεύοντο πρὸς τὴν Ποτείδαιαν
τρισχιλίοις μὲν ὁπλίταις ἑαυτῶν, χωρὶς δὲ τῶν
ξυμμάχων πολλοῖς, ἱππεῦσι δὲ ἑξακοσίοις
Μακεδόνων τοῖς μετὰ Φιλίππου καὶ Παυσανίου·
ἅμα δὲ νῆες παρέπλεον ἑβδομήκοντα. 5 Κατ' ὀλίγον δὲ προϊόντες τριταῖοι ἀφίκοντο ἐς Γίγωνον
καὶ ἐστρατοπεδεύσαντο.

---

brief review of Badian's book in *CR* 108 (1994) 338, P. A. Stadter endorses Badian's misinterpretation: "He rightly notes that kat' oligon (1.61.5) must refer to speed, not slowness (177–8)."

III

DIODOROS' PENTEKONTAETIA

THE OCCULT CAMPAIGN waged against Thucydides has its roots deeply embedded in Diodoros. Shakespeare's phrase (*W.T.* 4.3.26) has a very modern ring, "A snapper-up of unconsidered trifles." Scholars who profess to be students of Greek Historiography claim that they have found golden nuggets in Books 11 and 12, which confirm their highly imaginative reconstructions, without observing the most elementary rules of the discipline by appraising the record *in toto* or citing the bibliography of those who have.

In our section above on numerals, we raised the question whether the errors of Books 11 and 12, in what is the worst piece of historical writing preserved from Greek antiquity, could be traced to a faulty manuscript tradition.[1] The text, however, is primarily that of the Codex Patmius of the tenth or eleventh century, and the later codices have few variants. As we noted, in 12.5.2, we learn that Krison of Himera won the stadion in 448/7, and in 12.23.1 that he again won in 444/3; yet in 12.29.1, he won the same race τὸ δεύτερον in 440/39. In 12.35.4, we are told that Archidamos died in 434/3; yet later, he is leading an army into Boiotia (12.47.1) and invading Attika in 426 (12.52.1). In 12.1.5, Diodoros claims that Aristotle and Isokrates and his school flourished in 450–400 B.C. Again, repeating ourselves, we are told in 11.19.6 that the total of the army of Mardonios, which was left behind in Greece, was οὐκ ἐλάττων τῶν τετταράκοντα μυριάδων (400,000), in 11.28.4 πλείους τῶν εἴκοσι μυριάδων (200,000), and in 11.30.2 εἰς πεντήκοντα μυριάδας (500,000). In 12.38.2, Diodoros records a sum of money as 8,000 talents (τάλαντα σχεδὸν ὀκτακισχίλια); yet in 12.40.2 and 12.54.3, the

---

[1]There is no entry in our codices for the year 452/1 (11.90–91). The name of the archon occurs in *P.Oxy.* 2438.14.

164   THUCYDIDES' PENTEKONTAETIA AND OTHER ESSAYS

same sum has become 10,000 (τῶν μυρίων ταλάντων). The story of Themistokles—from a trial at Athens before his ostracism, flight, settlement at Magnesia, and death—is crowded into a single year, 471–470 (11.54–59). Incidentally, in 11.55.2, we are informed that the Athenian law of ostracism required an exile of five years (πενταετῆ). The exploits of Kimon, the capture of Eion, the discovery of the bones of Theseus with the resettlement of Skyros, and the Eurymedon campaign, are compressed within the year 470–469 (11.60–62). Under the year 464/3 (11.70), Diodoros records the revolt of Thasos, the resentment of the allies at Athens' imperialism, the attempt to colonize Amphipolis and the destruction of the colonists, and finally a "revolt" of Aigina, although we are assured that Aigina was not a member of the League. In 11.78 and 11.81, he has given accounts of "ghost" battles, which A. Andrewes has tried without much success to explain: *The Craft of the Ancient Historian* (1985) 189–197. Diodoros confuses the two campaigns of Kypros and Eurymedon, and quotes an epigram in connection with Eurymedon (11.62) which has to do with Kypros. Moreover, Kimon could not have fought at Kypros in the daytime and been at Eurymedon at nightfall, 125 miles away. He recounts the absurd story that Kimon tricked the Persian army into believing that rescue was at hand by transferring his forces into captured Persian ships dressed in Persian costume. Later, in 12.78, the record is filled with crass mistakes. In his account of events in his native Sicily, he wrongly telescopes (11.76 and 11.86) events that happened years later: so S. Berger, *Hermes* 117 (1989) 304 n. 2. As a catalogue of his slipshod methods, this is but the tip of the iceberg.

In addition to general appraisals of Diodoros, we have two detailed studies which treat his record of the Pentekontaetia: 1) Walther Kolbe, "Diodors Wert für die Geschichte der Pentekontaetie," *Hermes* 72 (1937) 241–269; 2) R. Meiggs, "The Use and Misuse of Diodorus," Appendix 2 pp. 447–458, *The*

III. DIODOROS' PENTEKONTAETIA

Athenian Empire (Oxford 1972).[2] See also the 1933 Tübingen dissertation of A. Scherr, *Diodors XI*. These studies establish that Diodoros has given us a clumsy compilation for which surely Ephoros cannot be blamed. No serious student of historiography would attempt to contradict the Thucydidean record on the Pentekontaetia with nothing more substantial than extracts from Diodoros to support his ratiocination.[3]

Of the "gold nuggets" mined out of Diodoros by D. Lewis, Badian, and others, the most prized has been that of Tolmides' campaign, as discussed above. From epigraphical sources, we conclude that the Athenians took Naupaktos for the express purpose of settling the Messenians there, and that the Messenians entered into a sympoliteia with the Lokrians. From archaeological reports, we know that Naupaktos had been occupied in the early part of the fifth century. The Athenians did not remain there, but later entered into an alliance with the combined settlement of the Messenians and Lokrians. The Spartans allowed the Messenians to depart en masse from their stronghold on Mount Ithome, which is a long way from any Peloponnesian port on the Korinthian gulf. It is reasonable to assume that the Messenians knew their destination and port of exit before they withdrew. Naupaktos had been taken, and the Athenians were prepared to transport the Messenians from some port to their ultimate destination. All of these conditions are met if we follow the Thucydidean scenario, which presupposes tripartite negotiations. It would be naive to assume that Thucydides had to tell his readers that the Athenians had a fleet and that in order to take

[2]Cf. G. T. Griffith, *Fifty Years (and Twelve) of Classical Scholarship* (Oxford 1968) 205, "Thus in the books where he owes much to Ephorus and nothing directly to Thucydides, there has appeared no cause to revise the received opinion that Diodorus contributes remarkably little to our knowledge of the period recorded by Thucydides himself."

[3]For Diodoros' defective history for the Roman period, see Eduard Meyer, "Untersuchungen über Diodor's römische Geschichte," *RM* 38 (1882) 610–627.

166 THUCYDIDES' PENTEKONTAETIA AND OTHER ESSAYS

Naupaktos and transport the Messenians, they had to make a periplous of the Peloponnesos.

The crowning argument against the Thucydidean scenario is advanced by Lewis (*CAH* V² [1992] 115 n. 71): "Those who maintain Thucydides' strict order and emend 1.103.1 have to assume an Athenian *periplous* to the Corinthian Gulf in 461 or so (even before the accession of Megara had given Athens Pegae), which has left no trace except this capture of Naupaktus."[4] This periplous Lewis finds in Diodoros 11.84.6–7 (Loeb):

> When all the other preparations for his expedition had been made, Tolmides set out to sea with fifty triremes and four thousand hoplites, and putting in at Methonê in Laconia, he took the place; and when the Lacedaemonians came to defend it, he withdrew, and cruising along the coast to Gytheium, which was a seaport of the Lacedaemonians, he seized it, burned the city and also the dockyards of the Lacedaemonians, and ravaged its territory. From here he set out to sea and sailed to Zacynthos which belonged to Cephallenia; he took the island and won over all the cities on Cephallenia, and then sailed across to the opposite mainland and put in at Naupactus. This city he likewise seized at the first assault and in it he settled the prominent Messenians whom the Lacedaemonians had allowed to go free under a truce.

Even an armchair historian will recognize that in a periplous around the Peloponnesos, Methone is far to the west of Gytheion. Moreover, if the Spartans were repulsing the large Athenian force at the southwestern tip of the Peloponnesos, they were hardly involved at Ithome. Nor is it likely that in an open state of war, they would enter into a pact with Tolmides to jeopardize their position in the Korinthian Gulf. What with fighting

---

[4]Lewis' objection to the emendation of the numeral is based on his mistaken assumption that ordinals were not transcribed as acrophonics. There is ample refutation in Meritt's studies in Attic epigraphy.

III. DIODOROS' PENTEKONTAETIA 167

the Athenians at Methone, hurrying back too late to defend Gytheion, then turning north to Ithome to wait for Tolmides to seize Naupaktos, all this presents a scenario, merely because Thucydides did not tell us there was a periplous, which has little to commend it. As Gomme observed (*HCT* 1.45), "Diodoros was a careless compiler and his inaccurate chronology is his own."

C. Falkner, *Historia* 34 (1994) 495–501, argues that Thucydides' νεώριον τῶν Λακεδαιμονίων, burned by Tolmides, was not at Gytheion. This view was earlier espoused by Niese, *NGG* 1906. 115, but rejected. We may dismiss Diodoros, who names Gytheion, but Pausanias, who conversed with the people of Gytheion (3.21.8), also reported that Tolmides burned the dockyards of Gytheion; so he found nothing to contradict the record. Gytheion remains the logical candidate for Thucydides' νεώριον until some substantive archaeological evidence is adduced to the contrary. Part of the ancient town is submerged because of the well-attested change in sea-level. Haussoullier in 1905 noted the remains of the quay and two ancient moles, as well as a submerged mosaic, as at Pylos. In any case, the essential feature is that the Lakonians had a port which must be on the Lakonian Gulf. The Lakedaimonians sent 16 ships to Salamis. If we reject Gytheion, we indict Diodoros as even more muddled than we have allowed.

Diodoros is the only author who assigns an archon date for a peace which he says was concluded by Kallias the Athenian with the Persians (12.4). His batting average is so low that a priori one would think that he cannot be right, and certainly no one should assign the date (449/8) with any confidence to Ephoros. Moreover, his passage must be appraised *in toto* including the terms he gives for the treaty. Strong arguments have been advanced for and against the historical reality of the treaty or treaties. R. Meiggs, *The Athenian Empire* (Oxford 1972) 598, wrote, "Statistically an article on the Peace of Callias can be expected every two years." Lewis (*CAH* V² 122–123) writes, "No

168 THUCYDIDES' PENTEKONTAETIA AND OTHER ESSAYS

topic in fifth-century history has provoked more continuous debate." No one seems to be completely persuasive.[5]

When Wade-Gery made the brilliant discovery that there was only one list on the right lateral face of the *lapis primus* of the quota-lists, that what had been taken to be a short list was in fact a "postscript" to List 1, he assumed that there must be a missing list with the aparchai of only fourteen years instead of fifteen being inscribed on this massive block of marble weighing over four tons. His position is still reflected in *IG* I³ (1981) 263: "Titulus anni 6 nunquam exstitit; in hoc anno (a. 449/8) propter pacem cum Persis a Callia ictam Athenienses tributum non collegerunt." The date was taken to be in accord with that of Diodoros for the Peace of Kallias. The war with the barbarian was over, and the empire was disbanded.

After a long debate with the *ATL*-D. Lewis group, we are prompted to return to the epigraphical evidence because of the following statement of Lewis, *CAH* V² (1992) 123: "The attempt of Pritchett 1964, 1966, 1967 (C 158–160) to find space for the eighth list on the back of a lost block attached to the top of the stela has been disproved by a new fragment of the top, Meritt 1972 (C 150) 403–5."

This statement is patently incorrect. Lewis and *IG* I³ omit reference to the illustrated article, "The Tormos of the *Lapis Primus*," *CSCA* 5 (1972) 153–159. We published a photograph (pl. 2) taken from the ceiling of the Epigraphical Museum, showing the projecting tormos, as well as one of the tormos on the Kittylos stele and a drawing of the tormos of the Mycenean gate. Students of sculpture are agreed that such projections were made to anchor capping members. Not only is the tormos dressed down with a chisel, but the mason polished a taenia or band of about three centimeters along the edge which would have permitted a

---

[5]How-Wells, 2 pp. 189–191, provide a good short summary of the ancient testimonia. See also C. W. Fornara, *Archaic Times to the End of the Peloponnesian War* (Baltimore 1977) no. 95.

III. DIODOROS' PENTEKONTAETIA

close-fitting contact surface; see the five photographs in the article, "The Top of the *Lapis Primus*," *GRBS* 7 (1966) 123–129, particularly figs. 2 and 3. The fragment published by Meritt exhibits the same tormos and polished taenia, and it is noteworthy that in spite of the rhetoric and the photographic equipment of the Agora, he publishes no head-on view. Why Lewis says the Meritt fragment disproves the theory of a capping member is inexplicable.

In connection with the tormos, there are two other noteworthy factors. 1. Pittakys, who provided the editio princeps of most of the stones before they were moved, stated that the surface was dressed to receive a γεῖσσον μετὰ ἀετώματος. 2. Pittakys reported that the stones of the *lapis primus* were in the area of the Propylaia, a low point on the acropolis, which means that the top of the monument was clearly visible from many places on the rock.[6] One cannot argue that the top was not meant to be seen. Aesthetically, the appearance of the *lapis primus* would have been enhanced if it had a sculptured relief on the obverse side, similar to that of the Kittylos stele which is thought to have had a statue of a Sphinx.

A second physical feature, one that is often ignored, is that by the *ATL*-Lewis reconstruction, their top list on the reverse side (*IG* I³ 266) does not begin at the top of the stone, which is lost, but 0.24 m. below the top, leaving by their theory an uninscribed surface which would have accommodated thirteen lines of text. Characteristically, Lewis, who offers a sketch of the layout of the stele in *CAH* V² 124, omits this feature. Meritt, *CP* 38 (1943) 236, offered the following desperate explanation:

> This upper space may have been left without inscription simply because the mason could not comfortably reach it. His ladder may

[6]This point was treated in detail in *The Liar School of Herodotos* 155–157, in response to an article (Lawton, *Hesperia* 61 [1992] 244–246) claiming that the top was not meant to be seen.

170 THUCYDIDES' PENTEKONTAETIA AND OTHER ESSAYS

have been too short, or the boxes and whatnot that formed his scaffolding may have been too low, or—within the range of possibility—the mason of 446/5 may have been a man of diminutive stature—say, five feet four—as contrasted with him of 441/0, who cut List 14 and who may have measured six feet three. Perhaps one man could reach the top of the stone and the other man could not.

I know of no inscription which has a text beginning so far below the top, and we can be sure that, if the experienced epigraphists who advocate such a position knew of one, they would have offered a photograph.

One hypothesis which will account for the alleged uninscribed surface is that the eighth list was inscribed on the reverse side, in part on the reverse of the capping member with its close-fitting join and in part on the surface above list 9.[7] If the empire was disbanded, and no tribute was collected, and there was no ἀρχή of the Hellenotamiai, it would have been incorrect to label the ninth, tenth, and subsequent lists as such. The tenth arche means the tenth list on the lapis primus. There was a fifteenth arche; so fifteen lists.

Historically, I do not believe that there was a *volte–face* in Athenian policy, whereby they could disband the empire in one year and re-assemble it in the next. It is easy to say that there was a peace which resulted in the dismemberment of the Delian League; but in the modern literature I have consulted, no explanation is offered as to why the numerous cities, once given their freedom (οἷα ἐλευθερίης γευσάμενοι), would be persuaded with unanimity to return to the fold and to render to Athens contributions in money, manpower, and ships, and that without

---

[7]No numeral was inscribed for the sixth list on the obverse side. For the restoration of the list on the right lateral side as No. 7, see Gomme, *CR* 54 (1940) 66; Pritchett, *Historia* 13 (1964) 130–131.

III. DIODOROS' PENTEKONTAETIA 171

leaving a trace. The condition of the world today affords many examples of dismemberment.

To support his theory of a Peace of Kallias in 449, Wade-Gery cited Thucydides' general statement about Ionia in 427 B.C. (3.38.2, ἀτειχίστου γὰρ οὔσης τῆς Ἰωνίας) and argued that these cities had their walls removed in 449 as a counter-concession in return for the withdrawal of Persian forces. Hornblower, on the Thucydidean passage, cites several scholars who concur, including Badian. In *War* 1 (1971) 62–66, I examined this hypothesis, and could find no archaeological evidence to support the claim. The problem has been examined afresh by Lisa Kallet-Marx, *Money, Expense and Naval Power in Thucydides' History* (Berkeley 1993) 140–143.

We place no credence on any position that relies on the flat-footed Diodoros alone for a date for the peace; nor do we believe that the *lapis primus* affords any evidence for such a date.[8] A discussion of Badian's theory that there were two Peaces of Kallias would take us far afield; it is rejected by C. W. Fornara and L. J. Samons, *Athens from Cleisthenes to Pericles* (1991).

---

[8]Stockton in *Historia* 8 (1959) 61–79, employed the fifth-century silence as his chief argument against the authenticity of the peace. He concluded that his argument would be stronger if he could assume the forgery of a document in the 80's of the fourth century. We now have not only the substantial article of Chr. Habicht, *Hermes* 89 (1961) 1–35, but in *The Liar School of Herodotos* (e.g. pp. 116–121, 339–341) we collected a mass of uncontested evidence about the faking and reconstruction of documents, particularly of the early period. We may be reminded that some who are the loudest in condemning Thucydides for the omission of the alleged peace are the same who, without the slightest topographical or archaeological research, claim he omitted a battle of Oinoa; see *Essays* chap. 1. However, with regard to omissions, it is well to be reminded that Thucydides' focus on the Pentekontaetia was the development of Athens' power; see L. Kallet-Marx, *Money, Expense, and Naval Power* chap. 2.

IV

THE SOLAR YEAR OF THUCYDIDES

W E FIRST DISCUSS three passages which are chrono-logically correct, but are placed out of strict chrono-logical order, one of which has been taken as the coup de grâce to the theory of the chronological sequence of the Pentekontaetia.

1. In 3.116, Thucydides records the eruption of Mount Etna. In the previous sentence (3.115.6), we have the phrase τελευτῶντος τοῦ χειμῶνος. Then Mount Etna erupted περὶ αὐτὸ τὸ ἔαρ τοῦτο. After this comes the usual formula for the end of the winter: Ἐρρύη δὲ περὶ αὐτὸ τὸ ἔαρ τοῦτο ὁ ῥύαξ τοῦ πυρὸς ἐκ τῆς Αἴτνης, ὥσπερ καὶ πρότερον. ... ταῦτα μὲν κατὰ τὸ χειμῶνα τοῦτον ἐγένετο, καὶ ἕκτον ἔτος τῷ πολέμῳ ἐτελεύτα τῷδε ὃν Θουκυδίδης ξυνέγραψεν. Gomme (HCT 3.704) explains:

In the previous sentence, 115.6, we are told of the arrival of Pythodoros in Sicily with a few Athenian ships τελευτῶντος τοῦ χειμῶνος, and of a small and unsuccessful action by him; then, περὶ αὐτὸ τὸ ἔαρ τοῦτο, Mt. Etna erupted. *After* this comes the usual formula about the end of the year, followed by the formula for the beginning of the next summer (iii.116.3, iv.1.1: see above, p. 700). The reason for this superficially illogical writing is clear: Thucydides did not want to begin a new 'book' with the mention of an incident, the eruption of Etna, which, worth recording for its own sake, had nothing to do with the war; it was best to tuck it away at the end of a 'book', even if that meant, strictly, putting it in its wrong year: especially here, since there is an interval of some length before the next event to be mentioned,

174 THUCYDIDES' PENTEKONTAETIA AND OTHER ESSAYS

which occurred in the spring (iv.2.1), but περὶ σίτου ἐκβολήν (1.1).[1]

2. Hornblower (1 pp. 235 and 290–291) believes that he has delivered the coup de grâce to the theory of chronological order when he observes that the historian wrote (2.31.3, tr. Loeb): "Later on in the course of the war still other invasions were made by the Athenians into Megaris every year." It seems pedantic to insist that an author violates his system when he clearly refers to an action as being repeated later.

3. In 4.50, Thucydides, writing of the winter of 425/4, tells of the arrest at Eion by Aristeides of a certain Persian named Artaphernes who was on his way from the king to Lakedaimon, concluding the episode with the statement (4.50.3, Loeb tr.):

τὸν δὲ ᾽Αρταφέρνη ὕστερον οἱ ᾽Αθηναῖοι ἀπο‾ στέλλουσι τριήρει ἐς ῎Εφεσον καὶ πρέσβεις ἅμα· οἳ πυθόμενοι αὐτόθι βασιλέα ᾽Αρταξέρξην τὸν Ξέρξου νεωστὶ τεθνηκότα (κατὰ γὰρ τοῦτον τὸν χρόνον ἐτελεύτησεν) ἐπ᾽ οἴκου ἀνεχώρησαν.

As for Artaphernes, the Athenians afterwards sent him to Ephesus in a trireme, together with some envoys; these, however, hearing there of the recent death of King Artaxerxes son of Xerxes—for he died about this time—returned to Athens.

It had been generally held that Artaxerxes died late in the winter of 425/4, but in 1983, M. W. Stolper, "The Death of Artaxerxes," *Archaeologische Mitteilungen aus Iran* 16. 223–226, published Babylonian documents which showed that Artaxerxes did not die before the winter of 424/3. On pp. 230–231, he writes:

---

[1]The passage was discussed by me in *ZPE* 62 (1986) 206.

IV. THE SOLAR YEAR OF THUCYDIDES

175

The most important issue is Thucydides. He is not in error, but he has been misunderstood. As Lewis suggests, Thucydides has introduced a chronological parenthesis. The arrest of Artaphernes was duly entered in the sequential narrative as the first event of 425/424 B.C. But the episode of Artaphernes and the Athenian mission to the Persian court proved to be without significant consequences or stages of development. Consequently, Thucydides narrates the whole episode at once, start to finish: Artaphernes was arrested in the winter before the eclipse; "later" he was sent as far as Ephesus, where the story ended. The parenthesis beginning "later" is actually fixed in time by reference to the king's death, which took place about a year later. Having completed the Artaphernes anecdote, Thucydides returns to his sequential narrative of the winter in which Artaphernes was arrested, then of the eclipse in March, 424. The date of the king's death is not the aim of the narration. It is an assumed datum which closes the parenthesis beginning with the word "later".

Andrewes, who knew of the existence of the Babylonian material but not its exact text, had written in part (*HCT* 5.13):

His '41st' year is a construct for the convenience of Babylonians who were not yet sure how to date their documents, and the ὕστερον of Thuc. iv.50.3 need not take us outside the limits of Thucydides' winter 425/4. It also makes it easier to suppose than an Athenian embassy visited Dareios, probably at Babylon, and concluded its business before the end of the Attic year 424/3 (Wade-Gery 209–10).

Without quoting Stolper, Badian devotes two pages to the sentence about Artaphernes in the light of the Babylonian evidence, claiming that the reference to the death of Artaxerxes may be deduced to substantiate his claims about Ithome and Drabeskos in the Pentekontaetia, concluding (p. 80):

It is now clear from several texts in the Murašû archive that Artaxerxes' death took place between late December and early February of 423 (or, to be precise, that this is when it was known in Babylonia). The section in Thucydides has been explained as "a chronological parenthesis" and must refer to some time not earlier than early 423, even though it is followed by events that precede it by a year or so. From a different point of view, we may say that Thucydides finishes off a story with a brief reference to its outcome, before going on with his main narrative.

The importance of this is that, if Thucydides will write like this even within the strictly chronological narrative of the war, he must surely be judged all the more likely to do so in his (clearly) not chronologically precise introductory book. His reference to the end of the Ithome war (1.103.1) and to Drabescus (1.100.3) should no longer be misinterpreted to fit in with a view of his technique that is now known to be mistaken.

A recent reviewer (P. A. Stadter) of Badian's book in *CR* 108 (1994) 338, writes:

> B. reaffirms (ch. 2) previous arguments that Thucydides' method (even in the body of his history, cf. 79–80 on 4.50.3) permitted notices out of chronological order, and rightly concludes that the Ithome settlement came in approximately 458/7, after the events of Thuc. 1.104–106, and that the disaster at Drabescus only occurred some years after the settlement of Ennea Hodoi, probably in 453/2.

We are in no position to question Stolper's interpretation of the Babylonian documents. We do note that in *AJP* 101 (1980) 93, Rahe had earlier questioned Stolper's observations, as reported in Stolper's Michigan dissertation, to which Stolper has responded (pp. 231–232) with a new collation about the damaged sign in question. We have no experience with cuneiform, and accept Stolper's position about the Babylonian texts and his appraisal of

IV. THE SOLAR YEAR OF THUCYDIDES   177

the Thucydidean passage, but note that in Attic epigraphy broken letters have a long history of controversy.

Gomme collects in *HCT* 3.704–705 two or three other passages where Thucydides, like all historians, decided that his usual temporal division of his narrative did not fit well with the division of events where a single operation runs over into the next season (e.g. 2.103.1–2). Sometimes in referring to places, he tells of events which had happened in their past: 3.34.1; 3.86.2; 5.4.2–4; etc. In our passage, he uses the adverb ὕστερον; it affords no parallel for the bare-bones, annalistic narrative of the Pentekontaetia.

What Badian does not tell us is that Diodoros has put the death of Artaxerxes under the year 425/4 (12.64.1), and that without the use of any adverb ὕστερον. Now Diodoros is the only authority to support Badian's contention that Tolmides in 458/7 interrupted his conquests to carry on negotiations with the Lakedaimonians and Messenians resulting in the undisturbed passage of the latter from distant Ithome to some port of exit, or the even stranger theory that the Thrakian tribes allowed the Athenian colonists to occupy the rich valleys of the lower Strymon and the entire Angites for thirteen years. Stolper's observations add one more deterrent to the reconstruction of the Pentekontaetia on the basis of Diodoros' narrative.

Key passages in the debate of Thucydides' summers and winters include the following:

1. **5.20.** Statement about the precision of his chronology (de Romilly's text):

> Αὗται αἱ σπονδαὶ ἐγένοντο τελευτῶντος τοῦ χειμῶνος ἅμα ἦρι ἐκ Διονυσίων εὐθὺς τῶν ἀστικῶν, αὐτόδεκα ἐτῶν διελθόντων καὶ ἡμερῶν ὀλίγων παρενεγκουσῶν ἢ ὡς τὸ πρῶτον ἡ ἐσβολὴ ἐς τὴν Ἀττικὴν καὶ ἡ ἀρχὴ τοῦ πολέμου τοῦδε ἐγένετο.

178 THUCYDIDES' PENTEKONTAETIA AND OTHER ESSAYS

Σκοπείτω δέ τις κατὰ τοὺς χρόνους καὶ μὴ τῶν ἑκασταχοῦ ἢ ἀρχόντων ἢ ἀπὸ τιμῆς τινος ἐς τὴν ἀπαρίθμησιν τῶν ὀνομάτων τὰ προγεγενημένα σημαινόντων πιστεύσας μᾶλλον. Οὐ γὰρ ἀκριβές ἐστιν, οἷς καὶ ἀρχομένοις καὶ μεσοῦσι καὶ ὅπως ἔτυχέ τῳ ἐπεγένετό τι. Κατὰ θέρη δὲ καὶ χειμῶνας ἀριθμῶν, ὥσπερ γέγραπται, εὑρήσει, ἐξ ἡμισείας ἑκατέρου τοῦ ἐνιαυτοῦ τὴν δύναμιν ἔχοντος, δέκα μὲν θέρη, ἴσους δὲ χειμῶνας τῷ πρώτῳ πολέμῳ τῷδε γεγενημένους.

2. **2.1.-2.2.1.** Beginning of war. Debate over numerals (see above under Numeral):

Ἄρχεται δὲ ὁ πόλεμος ἐνθένδε ἤδη Ἀθηναίων καὶ Πελοποννησίων καὶ τῶν ἑκατέροις ξυμμάχων, … καὶ γέγραπται ἑξῆς ὡς ἕκαστα ἐγίγνετο κατὰ θέρος καὶ χειμῶνα … Πυθοδώρου ἔτι δύο μῆνας ἄρχοντος Ἀθηναίοις, μετὰ τὴν ἐν Ποτειδαίᾳ μάχην μηνὶ ἕκτῳ καὶ ἅμα ἦρι ἀρχομένῳ.

3. **2.4.2.** The attack on Plataiai in darkness at the end of a month:

ἄπειροι μὲν ὄντες οἱ πλείους ἐν σκότῳ καὶ πηλῷ τῶν διόδων ᾗ χρὴ σωθῆναι (καὶ γὰρ τελευτῶντος τοῦ μηνὸς τὰ γιγνόμενα ἦν).

4. **4.118.12 and 119.1.** Date of armistice at opening of spring 423 B.C.:

τὴν <δ΄> ἐκεχειρίαν εἶναι ἐνιαυτόν, ἄρχειν δὲ τήνδε τὴν ἡμέραν, τετράδα ἐπὶ δέκα τοῦ Ἐλαφηβολιῶνος μηνός.… Ταῦτα ξυνέθεντο Λακεδαιμόνιοι καὶ ὤμοσαν καὶ οἱ ξύμμαχοι Ἀθηναίοις καὶ τοῖς

IV. THE SOLAR YEAR OF THUCYDIDES

179

ξυμμάχοις μηνὸς ἐν Λακεδαίμονι Γεραστίου δωδεκάτῃ.

5. 4.52.1. Solar eclipse of March 21 424 B.C.:

Τοῦ δ' ἐπιγιγνομένου θέρους εὐθὺς τοῦ τε ἡλίου ἐκλιπές τι ἐγένετο περὶ νουμηνίαν καὶ τοῦ αὐτοῦ μηνὸς ἱσταμένου ἔσεισεν.

6. 5.19.1. Calculations on dates in the Athenian festival calendar, focusing on the date of the Peace of Nikias in 422/1:

῎Αρχει δὲ τῶν σπονδῶν ἔφορος Πλειστόλας, ᾿Αρτεμισίου μηνὸς τετάρτη φθίνοντος, ἐν δὲ ᾿Αθήναις ἄρχων ᾿Αλκαῖος, ᾿Ελαφηβολιῶνος μηνὸς ἕκτη φθίνοντος. ῎Ωμνυον δὲ οἵδε καὶ ἐσπένδοντο.[2]

---

[2]The striking feature of the two equations in 4.118–119 and 5.19 is that at Athens in 423 B.C. the date was two days lower, but in 421 two days higher. E. Cavaignac, *REG* 57 (1944)51, writes: "Étant donné le caractère des deux peuples, il est certain que c'étaient les Spartiates qui employaient le second procédé" (= empirical observation). Dinsmoor, Meritt, and others assume that the Athenian calendar was correct. Any Greek state could have regulated its calendar empirically if it wished. In a year which begins with the first new moon after the solstice, the winter solstice would be observable in the middle of the year. If the eighth month begins before the winter solstice had been observed, that is adequate notice that an intercalary month is necessary. Alternatively, it is possible to use the rising of some star. At Athens, one of the principal functions of the eponymous archon was to regulate the festival calendar; see *IG* I³ 78 lines 53–54.

180   THUCYDIDES' PENTEKONTAETIA AND OTHER ESSAYS

7. **5.26.1 and 3.** End of war:

> Γέγραφε δὲ καὶ ταῦτα ὁ αὐτὸς Θουκυδίδης Ἀθηναῖος ἑξῆς, ὡς ἕκαστα ἐγένετο, κατὰ θέρη καὶ χειμῶνας, μέχρι οὗ τήν τε ἀρχὴν κατέπαυσαν τῶν Ἀθηναίων Λακεδαιμόνιοι καὶ οἱ ξύμμαχοι καὶ τὰ μακρὰ τείχη καὶ τὸν Πειραιᾶ κατέλαβον. ἔτη δὲ ἐς τοῦτο τὰ ξύμπαντα ἐγένοντο τῷ πολέμῳ ἑπτὰ καὶ εἴκοσι. ; ὥστε ξὺν τῷ πρώτῳ πολέμῳ τῷ δεκέτει καὶ τῇ μετ' αὐτὸν ὑπόπτῳ ἀνοκωχῇ καὶ τῷ ὕστερον ἐξ αὐτῆς πολέμῳ εὑρήσει τις τοσαῦτα ἔτη, λογιζόμενος κατὰ τοὺς χρόνους, καὶ ἡμέρας οὐ πολλὰς παρενεγκούσας.

8. The activities of the Lakedaimonian fleet in Asia Minor, which are narrated between the time of the winter solstice (8.39.1: περὶ ἡλίου τροπάς, December 24 412 B.C.) and the end of winter (8.60.3: ὁ χειμὼν ἐτελεύτα οὗτος), conclude with a treaty with Tissaphernes (8.58.1):

> Τρίτῳ καὶ δεκάτῳ ἔτει Δαρείου βασιλεύοντος, ἐφορεύοντος δὲ Ἀλεξιππίδα ἐν Λακεδαίμονι, ξυνθῆκαι ἐγένοντο ἐν Μαιάνδρου πεδίῳ Λακεδαιμονίων καὶ τῶν ξυμμάχων πρὸς Τισσαφέρνη καὶ Ἱεραμένη καὶ τοὺς Φαρνάκου παῖδας περὶ τῶν βασιλέως πραγμάτων καὶ Λακεδαιμονίων καὶ τῶν ξυμμάχων.

Dover, in *HCT* 4.20, attacking Gomme's system, claimed that Thucydides' statement of his chronology in 5.20 was not precise, that the intransitive παρενεγκουσῶν means "ten years plus a few days," citing Pohlenz. The invasion of Plataiai came after the be-

IV. THE SOLAR YEAR OF THUCYDIDES 181

ginning of spring 431 (2.2.1) and the treaty concluding the war came before the beginning of summer (5.20.1 and 5.24.2). In *ZPE* 62 (1986), "Thucydides' Statement on his Chronology," we collected the various uses of the word, concluding that Dover's translation was incorrect. I repeat two paragraphs (p. 209):

Wilamowitz (SPAW 1919.943) writes in part as follows: "der eigentümliche Gebrauch von παρενεγκεῖν kehrt 26,3 wieder; er bezeichnet besser als des geläufige διαφέρειν, dass die Tage neben der Rechnung etwas ausmachen, in Ansatx zu bringen sind; obs als Plus oder Minus, liegt nicht darin. Tatsächlich ist es ein Minus in beiden Fällen." He adds the important footnote, ignored by Pohlenz, "dass in παρενεγκεῖν ein komparatives Verhältnis durch παρά bezeichnet ist, so dass sich ἤ anschliessen kann, hätte ich nicht bezweifeln sollen." Similarly, in Kühner-Gerth, Gr. Gram. 2.302, under ἤ we read, "So auch zu erklären Th. 5,20 ἡμερῶν ὀλίγων παρενεγκουσῶν ἤ ὡς τὸ πρῶτον ἡ ἐσβολὴ ... ἐγένετο, mit einem Unterschiede weniger Tage von dem ersten Einfalle = wenige Tage mehr oder weniger nach dem ersten Einfalle."

Of the examples listed under "B. intr." in LSJ⁹ 1329, all except the Thucydidean ones are given the meaning "differ, vary." Add Dionysios Hal. 1.28.2 (τούτων ἡ γλῶσσα ὀλίγον παραφέρει) and E.A. Sophocles, Greek Lexicon, p.853. Moreover, the examples with a comparative (παραφέροντα ἤ κατ ' ἄλλον τρόπον δι- αλλάττοντα and π. παρά τι) clearly require this meaning. Wilamowitz and Kühner-Gerth are correct. Thucydides has said no more than "just ten years with the difference of a few days," as Graves, Herbst, and others have it. Having established his meaning with the intransitive use of παρενεγκεῖν and the comparative in 5.20.1, Thucydides merely repeats the phraseology in 5.26.3.

182 THUCYDIDES' PENTEKONTAETIA AND OTHER ESSAYS

Thus, we are spared the severe criticisms levelled at Thucydides by Andrewes.[3]

Since the publication of Gomme's position (HCT 3.699–715) that Thucydides reckoned by a solar year with definite dates for the beginning and end of seasons, there have been two serious allegations, in addition to the mistaken reference to "a few extra days," that Gomme's system would not work.

Invoking a theory of a "Dorian" calendar in accordance with the attested order of months at Kos, Meritt claimed (*Historia* 11 [1962] 436–446) that he could compute that the Peace of Nikias (4.117–118), dated according to the Athenian and Spartan calendars, could not fall within Gomme's time-frame. This theory of a Dorian calendar affording evidence for the Athenian one was

[3] I inadvertently attributed the passage to Andrewes instead of Dover. D. Lewis, *CAH* V² (1992) 14 n. 52, writes (omitting parentheses), "Meritt's successive tables of Julian equivalences for the late fifth century have been criticized by Pritchett on the ground that we cannot control the amount of irregular intercalation the Athenians may have indulged in, but see Dover, *HCT* IV 264–70." In the "Calendar of the Athenian Civic Administration," *Phoenix* 30 (1976) 337–356, we catalogued the irregularities which Meritt assumed for his calendar (esp. p. 350), which are in excess of anything that we had proposed. In turn, in "The hellenotamiai and Athenian Finance," *Historia* 26 (1977) 295–306, we responded to Dover's calendar which had been based on Meritt's equations in the *Athenian Financial Documents*, rejecting the theory of "clumsy bookkeeping," that the loans in question were inaccurate, that the Hellenotamiai held office for the Panathenaic year, and that Meritt's sequence of four ordinary years was correct. We maintain that all accounts are accurate with regard to the grantor and grantee alike, and that events, assigned by Thucydides to a late winter, did not fall in April, as Dover claims, but in early March. See, earlier, *The Choiseul Marble* chap. 9. In the same period, T. Drew-Bear and I ("*IG* I², 200: Affidavits," *REG* 86 [1973] 35–44) offered photographs and affidavits from Daux and Helly about a text which Lewis (*IG* I³ 285) persists in misreading without offering a supporting photograph.

IV. THE SOLAR YEAR OF THUCYDIDES   183

refuted in "Months in Dorian Calendars," *AJA* 50 (1946) 358–360, and *Historia* 13 (1964) 21–29.

The most serious charge that Thucydides did not use a fixed system for his summers and winters, advanced by Meritt, Lewis, Dover, Andrewes, Wenskus, and Hornblower, rests on the account of events in 8.39.1–8.60, including the treaty in the thirteenth year of King Dareios, which took place before the beginning of spring. It is claimed that Dareios' thirteenth year began on March 29 411 B.C. (Lewis, *Historia* 7 [1958] 392). The most detailed treatment is that of Andrewes in *HCT* 5.138–149. Waiving the possibility of an error in the numeral (ΔIII for ΔII), although similar errors are attested in Attic epigraphy, we treated the calendar for these events at length in *CP* 60 (1965) 259–261; *ZPE* 61 (1986) 205–207; and *Topography* 8 (1992) 55–57.

In the *CP* article, we noted that Parker-Duberstein claimed that there was a mistake in the Babylonian document, as was acknowledged by Andrewes in *Historia* 10 (1961) 2 n. 4; and we observed that Babylonian methods of dating need not be Persian ones, also quoting Parker-Duberstein, "There is no evidence in cuneiform tablets accepted as contemporary that Xerxes II was recognized as king in Babylonia."

The eminent chronologist, E. J. Bickerman, has now treated our passage in a special article, "Le comput des années de règne des Achéménides (Néh., I.2; II,1 et Thuc., VIII,58," *Revue Biblique* 88 (1981) 19–23. Bickerman has provided us with an analysis of how years were computed in the reign of the Achaemenidai, concluding, in a matter which concerns students of Thucydidean chronology, that the treaty given in Thucydides 8.58.1 was dated, not according to the Babylonian lunar calendar, but by the regnal year of the court at Sousa. Such was the conclusion also reached by me in *CP* 60 (1965) 259–260, but I lacked Bickerman's knowledge of Persian time-reckoning. Near the end of a Thucydidean winter (8.57.1 and 8.60.1) "in the plain of the Maiandros" at the mouth of the Kaystros, the treaty was ratified

184   THUCYDIDES' PENTEKONTAETIA AND OTHER ESSAYS

τρίτῳ καὶ δεκάτῳ ἔτει Δαρείου βασιλεύοντος. Bickerman writes:

> Darius II devint roi en janvier ou au début de février 423. La treiz-
> ième année de son règne commença donc quelques semaines avant
> le mois de mars de 411. Ainsi Néhémie et Tissapherne attestent l'un
> et l'autre l'usage de l'année royale, indépendante de l'année civile,
> à la cour de Suse.

Entirely apart from the date of the treaty in early February, it seems to me unlikely that the entire fleet of ninety-four ships remained inactive at Rhodes for eighty days (8.44.4). Wilamowitz and Gomme favored the emendation of 80 to 50. I defended palaeographically the emendation to 40: *CP* 60 (1965) 260.

Parenthetically, the observation may be made that the most serious charges against the Thucydidean chronology have been made on the basis of cuneiform Babylonian texts over which the Greek scholar has no control. We can debate the sanctity of numerals in the manuscript tradition, the correctness of toponyms, the restoration of the name of a month in an epigraphical text, and matters of syntax; but we are dependent upon others, both for the readings in cuneiform texts and for their validity. We observe that for one of the three Babylonian documents relating to the beginning of the reign of Dareios II, Parker-Duberstein claimed that the figure for the year was wrongly inscribed.

Turning to the calendar equations given in terms of both the Spartan and the Athenian calendars in 4.118–119 (424/3) and 5.19.1 (422/1), students of the fifth-century Athenian calendar will know that Meritt, using these equations first posited that there were four ordinary years in succession from 425/4 through 422/1, which he subsequently reduced to three by making 422/1 intercalary (*Hesperia* 33 [1964] 228), and yet again returned with

IV. THE SOLAR YEAR OF THUCYDIDES 185

McGregor (*Phoenix* 21 [1967] 85–91) to four,[4] in what he called the First Metonic Cycle. As explained in *War* 3.163–168; *Phoenix* 30 (1976) 337–356; and *The Choiseul Marble*, I regard Meritt's First Metonic Cycle with its highly irregular prytanies as only picturesque, but Dover (*HCT* 4.19) has used Meritt's date of 25 Elaphebolion in the fourth year to support his contention that Thucydides did not use regular seasons. This brings us to the problem of the epoch date for the so-called First Metonic Cycle.

I would remind the reader of the wide diversity of calendars. In *Revue Biblique* 88 (1981) 20, Bickerman writes:

> L'année royale commençait au 1er Thot et non le 1er Nisan dans les documents égyptiens dressés sous les Achéménides. De même, au IIIe s., les Ptolémées comptaient leurs années du jour de l'avènement et selon le calendrier macédonien tandis que leurs années dans le calendrier égyptien commençaient au 1er Thot, et l'année financière ne coïncidait ni avec l'année de la cour ni avec celle du calendrier égyptien. Un autre exemple: l'année séleucide ne commençait pas à la même date à Antioche et à Jérusalem ou dans les villages de Perse.

Until sometime after 407/6, the Athenians used two calendars, which were not coterminous,[5] one solar and the other lunar. The prytany, or bouleutic, calendar was roughly a solar one, regulating the administrative or official life of the city. Rents and

---

[4]As indicated in note 3, Lewis claimed a minimum of irregularities in the Meritt/Dover calendar. So far as regulating the festivals, which was the chief function of the festival calendar, they would be celebrated far out of season. In Dover's calendar, he has 28 Hekatombaion fall on 30 August 415 (*HCT* 4.268) as his primary equation, which is completely out of step with the *second* new moon after the solstice of 8/8 (Parker-Duberstein), or the first of 7/10 if we assume with Dover (4.270) that 415 had two Hekatombaions. Other equations in the Meritt/Dover reconstruction were rejected in *Historia* 26 (1977) 296–306.

[5]For details, see *BCH* 81 (1957) 269–301.

186 THUCYDIDES' PENTEKONTAETIA AND OTHER ESSAYS

taxes were paid according to this calendar; leases were made according to prytany dates. The archon's calendar was lunar, regulating the festivals. Before the merger,[6] the method of dating documents was regularly by the first secretary of the boule, whose name was often inscribed above the text in large letters The use of the archon's name was irregular until the two calendars were merged, when his name came to be required on all documents.[7] In Morocco today, the solar calendar is used in business life, while officially, the dating system runs according to the Islamic lunar year.[8] In *JS* 1989. 23–58, D. Knoepfler shows that the beginning of the year in the Chalkidike was in November/December; cf. *SEG* 39.579. Some believe that the Elean year began at the winter solstice; see A. E. Samuel, *Greek and Roman Chronology* (Munich 1972) 96. Bischoff thought that the year at Byzantion began with the autumnal equinox. We know that on the island of Euboia there was not a common calendar.

One wonders whether the Athenian archon list (Meiggs and Lewis no. 6; *IG* I³ 1031) is to be associated with the great calendar reform, when the two calendars were merged for their epoch dates and the archon became the sole eponymous official. It is commonly dated to 424/3 on the basis of Bradeen's reconstruction of a free-standing stele in four columns ending in 424/3, but the stele was reconstructed, Bradeen openly admits (p. 201), on Meritt's judgment of the letters c. 425: *Hesperia* 32 (1963) 187–

---

[6]According to Aristotle *Ath. Pol.* 32.1, Prytany 1.1 of 411/410 was due to fall on Skirophorion (XII) 14 of 412/411. For 407/6, see *The Choiseul Marble* p. 26.

[7]Writing in 1912, Schulthess (*RE* s.v. Grammateis 1714) stated: "Von den vor Ol. 93 (408/7) abgefaßten Psephismen nennen allerdings bloß 44 den Archon und Schreiber, 41 nur den Schreiber und bloß 5 nur den Archon. Daraus erhellt, daß in dieser Periode auf die Nennung des Schreibers größeres Gewicht gelegt wurde, als auf die des Archon."

[8]E. Westermarck, *Ritual and Belief in Morocco* 2 (London 1926) 150. For a separate financial year, which was different from the Makedonian or Egyptian regnal year, see A. E. Samuel, *Ptolemaic Chronology* (Munich 1962) 78.

IV. THE SOLAR YEAR OF THUCYDIDES 187

208. All fragments are broken on all sides. Dating by the script of a few letters has often proved to be erroneous by a couple of decades. Salutary are the comments of R. Stroud in *CSCA* 7 (1975) 292 n. 30 about the criterion of dating by letter-forms in a period where we have far more texts than in the last quarter of the fifth century:

> The need for scepticism regarding letter-form dates, even at Athens where there are so many fixed points, is vividly illustrated by the present case, where two of the most experienced Attic epigraphists of this century assigned to two joining fragments of the same stone dates which are as much as 36 years earlier and 74 years later than the true, archon year of the inscription. Wilhelm and Meritt differ from *each other* in letter-form dating by as much as 110 years on the same stone.

In *Essays in Greek History* chap. 1, I protested against some dates assigned to the work of the sculptor Hypatodoros on the basis of letter-forms. Our hypothetical date in no way contradicts the thesis advanced by R. Stroud in *Athens Comes of Age* (Princeton 1978) 32–33, that the archon-list was accurate and that the Athenians had records of many transactions. Indeed, the existence of the quota-lists and the fact that interest on loans was computed by the prytany year suggests that there were many public records kept on papyrus by the hellenotamiai and other public tamiai, as required by the elaborate system of auditing. All tamiai must have kept records dated by their term of office.

The Greek mathematicians and astronomers used the month names of the Athenian archon's calendar for months of the "artificial" calendars they reconstructed. In Ptolemy *Almagest* 8.3,[9] four observations are reported by Timocharis, "who ob-

---

[9]B. R. Goldstein and A. C. Bowen, "The Introduction of Dated Observations and Precise Measurement in Greek Astronomy," *Archive for History of Exact*

188 THUCYDIDES' PENTEKONTAETIA AND OTHER ESSAYS

served at Alexandria" (third century B.C.). These observations, made at Alexandria, are given in terms of the fixed Egyptian calendar, but also reported according to Athenian months and days in the Kallippic cyclic calendar.[10] G. J. Toomer (*Ptolemy's Almagest* [London 1984] 334 n. 65) writes in his translation of the work, "These and similar dates (pp. 335, 336, and 337) attributed to Timocharis must be dates in the *artificial* Metonic/Kalippic calendar" (italics supplied). Again, Ptolemy recorded three eclipses in terms of the Egyptian and Hipparchic calendars, the latter with Athenian archons and months, all observed at Babylon (4.11. H 340, H 341, and H 343). The Athenian archon list was used in the Greek astronomical world by astronomers, in their artificial calendars of cycles. According to Toomer, these calendars were solar ones starting with the summer solstice. For Euktemon's parapegma, in which Day 1 = Summer Solstice = June 27, see *BCH* 85 (1961) 32. Moreover, Hekatombaion (1) 1 in these artificial calendars could hardly coincide with that of the Athenian calendar, which observed irregular intercalations and even different intercalary months.[11] In the report of lunar eclipses at Babylon, the month is given by an Athenian month name, but no day of the Athenian month is stated. For the lunar occultations of fixed stars observed by Timocharis, both Athenian month names and days are given. B. R. Goldstein and A. C. Bowen, "On Early hellenistic Astronomy," *Centaurus* 32 (1989) 272–293, address this problem and show, as I understand them, that they were simply computed from Egyptian dates. This

---

Sciences 43 (1991) 93–132, collect 36 examples of reports in the *Almagest* of dated observations before Hipparchos.

[10]In my early chronological studies, I assumed that these were true Athenian dates, but was corrected by van der Waerden.

[11]See *The Choiseul Marble* p. 63. Fotheringham and A. E. Samuel believe that in Kallippos' artificial calendar, Skirophorion (XII) was regularly intercalated: see A. E. Samuel, *Greek and Roman Chronology* p. 47. In the calendar of Hipparchos, Poseidon (VI) was the intercalary month: *Almagest* 4.11. H 343.

IV. THE SOLAR YEAR OF THUCYDIDES 189

brings us to the crucial problem of what is generally regarded as the first fixed date for determining the epoch of an Athenian year in terms of a Julian date.

Several hundred years after the event, we have three different sources which record that Meton observed the summer solstice on Skirophorion (XII) 13 in the archon year 433/2 B.C.: 1) the Milesian parapegma of the late second century B.C., Diels and Rehm, *Sitz. der Berliner Akademie* 1904 92ff.;[12] 2) Ptolemy *Almagest* 3.1. H 205, tr. Toomer:[13]

> Furthermore if, because of its antiquity, we compare the summer solstice observed by the school of Meton and Euktemon (though somewhat crudely recorded) with the solstice which we determined as accurately as possible, we will get the same result. For that [solstice] is recorded as occurring in the year when Apseudes was archon at Athens, on Phamenoth 21 in the Egyptian calendar [−431 June 27], at dawn.[22]

In note 22, Toomer writes:

> The Egyptian date of this observation was not given by Meton himself, who dated it to Skirophorion 13 in his calendar, but is a later conversion (found in the Milesian parapegma of the late second century B.C., see Samuel, *Greek and Roman Chronology* 44 or Toomer [7] 338, but no doubt already made by Hipparchus.)

3) Diodoros 12.36 (Loeb tr.):

> In Athens Meton, the son of Pausanias, who had won fame for his study of the stars, revealed to the public his nineteen-year cycle,

[12]For the problem presented by the next eclipse recorded on the parapegma, see A. E. Samuel, *Greek and Roman Chronology* (Munich 1972) 45–46.

[13]In Toomer's notes, he reports that there may be scribal errors in recording alphabetical numerals (201, 213).

190   THUCYDIDES' PENTEKONTAETIA AND OTHER ESSAYS

as it is called, the beginning of which he fixed on the thirteenth day of the Athenian month of Scirophorion. In this number of years the stars accomplish their return to the same place in the heavens and conclude, as it were, the circuit of what may be called a Great Year; consequently it is called by some the Year of Meton. And we find that this man was astonishingly fortunate in this prediction which he published; for the stars complete both their movement and the effects they produce in accordance with his reckoning. Consequently, even down to our own day, the larger number of the Greeks use the nineteen-year cycle and are not cheated of the truth.

Two students of the history of Greek astronomy, A. C. Bowen and B. R. Goldstein, have now devoted a monograph-length study to "Meton of Athens and Astronomy in the Late Fifth Century B.C.," *A Scientific Humanist: Studies in Memory of Abraham Sachs* (ed. E. Leichty et alii, Philadelphia 1988) 39–80. Other studies are "Hipparchus' Treatment of Early Greek Astronomy: The Case of Eudoxus and the Length of Daytime," *Proceedings of the American Philosophical Society* 135 (1991) 233–254; "The Introduction of Dated Observations and Precise Measurement in Greek Astronomy," *Archive for History of Exact Sciences* 43 (1991) 93–132; and "Aristarchus, Thales, and Heraclitus on Solar Eclipses," *Physis: Rivista Internazionale di Storia della Scienza* (forthcoming).[14] Their works examine the conclusions of Neugebauer, van der Waerden, and Toomer.[15]

[14] I am greatly indebted to Professor Bowen for sending me reprints of these articles.

[15] I differ with these two scholars in my belief that in the Greek calendars, which omitted not the "30th" day of a hollow month called ἕνη καὶ νέα, but the "29th" day, the length of the lunar month was determined according to the last visibility of the moon, as in Egypt, and that the "day" was reckoned from the sunrise. We have the incontrovertible evidence of the ἡμερολόγιον from Rhodes that the 29th was omitted and Proklos tells us this was the case at Athens; see *The Choiseul Marble* 69–73; *CSCA* 9 (1976) 181–195; *ZPE* 41 (1981)

IV. THE SOLAR YEAR OF THUCYDIDES 191

Among their important conclusions are that seasons were not based on observations, that early parapegmata gave secular advice and omens. We extract the following from the first article listed above:

> However, if Skirophorion 13 is not properly reckoned in relation to the moon, then this date would appear to belong to the Athenian civil calendar, a calendar noted in the fifth century for being out of step with the moon. On this hypothesis, there is little hope of correlating the date, Skirophorion 13, directly with any particular Julian date, since there is no way to discover its relation to the actual occurrence of new moon on −431 June 17. Still, if Meton observed the summer solstice, the problem is to determine whether he did so on −431 Phamenoth 21. And this brings us back to the question of the equivalence of Skirophorion 13 and Phemenoth 21 in the year −431, a correlation which either involves mistaking the date of Meton's observation with a date for the occurrence of the summer solstice or presupposes that a civil date actually corresponds to one that is astronomical.
>
> In any case, this correlation is readily explained. Some centuries after Meton, someone using the Egyptian calendar computed that there was a summer solstice on −431 Phamenoth 21. He then identified this Egyptian date with the Athenian date for Meton's observation of a summer solstice in the same year. Whether he did this in ignorance of the fact that Skirohporion 13 was a proper lu-

---

145–148; *ZPE* 49 (1982) 243–266; *Philia Epe, Studies in Honor of G. Mylonas* 2 (1987) 179–199. Nilsson and Burkert believe that a sunrise calendar was used for secular matters, a sunset one for religious matters. Neugebauer concluded that in some periods astronomical texts and civil authorities used different epochs. Meritt denies that the Athenians had a true lunar calendar, and posits that day "21" or "22" was mechanically omitted in a hollow month according to the terminology used for the waning phase. For a summary of early literature, see Rehm, *RE* s.v. parapegma (1949) 1331ff.; and Sontheimer, s.v. Tageszeiten (1932) 2011–2023; *Der kleine Pauly* 5 (1975) 495–497.

192   THUCYDIDES' PENTEKONTAETIA AND OTHER ESSAYS

nar date or of the fact that Skirophorion 13 belongs to a civil calendar which was out of step with the moon (i.e., that Meton may not have observed the solstice on the right day), is indeterminable, though in either case the result is an error: all he probably had was the bare report that Meton observed the summer solstice on −431 Skirophorion 13, a report which he (uncritically?) took to mean that Meton observed the summer solstice on the right day and that this day was Skirophorion 13. Toomer suggests that this identification was made by Hipparchus; we agree and offer specific reasons.

...

If the date of Meton's observation, −431 Skirophorion 13, was identified with Phamenoth 21 in the manner we have suggested, then there remains little support for the view stated by Toomer and van der Waerden that Meton used or developed a lunar astronomical calendar which borrowed Athenian month names. As we see it, the only calendar Meton established was the zodiacal calendar of 365 days found in his parapegma, and he used the 19-year cycle to coordinate this zodiacal calendar and the Athenian civil calendar (which was lunar but erratic).

...

Consequently, these correlations were not really subject to observational control. Meton's parapegma was specifically indebted to the Babylonians in that it was organized according to a zodiacal calendar, since the division of the ecliptic into 12 signs of equal length was a Babylonian innovation. This zodiacal calendar was of 365 days, a year length which may be based on tradition rather than on contemporary observations of celestial phenomena. As for the division in this parapegma of the year into the four astronomical seasons, this too was probably not based on observations of the solstices and equinoxes and certainly should not be described as an

IV. THE SOLAR YEAR OF THUCYDIDES 193

account of solar anomaly: Meton's division simply adapts the solar theory found in Babylonian System A, that is, the rule that the ecliptic be divided into a fast and a slow zone, to the requirement that the year consist of 365 days or 12 months.

...

Moreover, no single observation would give the date of the solstice reliably. So, we think it more attractive to suppose that Meton did not observe the summer solstice in order to establish a starting point for his parapegma. Rather, his aim was to find out where the sun rose on the horizon on that day. In sum, we propose that in orienting a *heliotropion* to that part of the horizon where the sun rose on a predetermined date (which turned out to be Skirophorion 13 in the Athenian civil calendar), Meton hoped to determine an alignment.

We have in several publications since our collaboration with Neugebauer in 1947 vigorously denied that the Athenians used a Metonic Cycle, at least in the classical and Hellenistic periods according to the archon lists presented to us. We have also expressed unease about the use of the date Skirophorion 13 to obtain epoch dates for the archonships of 432/1 and 431/0 B.C., motivated by the fact that on Skirophorion (XII) 13 the festival calendar had 16/17 days to run to Skirophorion finem, whereas the new moon of July 17 (Hekatombaion 1) yielded twenty days, if we accept the equation Skirophorion 13 = June 26. However, there are cases, including the Choiseul Marble, where dates were subtracted at the end of the year to compensate for earlier intercalary days.

In *War* 3.163–168, we noted that according to the reconstructed calendars of Dinsmoor and Meritt, the new moons which began the years might fall on the first new moon before the solstice or the first or second after. Indeed by Meritt's tables, any given Julian day covered the range of 70 dates. We have

194   THUCYDIDES' PENTEKONTAETIA AND OTHER ESSAYS

stressed the incontestable assertion of Aristoxenos (4th century B.C.) *Harmonica* 2.37 (tr. Macan):

> "The fifth part of our science deals with the keys in which the scales are placed for the purpose of melody. No explanation has yet been offered of the manner in which those keys are to be found, or of the principle by which one must be guided in enunciating their number. The account of the keys given by the Harmonists closely resembles the observance of the days according to which, for example, the tenth day of the month at Corinth is the fifth day at Athens, and the sixth somewhere else."[16]

It is impressive that in two places where Thucydides gives the dates by month and day in the Spartan and Athenian calendars, the dates are different. Of the phrase νουμηνίᾳ κατὰ σελήνην in 2.28, Bower and Goldstein write, "His reason for writing κατὰ σελήνην is more likely that the civil calendar did not always begin with the first visibility of the moon."

S. Hornblower (1.235) writes, "Military conditions are the easy and obvious explanations for Th.'s system." I do not believe that the historian, writing of campaigns from Sicily to Asia Minor, from Rhodes to Byzantion and Kerkyra, from sea-level to mountainous terrain, inquired of the participants whether the seasons had changed and arranged his chronology accordingly. Nor do I believe that in 411 B.C., the "winter" had persisted on the sub-tropical island of Rhodes into mid-April (Andrewes) or mid-May (Wenskus) at a time today when Greek tabernas have brought out the menus in Swedish for the influx of such tourists. Nowhere does Thucydides give any indication of seasonal differences in one theater of warfare as against another.

---

[16]For other divergencies between the calendars of different city-states, see *Ancient Calendars on Stone* 327–328.

IV. THE SOLAR YEAR OF THUCYDIDES   195

Of two facts we can be certain: 1) Thucydides used a solar year of seasons, 2) he claimed accuracy for his system in comparison with others.

The first compelling questions to ask are, What were the prevalence and the nature of the solar calendars in use in his day? Bowen and Goldstein have brilliantly demonstrated at the close of their article on Meton that the reconstructed parapegmata of Meton and Euktemon were concerned with the same astronomical phenomena as found in a body of fifth-century literature devoted to specifying more precisely the relationship between the astral events and human life. Thus, they write of fifth-century Hippokratic treatises:

> Thus, one reads in *De aeribus* 1–2 what amounts to a prescription for the proper conduct of the medical art. The author begins by requiring that the physician understand the effect of each season of the year and of the seasonal changes. of hot and cold winds (πνεύματα) both universal and local, and of the quality of waters, so that on arriving in a particular town (πόλις) he will be able to know to what diseases the inhabitants are liable by observing how their town is situated in relation to the winds and the solar risings, the local waters and earth or soil, and their regimen. In general, he says, by knowing the circumstances and times of the changes of the seasons and the stellar risings and settings, the physician will be able to foretell what sort of year it will be and will accordingly be best equipped to handle particular cases successfully. And should someone think that such matters are μετεωρόλογα (literally, 'things appropriate to those who talk of what is high up in the air,' i.e., 'things fitting for astronomers'; but the sense may be sarcastic — t alking of things on high, i.e., of what is not down to earth, is the mark of a fool), the author states that reflection shows that astronomy (ἀστρονομίη) makes a major contribution to medicine, since human diseases and digestive organs (κοιλαί) change with the seasons. ...{The] *De nat. hom.* 7–8 supposes the seasons to influence health by affecting the bodily humors. As for whether the

196 THUCYDIDES' PENTEKONTAETIA AND OTHER ESSAYS

author of the *De aeribus* was either describing current medical practice or commending a way of practice which others adopted, the reader should consult the four statements of the general circumstances of an illness or 'constitutions' (καταστάσεις) listed in *De morbis popularibus*. These constitutions each begin with a statement of the predominating climatic circumstances during the time and at the place where the illness was contracted, and these climatic circumstances are defined by reference to those astral phenomena treated as most ominous by the author of the *De aeribus*. Thus, for example, the final constitution is specified climatically in terms of the visibility of Arcturus, the summer solstice, the autumnal equinox, and the heliacal rising of Sirius.

In sum, what we find in the medical and astronomical literature of the last half of the fifth century is the view that certain astronomical phenomena (among which are included, in particular, the summer solstice) are important in the course of human life not just for reckoning the days but because they signify important changes in the weather. This view eventually led to the emergence of a body of literature devoted to specifying more precisely the relationship between the astral events and the climatic changes they announce: several passages in Aristotle's *Meteorologica*, for example, aim to elaborate this connection.[17]

---

[17]Cf. G. Rechenhauer, *Thukydides und die hippokratische Medizin* (1991 = Spudasmata 47). There is a large literature on the question of whether Thucydides was familiar with the medical writers of his day as reflected in his vocabulary for the plague (Page) or whether his terms were in common daily usage (Parry). The most recent commentator on the question, T. E. Morgan, *TAPA* 124 (1994) 199, writes: "Using the computer-based *Thesaurus Linguae Graecae* (TLG), I examined the occurrence of all the terms used by Thucydides to describe the symptoms in *History* 2.49 and confirmed that Page was in almost all respects correct. There are at least five terms in Thucydides' description that occur only in the Hippocratean corpus and nowhere else in all of the pre-Thucydidean Greek literature that has survived to modern times."

IV. THE SOLAR YEAR OF THUCYDIDES 197

The author of the *De regimine* in the Hippocratic corpus, dated to the fifth century, writes (3.68), "I divide the year into four parts, the one most recognized by most men (ἅπερ μάλιστα γιγνώσκουσιν οἱ πολλοί), winter, spring, summer, and autumn: winter from the setting of the Pleiades to the vernal equinox, spring from the equinox to the rising of the Pleiades, summer from the Pleiades to the rising of Arcturus, and autumn from Arcturus to the setting of the Pleiades." The calendar of Theophrastos is studied in detail by Einarson and Link in their introduction (pp. xlvi-lix) to the Loeb *De causis plantarum* (1976). Euktemon, Thucydides, Theophrastos, Polybios (see *Choiseul Marble* 94–95; Walbank, *HCP* 2.640–641), and the author of the Hippokratic work all used a solar calendar with astronomical seasons. The Pythagoreans had a theory of four specific seasons (Diels, *Vorsokratiker* 1⁴ xlii). Gomme (*HCT* 3.706–708) collects several examples where term limits were given in astronomical terms. What Dicks (*CR* 84 [1970] 330) writes of Roman authors is equally true of Greeks: "The most cursory reading of, e.g., Virgil, Horace, and Ovid, not to mention Vitruvius and Pliny, will show that knowledge of risings and settings and of the signs and constellations of the zodiac formed part of the common stock of knowledge that a writer could assume was familiar to all his readers; this was just the type of material contained in the 'parapegmata' (astronomical calendars) which, originating probably in the last decades of the 5th century B.C., had a long history up to at least the 6th century A.D."

Solar years had widespread currency, not only among farmers, but in the contemporary literature. Agriculturists, botanists, and medical writers used solar years. In the solar years collected by Einarson/Link and others, winter regularly began with the morning setting of the Pleiades (c. November 8), autumn with the morning rising of Arcturus (c. September 14), and summer with the morning rising of the Pleiades (c. May 8),[18] but the

---

[18]For the variations of a few days, see *BCH* 85 (1961) 48; Gomme, *HCT* 3.710.

198 THUCYDIDES' PENTEKONTAETIA AND OTHER ESSAYS

indications of the beginning of spring are not so explicit. For Thucydides, the spring is formally part of his summer: 4.1.1–2, 117.1, 135.1 and 5.17.2. The autumn is also part of his summer: 2.31.1–32; 3.18.3–5, 100.2–102.7.

It remains to consider the solar year used by Thucydides. When I worked with van der Waerden (*BCH* 85 [1961] 17–52), we followed Gomme in postulating that the end of winter and the beginning of spring was marked by the evening rising of Arcturus (c. March 6) and, as we added, the beginning of winter by the morning setting of the Pleiades (November 8), both of which are attested. The solution hinges in great part on the number of months (Thucydides 2.2.1) remaining in the archonship of Pythodoros (432/1 B.C.) and the new moon to be assigned to his successor, Eythymos (Euthydemos), who entered office on Hekatombaion (I) νουμηνία. Chronologists believe that usually the epoch day of an archon's year was the first new moon after the solstice. Secondly, although we now believe that Meton had nothing to do with the civil calendar at Athens, the date attributed to him in late sources for his observation of the summer solstice is Skirophorion 13 (= June 26) of the year 433/2 B.C., which would have Pythodoros enter office on the next new moon, July 17. The new moons for Pythodoros' archonship then become: 7/17, 8/15, 9/14, 10/14, 11/12, 12/12, 1/10, 2/9, 3/10, 4/9, 5/9, 6/7. Pythodoros' archonship would end on July 5, and his successor begin office on the new moon of July 6, the first after the summer solstice. Since the beginning of spring in 431 is given in 2.2.1 as "x months" before the end of Pythorodos' archonship, Gomme read "x months" as "4" rather than "2" (codd.), as do de Romilly and Luschnat. Then, for Gomme the astronomical phenomenon in solar calendars which preceded these four months was the evening rising of Arcturus on March 6. One who rejects Gomme's solution rejects both the theory of the first new moon after the solstice as constituting the epoch date for Euthymos' archonship and the civil date for Meton's observation.

IV. THE SOLAR YEAR OF THUCYDIDES 199

J.D. Smart, in a volume replete with able articles, *Past Perspective*, ed. I. S. Moxon et alii (Cambridge 1986), pp. 19–35, has endorsed the theory of fixed astronomical seasons, but attributes the beginning of spring to the spring equinox, citing 4.52.1, where the question hinges on the meaning of εὐθύς. However, he reads "2 months" in 2.2.1 and has the year of Pythodoros end on 6 June, making the following year of Euthymos begin with the new moon of June 7,[19] before the summer solstice. Counting back twelve new moons from that of 7 June, we arrive at 6/17 for the epoch day of Pythodoros' archonship. An intercalary year would be out of the question. This gives two successive years when the archon's year began before the summer solstice.[20] Students of the Athenian calendar will know that in *IG* I[3] 364, the Panathenaia (Hekatombaion 28) of 433/2 B.C., falls between Prytany 1.13 and 1.37 (last day). Preceding two ordinary years, one might expect 433/2 to be intercalary. If so, it began on 5/30, considerably before the solstice. Any ultimate solution of the chronology will address the problem of the relation of the archon's calendar to that of the prytanies.

Whereas Rehm, in his study of parapegmata, collected twenty-three references to Greek and Roman parapegmata, including the oldest of Euktemon and Demokritos, we have no complete collection of solar years as adopted by various writers, including botanists and medical authors. Both ER Arcturus and Equinox are attested for spring. Since editors of the complete text of Thucydides, familiar with the manuscript tradition, regularly emend "2 months" to "4 months" in 2.2.1, apparently on the assumption that an alphabetical numeral δ´ was expanded to δύo, it may be noted that if an Athenian scribe caused the error,

---

[19]I adjust his dates by a few days in accordance with the tables of Parker-Duberstein.

[20]Smart, I believe, does not mention the problem of Meton's summer solstice, but the article he cites (Thompson, *Hermes* 96 [1969] 218 n. 1) rejects the equation, as had been my view following van der Waerden.

200 THUCYDIDES' PENTEKONTAETIA AND OTHER ESSAYS

he would have used acrophonics, and III might have been copied as II. Such errors with acrophonics are assumed for Attic epigraphy; see B. D. Meritt, *The Athenian Year* 112 and 161.

Our view is to favor a solution that has festivals fall in their more normal position, although countless vagaries may be cited in the Athenian festival calendar with its intercalary days and months. Of the two systems offered for "spring" in March, the prerequisite for a choice requires that Thucydides used a system which would be well known to his readers.[21] The fact that he nowhere explains it, though he defends it against other systems, and can assume that besides summers and winters there may be spring and autumn, is sufficient to show this. Our provisional choice is to follow Gomme and van der Waerden. In any case, the eclipse of 21 March 424 is within his summer. Waiving the matter of numerals, there is no event in Thucydides which contradicts either solar year.

Peasants and soldiers must have been familiar with solar years, as unquestionably were doctors and botanists. As we have noted, Athens, too, used a solar year which regulated the administrative and financial life of the city. We know that in a four-year period (426/5–423/2) the prytany calendar had 1464 days (4 X 366), and that where restoration is not a factor, the number of days in each prytany was fixed.[22] This was not an astronomical calendar, and

---

[21]It is important to note that the parapegmata of the astronomers (Euktemon, etc.) charted the solar zodiacal year. The scholiast to Aratos 752 (p. 478 Maass) states: δεξάμενοι τοίνυν οἱ μετὰ Μέτωνα ἀστρονόμοι πίνακας ἐν ταῖς πόλεσιν ἔθηκαν περὶ τῶν τοῦ ἡλίου περιφορῶν τῶν ἐννεακαιδεκαετηρίδων, ὅτι καθ᾽ ἕκαστον ἐνιαυτὸν τοιόσδε ἔσται χειμὼν καὶ τοιόνδε θέρος καὶ τοιόνδε φθινόπωρον καὶ τοιοίδε ἄνεμοι, καὶ πολλὰ πρὸς βιωφελεῖς χρείας τοῖς ἀνθρώποις. By contrast, the parapegma of *IG* II² 2782 marked the days of the Athenian month and was lunar. The two types were quite distinct. Thucydides followed the solar year.

[22]For the fifth-century prytany calendar, Dover (*HCT* 4.267) cites Lang, *Hesperia* 33 (1964) 146ff., and is followed by Lewis, *CAH* V² 14 n. 521. Cf. *IG* I³

IV. THE SOLAR YEAR OF THUCYDIDES   201

we can only speculate about its epoch date. Its year was dated by
the first secretary of the boule. In the Fasti presented by Hiller at
the end of *IG* I² , we see the frequency of the phrase ἐπὶ τῆς
βουλῆς ἧ ... πρῶτος ἐγραμμάτευε (last in 408/7), although
the archon's names appear, but less frequently. On the lapis
primus of the quota-lists, the years are dated by the first
secretary, although an archon's name is given in the prescript of
the first year (only). When the two calendars were made coterminous, the archon, not the first secretary, became the pivotal
factor in Athenian time-reckoning, which was ultimately extended to historians and the artificial calendars of astronomers
throughout the Greek world. Why the "first secretary" dating
was abandoned and the length of the prytany year changed, we
do not know, but it must have constituted a major calendaric
reform. The American Congress engages in heated debate about
daylight saving time; the change in Athens was much more dras-
tic, and the religious community prevailed over the financial.

If Thucydides asked a senior citizen, In what year did the
ekklesia authorize Tolmides' expedition?, he presumably would
have been told that it was when so-and-so was first secretary.

---

369. As explained in "Gaming Tables and *IG* I², 324," *Hesperia* 24 (1965) 131–
147, I did not accept a reconstruction of the stone which theorizes that the stele
had been damaged at the right margin before inscribing, thus reducing the
number of letters to be restored in the stoichedon text for eleven lines. Nor do I
accept computations which assume that the abacus operator placed pebbles in
the wrong column, subtracted instead of adding, neglected to place pebbles in
the proper column, and forgot to calculate the interest on some part of a sum.
As to the line critical for the festival calendar (*IG* I³ 369 line 79), I offered a
photograph in *AJP* 85 (1964) facing p. 40; and I do not believe that the *editio
tertia* text is correct, or that the restoration of the line is guaranteed, as Dover's
reconstruction requires. For the calculations of the abacus operator, see
Pritchett and Neugebauer, *The Calendars of Athens* (1947) 95–105. I do not believe that we are in a position to gain from inscriptions more than a discon-
nected and partial view of the two Athenian calendars.

Such a calendar applied only to Athens. If he had asked the skipper of Themistokles' ship in what year did he sail, it is difficult to imagine what the answer would have been.

We often hear laments that Thucydides did not use the archon's calendar. A response may be made that this lunar calendar with irregular intercalation gave a wide variety of dates for any day in our Julian calendar. Meritt's tables show three ordinary years in a row and two intercalary ones. For the fifth century, he was firm in his conviction that there were four successive ordinary years. In the Pentekontaetia, Thucydides sought only to arrange events in order. His task was similar to that of one writing a history of the First World War today without the use of Julian dates by anyone he interrogated, assuming that there were few written sources.

IV. THE SOLAR YEAR OF THUCYDIDES

APPENDIX

We give below the more important of the dates of the festival calendar preserved from ancient sources:

YEAR	DATE AND TESTIMONIA
433/2.	Hekatombaion (I) 28 falls between Prytany 1 13 and 1 37.
	IG I³ 364
	Skirophorion (XII) 13 = Summer solstice.
	Milesian parapegma, etc. Accepted by Bowen and Goldstein; van der Waerden and Toomer do not believe this is a date in the Athenian civil calendar.
424/3.	Elaphebolion (IX) 14 = Gerastios 12 (at Sparta).
	Thucydides 4.118–119
423–2.	Month restored as Hekatombaion (Meritt) or Metageitnion (Pritchett*) [2]3 = Prytany [I ?]
	IG I³ 369 line 58
	Month restored as Skirophorion (Meritt) or Hekatombaion (Pritchett*) 23 = Prytany X 20.
	IG I³ 369 line 79

* See *Historia* 26 (1977) 303–304.

YEAR	DATE AND TESTIMONIA
422/1.	Elaphebolion (IX) 25 = Artemision 27 (at Sparta). Thucydides 5.19
Unknown year c. 425–415 (?)	Intercalary Hekatombaion. *IG* I³ 78 lines 53–54
414/3.	Gamelion (VII) 7 and 25 = Prytany VII. *IG* I³ 430
412/1.	Skirophorion (XII) 14 = Prytany I 1. Aristotle *Ath. Pol.* 32.1. See *ZPE* 49 (1982) 257.

Crucial considerations for any effort to obtain Julian dates are 1) the new moon for any archon's year and 2), equally important for the financial records, the epoch date of the office of Hellenotamiai.

V

AETIOLOGY SANS TOPOGRAPHY

A S A STUDENT of Greek historiography, I have commented from time to time on the importance of an accurate knowledge of topography in the study of ancient Greek history.[1] A volume (Noel Robertson, *Festivals and Legends* [Toronto 1992]) has been published in which the thesis is developed that the accounts of early battles and wars, recorded in our sources, are but legends developed from festivals (originally funeral games) associated with ancient monuments of heroes. "A putative tomb is requisite to the festival site" (p. xvi). The claim is made that the monument and the festival inspired the "aetiology." One invents a monument, assigns a festival to the site

---

[1]See, for example, chapter 10 ("Chimney Corner Topography") of *Topography* 3.347–369, devoted to examining N. Robertson's thesis in *JHS* 96 (1976) 100–120, that Herodotos was mistaken in describing the route used by Xerxes in 480 B.C. in advancing on Tempe. Again, in *War* 4.94 n. 1, we commented on the same author's penchant for misinterpreting ancient texts and, more importantly, misrepresenting the opinions of other scholars, usually without quotation marks. A conspicuous example in the present work may be found on p. 18 n. 53, where Hedrick's position about the temple and cult statue of Apollo is misrepresented. On the same page, Robertson says the Demosion Sema was "on the Academy road." This road has been excavated in many places and has yielded but a single fragment of a Demosion Sema inscription built into a Late Roman tomb. The Demosion Sema was to the east. For Robertson's attempt to explain the First Sacred War as a myth (*CQ* 72 [1978] 38-73), see G. A. Lehmann, *Historia* 29 (1980) 242–246. For the site of Krisa, see Braun in S. Lauffer, *Griechenland* (Munich 1989) 353–354. In baseball, three strikes and you are out; our profession seems to have no limits. We add that we do not maintain that the historicity of the Sacred War may not be challenged, only that Robertson has not touched the main issues, which are studied by J. Davies in S. Hornblower's *Greek Historiography* (1994) 193–212.

of the monument, and then alleges that amidst their sacrifices and songs and dances, the performers created tales about battles and wars which had never occurred.

Robertson writes (p. xiv):

> Or consider some early battles and wars: Hysiae, Thyrea, the Messenian wars, the ordeal of Phigaleia. Each is generally accepted, and all are usually combined as the history of unfolding relations between Sparta, Argos, and other places. Yet these are local legends of independent origin; behind each is a local festival. The several stories changed with time, from myth or legend to a more chauvinistic episode. Local conditions changed as well, for these festivals were all conducted in border areas. By tracing the changes, we can reach a truer understanding of the early Peloponnesus.

A triple process is involved. 1) One designates a site for the tomb of an imaginary hero of the Dark Age and funeral games in his honor. 2) The celebrants forget the original occasion for the monument and the festival. 3) The celebrants invent the tales which got into Herodotos, the elegiac poets, and later writers. Phigaleia is something of an exception; a conversion of a monument of a Dark Age hero into a polyandrion takes place in the 360's.

The four battles or wars cited by Robertson belong to places in the Peloponnesos which I have treated in my topographical studies. In order to make his thesis work, N. Robertson is sharply critical of my topographical identifications. In this reply, I attempt to cut through the mythhistorical jungle about the rituals and focus on the topography and aetiology. I have taken the opportunity to revisit the sites and to expand on my previous discussions.

I discuss Robertson's Peloponnesian chapters under the following headings:

V. AETIOLOGY SANS TOPOGRAPHY

1. Kenchreai and the Battle of Hysiai
2. Thyreatis and the Battle of Champions
3. Phigaleia and the Oresthasians
4. The Ithomaia and the Messenian Wars

1. KENCHREAI AND THE BATTLE OF HYSIAI

In a section titled, "A Festival of Cenchreae and the Battle of Hysiae" in his volume *Festivals and Legends* (Toronto 1992) 208–216, Noel Robertson, after postulating an unattested festival of Hermes and a memorial of Argos at the Argive town of Kenchreai, claims that he can show that the battle of Hysiai is a myth and not an historical event.

I take up his treatment under the following headings:

1. The Polyandria at Kenchreai
2. Trochos
3. The Myth
4. The Topography

1. The Polyandria at Kenchreai.[2] Robertson writes (p. 212), "What we know otherwise of Argive burials, both historical and legendary, indicates that Argos like most other cities preferred to bring home the dead. Second, had the Argives chosen for once to bury their dead on the battlefield, like the Spartans, they could easily have done so, for this was an Argive victory in Argive territory." There are no references to back up these generalizations.

---

[2]For Pausanias' use of the plural form polyandria, see Bölte, *RE* s.v. Kenchreai (1921) 166.60–62.

208 THUCYDIDES' PENTEKONTAETIA AND OTHER ESSAYS

What we know about Argive warfare burials is the following:

1. After Tanagra (457 B.C.?), the Argives did not bring home the dead. Not only does Pausanias tell us that the Argives who fought for Athens were buried in the Kerameikos (2.29.7–9), but the epigraphical text for the Argive dead at Tanagra is published in the well-known handbook of Meiggs and Lewis (*GHI* no. 35). The text has been published more recently by D. W. Bradeen, *The Athenian Agora* 17 no. 4 (= *IG* I³ 1149).[3]

2. Although Pausanias was shown the graves of many legendary figures at Argos, as well as a cenotaph (τάφος κενός), for the Argive dead from Troy (2.20.6) and the grave of the Argive women who fought with Dionysos against Perseus (2.22.1), a legend known to us from the late sixth-century work of Nonnus of Egypt (47.474–741),[4] the only historical polyandrion he reported was that for the Argives who sailed to Syrakuse with the Athenians (2.22.9). This grave could hardly have contained their bodies, but must have marked their ashes, or was a cenotaph.

3. Kritsas, *Stele Kontoleon* (1980) 497–510, publishes an Argive casualty list of about 400 B.C., found near the ancient agora, and reviews the evidence for Argive battles of the period (= *SEG*

---

[3]See *War* 4.181–182.

[4]Pausanias observed the τάφοι of many legendary or semi-legendary figures at Argos: Choreia (2.20.4), Epimenides (2.21.3), Gorgophone (2.21.7), Likymnios (2.22.8), Linos, son of Apollo (2.19.8), Pelasgos (2.22.1), Phoroneus (2.20.3), Talaos (2.21.2), and Thyestes (2.18.1). In addition to these nine, he recorded the μνήματα of Danaos (2.20.6), Kerdo (2.21.1), Prometheus (2.19.8), and Sakadas (2.22.8). In the *Liar School of Herodotos*, I collected references to a considerable body of objects in temples which priests passed off as historical dedications (339–324). Cf. L. Casson, *Travels in the Ancient World* (London 1974) 240–252. The fabrication or reconstruction of epigraphical texts comes early (116–120) and probably continued throughout antiquity (cf. 340 n. 295).

V. AETIOLOGY SANS TOPOGRAPHY 209

29.361). It has been suggested that the list is from the poly-andrion of the dead in Sikily (see *War* 4.141; *SEG* 33.293).

4. Most importantly, Pausanias, in his detailed account of the monuments of Argos, mentions no Demosion Sema. The poly-andrion for the Argives from Sikily was near the gymnasion, but no other military graves are mentioned.

Although Hysiai was clearly regarded as being in the Argolid in later times, its status in 669 B.C. is unknown, except that one may presume that it was friendly to Argos. For Pausanias' date of the battle, see A. A. Mosshammer, *The Chronicle of Eusebius and Greek Chronographic Tradition* (1979) 224 and n. 8. Earlier, Pausanias (2.36.4; 3.7.4; 4.14.3) reports that Asine joined with Nikandros of Sparta in a war against Argos. It would be a mistake to speak of eighth-century Asine as "Argive" in the sense of being allied with Argos. Asine, southeast of Nauplia, is much closer to Argos than is Hysiai. Incidentally, Pausanias's account has the support of archaeology, for Asine was destroyed in the late eighth century.[5] If Asine was independent in the eighth century, Hysiai may have been in the first half of the seventh. Pausanias (8.27.1) reports that at some period earlier than the founding of Megalopolis, Argos took over Hysiai, along with Tiryns and Mykenai, which would mean that they were earlier independent. Mykenai sent citizens to Thermopylai (Herodotos 7.202) and Plataiai (9.28), and was not taken and destroyed by Argos until 468 B.C. Both Thucydides (5.83.2) and Diodoros (12.81.1) call Hysiai a χωρίον. Diodoros adds τὸ φρούριον κατέσκαψαν. Apollodoros (i.e. Strabo 9.2.12.404 and Stephanos s.v. ῾Υσία) uses the term κώμη. Lolling, in the 1883 Baedeker, measured the wall as 52 paces, which means that it was a place of refuge, not the

---

[5]See G. L. Huxley, *Early Sparta* (London 1962) 21, and W. G. Forrest, *A History of Sparta* (London 1968) 36. For recent excavations by the Swedes at Asine, see *JHS Reports* 1990–91 21; 1993–94 15–16.

210   THUCYDIDES' PENTEKONTAETIA AND OTHER ESSAYS

"akropolis" of a polis. This small walled akropolis of Hysiai, of polygonal masonry resting upon a foundation of ashlar masonry bonded with mortar, lies to the left of the road descending on Achladokampos on a rocky knoll on the western slopes of Mount Kreion with a church of the Panagia: see Papachatzes, 2 p. 183 fig. 193. Unfortunately, there has been no archaeological activity here, which might be rewarding. To the best of my knowledge, no remains have been found in this upper valley of Achladokampos. Kenchreai, on the other hand, lies higher, but on the eastern side of the same mountain, about two kilometers north of a ridge which looks down on part of the Argive plain around Lerna, north of the pass which has been dramatically altered in building the new highway running to Tripolis. It is about seven kilometers between the two sites. Kenchreai marks the ἐσχατιά of the mountains rimming the Argive plain; Hysiai is in a separate valley. The remains of the dead of the battle of Hysiai were taken to the nearest site that we can be sure had an organized civic community and a temple (at least in later times).

Customs about burial varied; see *War* 4.249ff. After the battle of Delion, for example, although the nearby sanctuary of Apollo was in Boiotian territory, the victorious Boiotians of Thespiai transported the bodies, not to a Demosion Sema, but to a position about 1,200 yards east of the city alongside the road which led to Thebes. Robertson has laid no foundation for discrediting Pausanias about the polyandria.

2. **Trochos.** Of the landmark called Trochos, Pausanias says that "Kenchreai is to the right of what is called Trochos" (ἐν δεξιᾷ τοῦ ὀνοματοζομένου Τροχου). The exemplar of Niccolo Niccoli (= all codd.) accented the word as τροχοῦ. The phrase τῷ χωρίῳ in the following sentence applies to Kenchreai, not to Trochos. We have no other information, and must turn to the topography.

V. AETIOLOGY SANS TOPOGRAPHY 211

Robertson writes (212–213), "Pausanias would not leave his readers in the dark about the *Wheel*, strange work of nature or of man. The term must be self-explanatory. Sibelis set matters right with a change of accent: Τρόχου, 'Running place,' 'Racecourse'. ... We may still ask why the landmark was called τρόχος rather than δρόμος ... The answer must be that τρόχος was the Argive term. The Argive hero Τροχίλος proves it so."[6]

Trochilos, legendary son of the first priestess of Hera in Argos, is well known as the inventor of the chariot (ἅρμα); see von Geisau, *RE* s.v. Trochilos (1939) 588–590. By this association, the alleged "racecourse" at Kenchreai is one for ἅρματα. We may anticipate our comments on the topography by saying that one may look in vain on the high slopes of Mount Kreion[7] for any physical feature which would have accommodated a chariot racetrack. As to Trochos being an "Argive" term, it is found in

[6]This etymological explanation for the Trochos accords with the characterization of the *aitia* of games found in Hyginus, as given by M. Grant, *The Myths of Hyginus* (Lawrence 1960) 6: "In many of these instances the point hangs on etymology, though it is often of the feeblest kind." In any case, since Trochilos is associated with ἅρματα, the topographical feature at Kenchreai required by Robertson's αἴτιον is a chariot race-track.

[7]The mountain on which Kenchreai is situated is often referred to as Chaon. But for Pausanias (2.24.6), Chaon was the mountain rising above Kephalari, the springs of the Erasinos. The name of Kenchreai's mountain is to be found in the partial lacuna of the text of Strabo. Strabo (8.6.18.376) says there were two mountains between Tegea and Argos: διὰ τοῦ Παρθενίου ὄρους καὶ τοῦ Κρεοπώλου (Budé text). In Baladié's critical apparatus, we see that the reading is corrupt, and the emendation rejected by a number of scholars. A Κρεῖον (= "carving dish," Homer) ὄρος for the Argolid is attested in Kallimachos *Hymn* 5.40 with scholion, and, not otherwise identified, would seem to be the candidate sharing Κρεο in common. Robertson (p. 209) had Kenchreai's mountain as Artemision! The name on the Greek Army map is Psilo Lithari.

212   THUCYDIDES' PENTEKONTAETIA AND OTHER ESSAYS

fifth-century Attic. I find neither trochos nor dromos in Argive inscriptions, although σταδιοδρόμος occurs in the Argive text *IG* IV.1508 B line 4.

Robertson does not understand the fundamentals of textual criticism. Modern textual critics do not adopt an emendation simply because a nineteenth-century scholar proposed it, be it Sibelis, Cobet, Madvig, or whosoever. According to Hitzig's critical apparatus (1899), Sibelis, Schubart and Walz, Dindorf, and Schubart read Τρόχου, other editors up to that time and the codd., Τροχοῦ.[8] We weigh their reasons for the emendation, and in this case the only criteria we have are the topography and the use of the words in other contexts. Normally, one follows the codices unless evidence is adduced for an emendation.

D. Page in his commentary on Euripides *Med.* 46 writes:

> 46. τρόχων or τροχῶν? As Eur. did not use accents, it was perhaps as difficult for a fourth century B.C. reader as for us to decide. Ammonius (grammaticus, A.D. circ. 100) quoting Truphon (grammaticus, saec. i A.C.) distinguished τροχῶν (hoops) from τρόχων (runnings) and gave *Med.* 46 as his example of τροχῶν (v. Elmsley, who is clearly right in this); there have always been two opinions about the word here (cf. Photius τρόχον, δρόμον. Εὐριπίδης Μηδείᾳ, ἄλλοι δὲ παῖδες ἐκ τροχῶν πεπαυμένοι), and probably always will be: I prefer τρόχων. For ἐκ cf. S. *El.* 231 ἐκ καμάτων ἀποπαύομαι: for the whole phrase cf. ἐκ τρόχων πεπαυμένοι, *Alope, fr.* 105; Aristoph. *fr.* 637 K. ἐβάδιζέ μοι τὸ μειράκιον ἐξ ἀποτρόχων.

---

[8] Both words are associated with τρέχω. For the etymology, see P. Chantraine, *Dictionnaire étymologique* 1135.

V. AETIOLOGY SANS TOPOGRAPHY 213

The lack of accents does not apply to the time of Pausanias, although the weight to be given to the exemplar of Niccolo Niccoli (τροχοῦ) is another matter.

In turn on Sophokles *Ant.* 1065, Jebb comments,

> —τρόχους = δρόμους, 'courses.' The MS. τροχούς = 'runners,' *i.e.*, κύκλους, wheels. The authority for this Attic distinction goes back at least to the Augustan age: see Chandler § 332 n. 1 (2nd ed.), who cites Ammonius p. 137, τροχοὶ ὀξυτόνως καὶ τρόχοι βαρυτόνως διαφέροισι παρὰ τοῖς ᾿Αττικοῖς. φησὶ Τρύφων (in the Augustan age) ἐν δευτέρᾳ περὶ ᾿Αττικῆς προσῳδίας. τοὺς μὲν γὰρ περιφερεῖς τροχοὺς ὁμοίως ἡμῖν προφέρονται ὀξυτονοῦντες· τρόχους δὲ βαρυτόνως λέγουσι τοὺς δρόμους. This passage helps to explain why our MSS. all give τροχούς here. When Ammonius wrote (towards the end of the 4th cent. A.D.) τρόχος, 'course,' was known only as an Atticism, while τροχός, 'wheel,' was a common word.

The confusion about the two words is illustrated in modern texts of Pausanias. Musti in his 1986 edition reads Τρόχου, but translates "la Ruota." Likewise, the Loeb reads Τρόχου, which is translated as "the Wheel."[9]

3. The Myth. Robertson accepts without argumentation the hypothesis that festivals were given a mythical origin.[10] Here his

---

[9]One well-attested "Circle"(κύκλος) was a plot of land, the "Sacred Orgas" marked off in a circle with stone stelai, the boundaries of which had been disputed by the Athenians and Megarians: Didymos *Commentary on Demosthenes* col. 13.57; *IG* II² 204; P. Harding, *Androtion* (Oxford 1994) frg. 30.

[10]Hammond, in *CAH²* 3.1 (1982) 713, writes, "In the eighth century itself there was a strong sense of the past (the archaeological evidence also attests this), and the traditions then current were collected and formalized not only about gods and heroes, as Herodotus indicated (II.53.2), but also about peoples

214 THUCYDIDES' PENTEKONTAETIA AND OTHER ESSAYS

position is that after a pretended festival was created at Kenchreai, the "battle of Hysiai" was developed from it. As to why the battle was at Hysiai and between Sparta and Argos, he says not a word. Since no festival is attested for Kenchreai, he creates one out of thin air from the myth of Io. We extract the kernel of his presentation (214–216):

> No cult or festival of Cenchreae is directly attested, except perhaps a cult of Asclepius. But a famous episode in the myth of Io, the slaying of Argus by Hermes, takes place at Cenchreae. Like other elements of the myth, this is *undoubtedly* (italics supplied) a ritual *aition*, and the background is most likely an agonistic festival of Hermes.
>
> In *Prometheus Vinctus* the maiden Io is summoned by insistent dreams to Lerna, to its 'deep meadow' and its 'pastures and stalls,' so that Zeus can have his way with her. When in due curse she is expelled from home, she rushes in cow form to 'the spring of Lerna,' there presumably to mate. And the impulse takes her farther, to 'the fresh stream of Cenchreae.' Argus, meanwhile, the ever-watchful cowherd, follows close upon her tracks, until he is suddenly killed. Then the gadfly comes, and drives her across the world. Io's narrative, brief and excited though it is, indicates that Argus was killed at Cenchreae. Outside the myth of Io, the

and places." It is one thing to say that early festivals had foundation legends and quite another to postulate that such legends were created for all ceremonies, including military processions and games, in historical times. At the least, we want documentation before we attribute legends willy-nilly. Cities doubtless enhanced their glory by appropriating and inventing myths, and the Argolid is the province which excels all others in extensive and famous cycles of myths (M. P. Nilsson, *The Mycenaean Origin of Greek Mythology* [Berkeley 1932] 191), which have been traced to Minoan and Mycenaean times, but there is no major or minor myth relating to Hysiai, nor has Robertson adduced anything in mythology which would form the basis for fabricating a legend about a battle between historical states in historical times.

V. AETIOLOGY SANS TOPOGRAPHY

watchful cowherd is better spoken of. Argus killed the bull that ravaged Arcadia, and also a satyr who reived Arcadian herds. This is a very old tradition, for Argus' costume, so variously rendered in later art and literature, was at first the hide of the Arcadian bull. The story belongs to a setting where Argive pasture land meets Arcadian, i.e., the road to Tegea. ... Hermes as a pastoral god has more to do as a rule with sheep and goats: the smaller animals are more extensively pastured. But the best hides for leather are from cattle that are pastured in the mountains, for wind and weather toughen the skin. Therefore Hermes in the *Homeric Hymn* drives the cattle far afield, up hill and down dale, and when he slaughters them, he takes particular care with the hides — afterwards Apollo marvels at his handiwork. As for Argus, the bull's hide he wears is emblematic. ... Thus the myth of Argus derives from a festival of Hermes that promoted leather making. Cenchreae, in good mountain pasture not far from Argos, was the place for such a festival. At the festival site there was some memorial of Argus, *no doubt* (italics supplied) a grave. But in Pausanias' day the festival was long forgotten; the very town of Cenchreae may have disappeared. It was easy to regard the monument of Argus as a monument to other heroes, Argive soldiers who fell in battle. So it was at Thyrea: the monument of Othryades became a mass burial of the champions.[11]

[11]Throughout his book, Robertson uses such terms as "no doubt," "doubtless," "as plain as day," "obvious," "plainly," etc. They always signify that he has not one bit of evidence. The oft-repeated phrase "It is easy to suppose" means it is easy to suppose if one closes one's eyes. On p. 13, he writes, "It is easy to suppose that the main elements of that famous fountain-house were brought there and reassembled in the Roman period." The Ares temple cited in order to make it easy to suppose had Roman foundations with Roman sherds and Roman lettering to reassemble the blocks. The SE fountain-house had no signs of reuse.

216 THUCYDIDES' PENTEKONTAETIA AND OTHER ESSAYS

Robertson misinterprets the *Prometheus* passage, which contains the only reference to Kenchreai in tragedy, in several particulars. We give West's text of lines 673–681 with the translation of H. W. Smyth:

> εὐθὺς δὲ μορφὴ καὶ φρένες διάστροφοι
> ἦσαν, κεραστὶς δ᾽, ὡς ὁρᾶτ᾽, ὀξυστόμωι
> 675 μύωπι χρισθεῖσ᾽ ἐμμανεῖ σκιρτήματι
> ἦισσον πρὸς εὔποτόν τε Κερχνείας ῥέος
> Λέρνης τε κρήνην· βουκόλος δὲ γηγενής
> ἄκρατος ὀργὴν Ἄργος ὡμάρτει, πυκνοῖς
> ὄσσοις δεδορκώς, τοὺς ἐμοὺς κατὰ στίβους.
> 680 ἀπροσδόκητος δ᾽ αὐτὸν ταἰφνίδιοςϯ μόρος
> τοῦ ζῆν ἀπεστέρησεν.

Forthwith my form and mind were distorted, and with horns, as ye see, upon my front, stung by a sharp-fanged gad-fly I rushed with frantic bounds to Cerchnea's sweet stream and Lerna's spring. But the earth-born herdsman, untempered in his rage, even Argus, followed ever close upon me, peering with his many eyes upon my steps. But a sudden death reft him of life unawares.

Clearly, Io comes first to Kenchreai, then to Lerna. Io's goal was Lerna (line 652). It is only after reaching Lerna's springs that death befell Argos. Aischylos does not attribute the death of Argos to Hermes; that idea is found in other sources and often portrayed in art. Moreover, Io is not stopping at Kenchreai and Lerna to mate with Zeus, as Robertson has it; J. E. Harry suggests that in her torment Io sought water for drink and coolness. A. Smyth (*CR* 35 [1921] 99) translates, "I rushed to the rivulet of Cerchneia, so cool and clear to drink." Moreover, the gad-fly appears before she reaches Kenchreai. Robertson completely misrepresents the *Prometheus* passage, which he does not reproduce.

V. AETIOLOGY SANS TOPOGRAPHY 217

There is no basis for associating either Argos or Hermes with Kenchreai.[12]

The festival Robertson creates was one for cattle breeders, or, more specifically, for those who tanned the skin of cattle, "leather makers," βυρσοδέψαι. Argos, we are told, was chosen as patron because he killed a ταῦρος that ravaged Arkadia. The only reference to Arkadia in the enormous Argos saga seems to be the Apollodoros reference (2.1.2), where the hide is that of the slain ταῦρος: ὑπερβάλλων δὲ δυνάμει τὸν μὲν τὴν Ἀρκαδίαν λυμαινόμενον ταῦρον ἀνελὼν τὴν τούτου δορὰν ἠμφιέσατο. The scholiast of Euripides *Phoin.* 1116 refers to Argos simply as clad in a hide (βύρσα); see Engelmann in Roscher, *Lexikon* 1.1.538 col. 2 lines 28–33. Wernicke in *RE* s.v. Argos 18 (1895) 794, says that in art Argos wore a panther's skin (lines 30, 49 ["sein Attribut häufig das Pantherfell"], and 61. Yalouris in *LIMC* 5.1 (1990) also has him clad in a panther skin ("peau de panthère," 665 col. 1) or, more often, "peau de bête."[13] This one late reference in Apollodoros to a tauros is a very thin thread to make Argos into the patron of bull-keepers.[14]

---

[12]Hermes was the mythological inventor of wrestling, the sire of the palaestra, the personified god of wrestling; so M. B. Poliakoff, *Combat Sports in the Ancient World* (New Haven 1987) 12–13, 166 n. 15.

[13]For a catalogue of vase-paintings of Argos, see also D. J. Mastronarde, *Euripides Phoenissae* (Cambridge 1994) 463. Robertson offers no documentation for his statement that the earliest representations of Argos show him clad in a bull's hide, nor does he explain why the Apollodoros reference is earlier than legends which have Argos with eyes.

[14]Robertson is weak on mythology. He knows nothing of the passage in Aischylos, *Suppl.* 303ff., where Argos is called πανόπτης, and it is clear that Hera appointed Argos to *prevent* Zeus copulating with Io. In their commentary on this passage in the *Suppliants*, H. Friis Johansen and E. W. Whittle collect the numerous passages in the literature where Argos is credited with a varying number of eyes.

218   THUCYDIDES' PENTEKONTAETIA AND OTHER ESSAYS

A. B. Cook, "Animal Worship in the Mycenean Age," *JHS* 14 (1894) 125 n. 250, explains that "Argos of the hundred eyes was a leopard," the spots on the leopard's skin becoming eyes.[15] Robertson (215 n. 22) cites three vases as having Argos with the hide of a bull. His "*ARV²* 579.84" reference is to a vase illustrated in *AJA* 21 (1917) 52 fig. 6. The skin is covered with spots (= eyes) and does not have hoofs, being the hide of a leopard or panther. A second example is "*ABV* 148.2" ("Near Exekias"). This is illustrated in J. Overbeck, *Atlas der griechischen Kunstmythologie* 2 (Leipzig 1873) pl. 7.9, where the hide tied across the chest has claws, which bulls do not have. Incidentally, on Overbeck's same page (no. 7.13), we again have the leopard's skin dotted with spots. Only Robertson's third example ("*ARV²* 1409.9") is correct. This is illustrated in Overbeck, no. 7.16. Here the hide is tied across the shoulders and extends to the feet of the seated figure. The animal is cloven-footed with a tail. The exceptional nature of this hide in the Io legend has not gone unnoticed.[16] Jane Harrison, *CR* 7 (1893) 76, regarded it as being derived from the Argos of the legend of the Argonauts, thus taking the Argos of the Io legend as identical with that of the Argonauts. The Argos who was the builder of the ship of the Argonauts is given a bull's hide in Apollonios Rhodios 1.324: "Argus, son of Arestor, had cast round his shoulders the hide of a bull reaching to his feet, with the black hair upon it" (Loeb tr.). Hyginus, in listing the Argonauts, describes the same hero as an "Argive clad in a black, hairy bull's hide" (hic fuit Argiuus, pelle taurina lanugine nigra adopertus): page 16 line 2 of H. I. Rose, *Hygini Fabulae* (1934).

---

[15]Wotke and Jereb have long articles on the panther in *RE* 18.3 (1983) 747–776. See also Richter in *Der kleine Pauly* 4 (1972) 475–477. They do not discuss Argos; but no Greek festival had a foundation legend arising from the sacrifice of panthers.

[16]For an "error" on the part of another painter, see Overbeck, pl. 7.10, where Io is drawn as a bull (cf. Hoppin, *HSCP* 12 [1901] 338).

V. AETIOLOGY SANS TOPOGRAPHY

Rather than assigning the two legends to the same hero, A. B. Cook, *Zeus* 1.459, writes of the same vase, "It seems wise, therefore, to suppose that he wore a bull-skin in order to assimilate himself to the Argive bull-god Zeus." The Argos, surnamed Panoptes, son of Agenor, is to be distinguished from Argos, son of Zeus and Niobe, the third king of Argos, and from the builder of the Argo. The Argos of the Io myth is Panoptes, as designated in Aischylos and throughout the literature down to Ovid, and portrayed in art with the panther's skin. The Io myth affords no evidence for cattle breeding (or leopard breeding) at Kenchreai.

In W. Smith's *Dictionary of Greek and Roman Biography and Mythology* 1 (1873) 282, the author distinguishes three heroes by the name of Argus: in the *RE* (1895), Wernicke isolates ten mythical personages (nos. 18–27), and in *Der kleine Pauly* 1 (1964) 540–541, Hiller makes half-a-dozen distinctions. All distinguish the Argos of the Io legend from that of the Argonauts. Ancient vase painters may not have observed such rigid categories, and our literary sources give different genealogies.[17] In Aristophanes *Eccl.* 76, Argos is given a διφθέρα, which the most recent commentator, R. G. Ussher (1973), takes to be a goat-skin. In any case, Robertson's treatment of Argos is completely muddled, building a house of cards by extracting one passage here and another there. We add that we have not studied all the vases listed in *LIMC* nor the bibliography there.

"The story belongs to a setting where Argive pasture land meets Arkadian, i.e., the road to Tegea." This is nonsense. Kenchreai is separated from Tegea by Mount Kreion and Mount Parthenion. To refer to this region as Arkadian "pasture-land" meeting Argive is absurd. A hike from Kenchreai to Tegea is recommended.

---

[17]Cf. Apollodoros 2.1.3 (Loeb tr.): "Pherecydes says that this Argus was a son of Arestor; but Asclepiades says that he was a son of Inachus, and Cercops says that he was a son of Argus and Ismene, daughter of Asopus; but Acusilaus says that he was earth-born."

220 THUCYDIDES' PENTEKONTAETIA AND OTHER ESSAYS

I have seen a herd of cattle on a lovely glen on Mount Kallidromos where there is a high upland plain with a lake surrounded by grass on the trail between Nevropolis and Anavra, and a herdsman with a small herd of animals on a grassy plateau in Akarnania; but cattle do not graze on the valonia oak and mountain shrubs, nor do they climb trees, nor are they pastured on steep mountain slopes. There are goats today on Mount Kreion and many on Mount Parthenion, but we can be sure that Kenchreai was not founded by tanners of cattle.[18]

The basis for Robertson's attribution of Hermes as the patron deity of the alleged cattle-tanners of Kenchreai is found in the *Homeric Hymn to Hermes*. Here the child Hermes steals twelve πόρτιες, a hundred βόες ἄζυγες, and a bull from Apollo. The theft of the cattle is followed by a contest of litigious minds, and the reconciliation of Hermes and Apollo by an exchange of gifts. T. W. Allen, W. R. Halliday, and E. E. Sikes, in their second edition of the *Homeric Hymns* (Amsterdam 1963) 270, write, "Both were patrons of flocks and herds (Apollo rather God of cattle, Hermes of sheep)." There are two lines which suggest tanning to Robertson. On line 124, Hephaistos spreads out the hides on the rugged rock (καταστυφέλῳ ἐνὶ πέτρῃ), where, the poet continues, they remained for many ages. Secondly, in lines 403–405, we are told that Apollo, having reached a ford of the Alpheios and a cave at sandy Pylos, saw "the hides on the sheer rock" (ἰδὼν ... βοείας πέτρῃ ἐπ᾽ ἠλιβάτῳ). W. Burkert, *Homo Necans* (Berkeley 1983) 15 n. 13, comments, "In the myth, the skins apparently turned to stone." It is well known that most scholars suggest the "hides" were a stalactite formation in a cave,

---

[18]As noted in *War* 5.202–203, a convoy of 230 merchant ships laden with grain and hides from the Bosporos was captured by Philip in 340 B.C. In the context of a commentary on the entry βύρσαι Σικελικαί in the Eleusinian records of 408/7 B.C. (*IG* I³.386/7), W. Habermann, *Münstersche Beiträge zur antiken Handelsgeschichte* 6 (1987) 89–113, has given a lengthy study on trade in hides, but there is nothing to suggest that Kenchreai or Argos was a center.

V. AETIOLOGY SANS TOPOGRAPHY 221

and that the Pylos reference played a major role in the early debate on the location of Nestor's Pylos. The thread which makes Hermes the God of tanners at Kenchreai is even thinner than that for a statue of Argos. We now have the lengthy study of Hermes in *LIMC* V.1 (1990) 285–387, not cited by Robertson. Under "Hermes et les troupeaux," Hermes is generally portrayed with a ram (bélier), but sometimes as an ox-driver (bouvier). There is no representation suggesting tanning.

We noted above that in order to hypothesize a festival of Hermes at Kenchreai, Robertson placed the scene of the combat between Hermes and Argos at the site, grossly misinterpreting the *Prometheus* passage, which has the scene after Kenchreai and Lerna. Hoppin (*HSCP* 12 [1901] 339) noted that in the six vase paintings of the scene which he studied a grove was represented as indicated by the presence of bushes or a tree. Now, Apollodoros (2.1.3) puts the scene in the grove of the Mycenaeans (ἐν τῷ Μυκηναίων ἄλσει), which Hoppin suggests was the sacred temenos of the Argive Heraion. Apollodoros had before him a number of early sources, including Pherekydes and Akusilaos of Argos. Pliny (*NH* 16.239) and apparently Sophokles (*Elek.* 4) have the scene at Argos or the plain of Argos. Lucian (*DDeor.* 7[3] 207) gives Nemea. Hoppin adduces evidence for the grove of Io in the island of Euboia; but this is not necessarily the scene of the combat, as I understand it. There is no tradition for Kenchreai, which alone puts the *coup de mort* on Robertson's creation. "The grove of the Mycenaeans" is a long way from Kenchreai.

4. The Topography. My initial interest in the topography of Kenchreai, as suggested by the title of the chapter in *Topography* 3, "The Road from Argos to Hysiai via Kenchreai," was only in the road.[19] One thrust of the study was to discredit the idea that

---

[19]More recently, Pikoulas, *Praktika tou B' Topikou Synedriou Argolikon Spoudon* (Athens 1989) 296–297, has determined that this road past Kenchreai

222 THUCYDIDES' PENTEKONTAETIA AND OTHER ESSAYS

Pausanias' polyandria at Kenchreai for the battle of Hysiai were the striking pyramid called Helleniko, about two and a half kilometers west of the springs of Kephalari, following in this respect Bölte, *RE* s.v. Kenchreai 1 (1921) 165–167.[20] The ruins at Sta Nera were succinctly described by Bölte, 166.39–46, as follows:

> Hier sind deutliche Spuren einer antiken Siedlung festgestellet worden: die Ruinen eines kleinen Gebäudes aus großen Quadern (Boblaye 47), ein Stück polygonischen Gemäuers, hellenische Fundamente und alte Werkstücke (Ross 145), Marmorplatten und Säulentrommeln (Bädeker 344), endlich zahlreiche antike Scherben (nach Mitteilung von Frickenhaus).

Roads. Robertson's knowledge of roads of the Peloponnesos (210–211) is limited to that of modern automobile maps,[21] ignoring the travelers, Baedeker, Guide Joanne, Loring, and recent investigations. Loring, in his end-map in *JHS* 15 (1885), marked in red two principal roads leading out of Sparta, one up the valley of the Sarandapotamos (= Pausanias' Alpheios), the other leading to Thyrea via Ayios Petros and Pausanias' road from Argos. The latter was probably the route used in the eighth century B.C. when the Spartans went to the aid of Asine, southeast of Nauplia at modern Tolon (see above). When the Spartan Kleomenes in-

---

runs, not only to Argos, but to Oinoa in the Charadra valley. Pikoulas, interviewing shepherds and natives in his quest for wheel-ruts, is preparing a study of the roads of the Peloponnesos which will supersede prior studies.

[20]Confusion about the pyramid persists. In S. Lauffer, *Griechenland. Lexicon* (Munich 1989) 275, we read: "Die in dieser Schlacht gefallenen Argiver sollen in einem Massengrab (Polyandrion), der sog. *Pyramide* von Kenchreai beim heutigen Ort Helleniko, ca. 3. km. nördl. von Achladokampos, bestattet worden sein." Helleniko is not three kilometers north of Achladokampos. Helena Fracchia, "The Peloponnesian Pyramids Reconsidered," *AJA* 89 (1985) 683–689, gives a recent report on Helleniko.

[21]"To reach Hysiai the Spartans must pass Tegea" (p. 211, etc.).

V. AETIOLOGY SANS TOPOGRAPHY 223

vaded Argos c. 496 B.C., he came to Thyrea by land, then by ship to Tiryns, and at the Heraion received the omen which caused him to retire from Argolis: Herodotos 6.81. The Heraion is about five miles northeast of Argos. Once one has descended the northern side of Mount Zavitza, by the road studied in *Topography* 7 chapter 7 (with photographs and map), one strikes the old Turkish khan (7 pl. 166), and is in the lower valley of Achladokampos. The railroad uses this valley, passing the sites of Elaious, mentioned by Apollodoros in connection with Herakles' slaying of the Lerna hydra (7 p. 172), Belanidia, and Achladokampos. Any valley used by a Greek railroad would be easy going for an army.[22] Parenthetically, on coming from Sparta, once one reaches Pausanias' herms at the Lakonia/Argos frontier (*Topography* 6, chapter 6 with photographs) near Ayios Petros, the terrain suggests to me that it would have been easy to strike northwards to Achladokampos, rather than to descend to Thyrea; but I have never hiked it. On the other hand, if the Spartans used the valley of the Sarandapotamos to reach Hysiai, I judge that it would have been easy to by-pass Tegea, if we assume that seventh-century Tegea was located at the temple of Athena Alea and the museum near the modern highway, several kilometers removed from the river. Xenophon tells us that a Spartan army went north passing a hostile Korinth, and earlier Tolmides reached Chaironeia passing Thebes. We anticipate that the whole road structure of the Peloponnesos will be put on a firm basis by

[22]In 417 B.C., Thucydides (5.83.1–2) relates that the Lakedaimonians marched on Argos, demolished the walls, and then seized Hysiai, before withdrawing home. To seize Hysiai from Argos, they could have marched through Kenchreai, but an easier route, if they were at Lerna, is up the valley of the Xavrio to Achladokampos along the line of the Argos-Tripolis railroad. By the railroad it is 6 miles from Argos to Myloi (Lerna). In the *Handbook of Greece* (1920) 719, Myloi is described as the port of Tripolis. The railroad carried goods between the two places. From Myloi to the station of Achladokampos is 13 1/2 miles.

224 THUCYDIDES' PENTEKONTAETIA AND OTHER ESSAYS

the investigations of Pikoulas. One may ignore Robertson's strictures as due to ignorance of topography. Sparta did not have to conquer Tegea to reach Argos or Hysiai, particularly if Spartans were in control of Thyreatis, as Herodotos tells us they were at the time of the battle of Champions.

Being the only scholar in the literature who has suggested, and that only in passing since my interest was in the road, that Trochos might be a race course, I find it anomalous that Robertson has adopted the same solution, since he rejects the two reasons for my suggestion. I noted (*Topography* 3.66) that there was a rather level oval-shaped area, extending eastwards from the road to the gorge descending towards Lerna. Robertson (213 n. 14) objects to the word "oval," informing us that racing is in a straight line.[23] Since Greek race-courses have a tribunal on one side and "standing place" for spectators at some part,[24] I considered that more than a straight line was required. Secondly, I quoted authorities who noted that excavations had shown that early town-plans reveal the presence of tracks to be used for racing, citing H. Robinson for Athens and Korinth, and Dyer for Chaironeia, and Pausanias for Sparta (καλοῦσι δὲ Λακεδαιμόνιοι Δρόμον ...). To this, Robertson (214 n. 19) objects that the parallels are not apposite for Kenchreai. In his denigrating fashion, he has disposed to his satisfaction of the only topographical feature which might allow for a race course. From his association of the trochos with Trochilos, and his recognition

---

[23]Euripides *Hipp.* 1133 reads: τὸν ἀμφὶ Λίμνας τρόχον κατέχων ποδὶ γυμάδος ἵππου. One did not run around Limnai in a straight line.

[24]See now D. G. Romano, *Athletics and Mathematics in Archaic Corinth: The Origins of the Greek Stadion* (Philadelphia 1993). Robertson cites as an example the racing instituted by the Ten Thousand when they reached Trapezos, as narrated at the close of the fourth book of Xenophon's *Anabasis*. It is true that there was a horse race, but all was witnessed by the entire army (καλὴ θέα). Such races were common in the army of Alexander, but this has nothing to do with festivals, an idea which is the thrust of Robertson's presentation.

V. AETIOLOGY SANS TOPOGRAPHY 225

of the fact that "Trochilos is an exponent of chariot racing" (p. 213), one may deduce that Robertson envisages some form of a hippodrome. He gives no clue as to where it is to be found on Mount Kreion or what shape it ought to have.

Because of Robertson's strictures, I revisited Kenchreai in 1995 to inspect the area more closely. Since my last visit seventeen years ago, a monastery has been constructed about one hundred meters northeast of the church of Ayia Paraskevi. The fields are farmed by natives from Achladokampos and disclose a wide scattering of sherds. The farmers directed us to a large flat-top circular hill, which they call the kastro. It is situated about one kilometer east of the springs, overlooking the gorge on the eastern side. Ancient roof-tiles and pottery are dispersed over a wide area. We envisage Kenchreai as a village with scattered houses. The kastro hill with its steep sides could have served as a place of refuge. Pausanias tells us that Kenchreai was to the right of the Trochos: ἐπανελθοῦσι δὲ ἐς τὴν ἐπὶ Τεγέας ὁδόν ἐστιν ἐν δεξιᾷ τοῦ ὀνομαζομένου Τρόχου Κεγχρεαί. Since the kastro is part of the ancient site, the likely candidate for the Trochos would seem to be the mountain which rises on the eastern side of the gorge, hardly the gorge itself. The limestone of this mountain is honeycombed with caves. Whereas Strabo says there are two mountains between Argos and Tegea, there are in fact three. The gorge separates Mount Kreion from Trochos, the lowest of the three, Parthenion being the third.

Closer inspection reveals nothing within many kilometers which could be a candidate for a race-course or a hippodrome.

I mention briefly Robertson's discussion of Pausanias' sources for Hysiai: "His memory plays him false ... Pausanias first learned of the battle of Hysiae from an Argive informant ... As for the date ... perhaps he looked it up afterwards in a book ... Pausanias' source asserted that Hysiae was an Argive counterstroke" and on to Pheidon and Ephoros ("There can be little doubt that Pausanias' date is also an inference from Ephorus"), concluding, "The only impediment to dismissing Hysiae as an

226 THUCYDIDES' PENTEKONTAETIA AND OTHER ESSAYS

outright fiction is those graves at Cenchreae." There is no reference to the studies of Pausanias' sources by Frazer, Daux, Habicht, Regenbogen (in his monograph-length study in *RE* Suppl. VIII), etc., or to separate articles such as G. Pasquali, "Die schriftstellerische Form des Pausanias," *Hermes* 48 (1913) 161–223. Pausanias combined what he had seen with what he had read.[25] In addition to Herodotos, Thucydides, and Xenophon, he refers to Anaximenes, Antiochos of Syrakuse, Charon of Lampsakos, Ktesias, Hekataios, Hieronymos of Kardia, Myron of Priene, Philistos, Polybios, Theopompos, and several local historians. For the Argolid, he refers four times (1.13.8; 2.19.5; 2.22.2; 2.23.8) to what was a versified history of Argos by Lykeas, dated in the time of Kallimachos (so Kroll, *RE* s.v. Lykeas 2 [1927] 2266), about whom nothing further is known. He calls Lykeas "the local antiquary" (ὁ τῶν ἐπιχωρίων ἐξηγητής). But he never refers to Ephoros, as Robertson would have it.[26]

The date given by Pausanias for the battle of Hysiai rests in part on the Elean register of Olympic victors (2.24.7). This register had been published many years earlier by Hippias of Elis (Plutarch *Numa* 1) and copies may have been in common circulation. He often refers to it. In 6.13.10, after consulting the register, he writes, ταῦτα μὲν δὴ οὕτως ἔχοντα ἴστω τις ("You may take my statements as accurate," Loeb). G. Huxley, *Early Sparta* (London 1962) 29, writes, "The lists form the most important part of the framework of early Greek chronology, and where they can be checked prove themselves a reliable guide to the events of the eighth and seventh centuries." Pausanias did his research, and we can affirm that the attacks on him in recent times which concern Kenchreai exhibit an unfamiliarity with the

---

[25]No student of the sources of Pausanias should neglect the study by C. Habicht, *Pausanias' Guide to Ancient Greece* (Berkeley 1985) 96ff.

[26]If Diodoros referred to Hysiai in the lost book 7, as G. Huxley suggests (*Early Sparta* 131 n. 394), the reference must derive from a tradition different from that used by Pausanias.

V. AETIOLOGY SANS TOPOGRAPHY

topography,[27] and in the case of Robertson a misunderstanding of the mythology as well.

When I first visited the site, shepherds reported that in excavating the site of the modern church of Ayia Paraskevi, illustrated in *Topography* 3 pl. 35, they had discovered the foundations of a temple and a great quantity of bones; see *Topography* 3.63. We have no archaeological report. The testimonia of the travelers about the remains at Kenchreai were presented in *Topography* 3.59–61. The *Guide-Joanne, Grèce* 2.234, for example, reported, "une chapelle avec des restes de murs polygonaux, de colonnes de marbre et autres restes antiques."[28] Just as the various demes of Attika were mini-poleis with their calendars of festivals, so Kenchreai must have celebrated minor festivals of its own as part of its religious life. Kenchrias was the son of Peirene by Poseidon. Peirene, in turn, was the daughter of Acheloos. In giving the genealogy (2.2.3), Pausanias says that there was a hieron and agalma of Poseidon at Lechaion. Peirene was regarded as the nymph of the springs at Korinth, believed to have arisen out of the tears which she shed in her grief at the death of her son Kenchrias. Located at powerful springs which drained down to Lerna, our kome of Kenchreai might be expected to have festivals celebrating these deities. Such festivals had nothing to do with the battle of Hysiai.

By conflating different legends, by grossly misinterpreting the *Prometheus* passage, by postulating that Kenchreai on Mount Kreion was a settlement of βυρσοδέψαι, by invoking the name of Trochilos to explain the Trochos, i.e. a hippodrome where none could possibly exist, by giving references to vase-paintings which belie his interpretation, N. Robertson creates a mytholiterary jungle, written in flyting style and having nothing in the world

[27]For T. Kelly, see *Topography* 3.71–74.

[28]Frazer (3.212) reported a "large ruined khan," evidence for the use of the road.

228 THUCYDIDES' PENTEKONTAETIA AND OTHER ESSAYS

to do with history or the battle of Hysiai. The conclusion (p. 216) that the battle sprang from "some memorial of Argus" is sublime.

2. THYREATIS AND BATTLE OF CHAMPIONS

Claiming disagreements with modern historians of Sparta and of Greek history in general, Robertson alleges in his chapter 8 that he can disprove the historicity of the Battle of Champions between Argos and Sparta. He claims that the account of the battle was a legend which sprang from an unmarked grave and the festival of Parparonia, invoking the word *aition*, familiar to us now from his other studies as a buzzword for indicting the historical record.

Citing (pp. 181–184) sources from Herodotos to late chronographers, he notes that they give different dates for the battle: "Herodotus and the later vulgate discredit each other ... In other words, it was a popular legend which historians situated in time according to their own lights." "The connection (with Lydia) can be attributed to Herodotus himself ... so as to form a climax." Etc. A significant omission in his pages 181–184 is Thucydides 5.41, where the Argives in 420 B.C. propose the idea of holding a battle between champions "as once before" in the matter of Kynourian territory.[29] Virtually every historian and every commentator on Herodotos and Thucydides refers to the connection between Herodotos 1.82 and Thucydides 5.41. Our two best historians alluded to the battle, as did the Lakedaimonian historian Sosibios (Athenaios 15.678 = Jacoby, *FGrH* 595 frg. 5). Chronol-

---

[29]It is only near the end of his chapter in a footnote (n. 62) that Robertson refers to Thucydides. The proposition made by the Argives was a renewal of an old practice of judicial combat. Times had changed, and the Lakedaimonians regarded the idea as absurd, but agreed to the condition. Neither the Argives nor the Lakedaimonians nor Thucydides challenged the historicity of the battle. Robertson attributes the attitude of the Spartans to Thucydides' invention: "Thucydides' attribution of τὸ δέον as he conceived it."

V. AETIOLOGY SANS TOPOGRAPHY

ogists used different king-lists, different lengths for a generation; the absolute dates are attributable to the heortologists. Opinions may differ about a date, but this difference in no way disproves the reality of the event in question. Since Xenophon differs with Diodoros, and Polybios with Plutarch, about dates, one could dismiss much of Greek history by this extremely superficial method, which is the only one adduced by Robertson. The testimonia on the date of the Battle of Thyrea are collected by A. A. Mosshammer, *The Chronicle of Eusebius and Greek Chronographic Tradition* (1979) 205–208, 223–224. The article of Kohlmann on Othryades in *RM* 29 (1874) 463–480 is still valuable.

Since the exact site of the Battle of Champions is attested only by Pausanias on his road from Argos to Sparta, Robertson's next step, after dismissing Herodotos and the historical sources because of a diversity of chronology, is to discredit the topographical reconstruction which I have proposed for Pausanias' itinerary of the Thyreatis in his effort to show that the site proposed for the Battle of Champions is impossible, and, in any case, that Pausanias is mistaken about the identification, claiming that no battle could have occurred where he sites it. The sites are not taken up seriatim, nor is any walled site in the Thyreatis identified with any of Pausanias' toponyms. Robertson ignores the problem of the roads over Mount Zavitza (= Parparos), which separates the district of Lerna from the plain of Astros, as well as all reports of travelers; Pausanias listed his sites according to roads. Indeed, Robertson's ignorance of Pausanias' practice is inexplicable; he offers a page of ridicule (197) to the idea that Pausanias, after reaching one frontier, would backtrack to describe a road to another frontier. Pausanias' practice is well-known and is illustrated on the various maps of Papachatzes' edition.[30] For Argos, for example, see his vol. 2 pp. 12–13. Pausanias leaves the Deiras gate of Argos and goes up the Charadros to Oinoa. He

---

[30]Pausanias' procedure was explained in *Topography* 3.139 n. 84.

230 THUCYDIDES' PENTEKONTAETIA AND OTHER ESSAYS

then backtracks to the junction of the Charadros and the Inachos to proceed to Orneai and Phleious. And so throughout.

We briefly review the evidence for two well-marked kalderimi roads over Mount Zavitza and our suggestions about the walled sites to be associated with Pausanias' toponyms. Since we can correlate ruins with toponyms only on the assumption of a lacuna in the text, we comment first on the condition of the fifteenth-century exemplar. To correct Robertson's misconceptions, we give references to photographs, which are self explanatory Although we disagree on some identifications, we single out the important work of P. B. Phaklares, published as a Thessaloniki dissertation in 1985, then revised and republished under the same title of *Archaia Kynouria* in 1990 (Athens).

Before turning to Robertson's aetiology for the festival of the Parparonia, we treat the topography under the following headings:

    1. Lacunae in the exemplar of Pausanias
    2. Two roads over Mount Zavitza (= Parparos)
    3. Sites
        a. Plain of Astros
            1. Ayios Andreas
            2. Great estate of Herodes Atticus at Loukou
        b. On road from Lerna to frontier (out of order)
            1. Neris
            2. Eva
            3. Herms at frontier
            4. Anthene
            5. Battle of Champions and cenotaph inscription

1. Lacunae in the exemplar of Pausanias. Attested lacunae are demonstrated by a break either in the syntax or of the contents; they cannot be contested. Our proposal for a lacuna at the end of 2.38.4 rests on two considerations: the sites which we know on the

V. AETIOLOGY SANS TOPOGRAPHY   231

evidence of walls and sherds were in existence when Pausanias went through, and the two roads marked with retaining walls and pavement which we believe duplicated his routes.

Parenthetically, we note that in two articles titled, "The Plain of Astros. A Survey," Y. Goester, *Newsletter Netherlands Institute at Athens* 4 (1991) 55, and *Pharos* 1 (1993) 55, has misunderstood my position about the phrase ἔστιν ἐν ἀριστερᾷ μὲν καθή-κουσα ἐπὶ θάλασσαν καὶ δένδρα ἐλαίας μάλιστα ἀγαθὴ τρέφειν γῆ in Pausanias 2.38.4. After proceeding through the Anigraia along the coast by a narrow and difficult road, Pausanias descends on the plain of Astros, reaching a tract "on his left which extends to the sea; it is fertile in trees, especially the olive." Pausanias' practice was to go to the border. I have suggested that at the end of the phrase there is a lacuna, that he proceeded to the estate of Herodes Atticus and then to Ayios Andreas and the border,[31] before returning to the principal Argos-Sparta road at 2.38.5: ἰόντι δὲ ἄνω πρὸς τὴν ἤπειρον ... αὐτῆς (vel αὐτῶν) χωρίον ἐστίν (codd.). Hitzig has two notes in his critical apparatus: "ἀπ᾽ αὐτῆς emendatio est Bursiani," and "virgulas delevi, quas edd. praeter A X ante et post ἐλαίας μάλιστα ponunt." For αὐτῆς, I proposed ἐκ Λέρνης, comparing the beginning of 2.38.4.

We repeat the contents of our observations about lacunae in the codices, as presented in *Topography* 6.97–98:

---

[31]According to the map of Papachatzes (2 p. 309), Tyros, south of Ayios Andreas, was Argive in Pausanias' time. In his Lakonian itinerary, Pausanias goes north only to Prasiai, which suggests that the boundary was the river of Leonidion (Daphnon). At the time of the text inscribed on the Lysander monument at Delphi (*SEG* 23.324a, c. 400 B.C.), Tyros was Lakedaimonian. One would expect Pausanias to mention the site with its well-preserved walls and towers as well as a small temple (Phaklares, 1990 pl. 61; see also his note 462). Since Pausanias regularly went to the border, the theory of a lacuna would account for the omission of Tyros.

232 THUCYDIDES' PENTEKONTAETIA AND OTHER ESSAYS

In the *RE* article on Pausanias (Suppl. 8 [1956] 1009), Regenbogen writes, "Die Hss. sind samt und sonders jung und durch viele grössere und kleinere Lücken entstellt. Das scheint schon im 6. Jhdt. in der Hs. des Stephanos von Byzanz so gewesen zu sein." Hitzig, in the first volume of the Hitzig-Bluemner commentary on Pausanias (1896), offers a study of individual manuscripts, noting "grösser Lücken," as in the Leiden codex (p. v). He summarizes his study with the observation (xvi-xvii): "Die Sache liegt eben doch so, dass wir einen Text haben, der neben einer grossen Zahl von meist unheilbaren Lücken eine schwere Menge von Vehlern enthält, die nicht der Verfasser verschuldet hat. Pausanias ist nicht den besten Kopisten in die Hände gefallen, und unsere Hss. sind alle jungen Datums." F. A. Hall (*A Companion to Classical Texts* [Oxford 1913] 256), in his catalogue of classical texts, under the entry for Pausanias, observes, "The MSS are numerous but late. The condition of the text is unsound owing to the number of lacunae." The study of the text was placed on a new footing by A. Diller's demonstration in two articles ("Pausanias in the Middle Ages," *TAPA* 87 [1956] 84–97; "The Manuscripts of Pausanias," 88 [1957] 169–188) that all of our manuscripts derive from a codex which in 1418 was in possession of Niccolò Niccoli of Florence. This single exemplar was preserved in the convent of St. Mary in Florence for a century or so and then disappeared. Since the omissions in manuscripts are crucial for their classification, Diller (notes 9, 40, 56, 59, 61 of the 1957 article) lists numerous examples. Earlier, he had recorded (*TAPA* 67 [1936] 234) instances of the omission of single lines in the archetype. In the Rocha-Pereira text, there are thirty cases where the editor has marked a gap in the text by triple asterisks. In some cases, there is a change in the subject matter, as appears to be the case, for example, in 3.25.1; 6.13.4; 6.19.8; 8.21.3; 9.8.5.

As one descends the Anigraia and continuing until one reaches the estate of Herodes Atticus, situated above the right bank of the Tanos, one would have on his left the olive grove. Rather than

V. AETIOLOGY SANS TOPOGRAPHY 233

constituting an objection to the theory of a lacuna, the phrase confirms it for those who believe that Pausanias would have continued by mentioning Herodes' great estate.

After his ascent on a road leading to Sparta which is distinguished from the coastal road (ἰόντι δὲ ἄνω πρὸς τὴν ἤπειρον; we stress the phrase πρὸς τὴν ἤπειρον), Pausanias enumerates in order: 1) the site of the Battle of Champions, 2) Anthene, 3) Neris, 4) Eva, and 5) the herms at the Argive-Lakonian border. In the mountains looking down on the plain of Astros, we have two sites with the remains of walls, 1) the ruins called Helleniko about five miles from Astros on the modern road to Ayios Joannes and Ayios Petros; 2) the ruins called Tsorovos on the southern slopes of Mount Zavitza three kilometers above the Tanos river and the town of Kato Doliana.

2. Two Roads over Mount Zavitza (= Parparos). From Lerna to the Lakonian border there were in pre-automobile days, two well-attested roads, marked by retaining walls and lithostrotos or kalderimi pavement over long stretches of several kilometers.

A. Pausanias' Anigraia starts at modern Kiveri and runs high along the coast past Dine, mentioned by Pausanias, to the plain of Astros. In *Topography* 3.105–106, with photographs in pls. 56–66, I offered descriptions of the road given by Lolling, Frazer (3.306), and the *Guide Joanne*. Continuation of the route through the level plain of Astros would present no problem. At 2.36.5–6, Pausanias leaves Asine and crosses over by sea to Lerna, whence he works his way back to Nauplia, which he reaches at 2.38.2–3; see Frazer on 2.36.6. At 2.38.4, he resumes his southwards itinerary towards the Lakonian frontier with the statement, ἔστι δὲ ἐκ Λέρνης καὶ ἑτέρα ... ὁδός. This is often translated, "From Lerna there is another road," but ἑτέρα means "one of two." Out of Lerna there is a road which is one of two. See Gildersleeve, *SCG* 587ff. The English idiom is with the plural, "one of two roads." The text requires that ἐκ Λέρνης there are two roads, i.e., one along the coast, the other inland.

234 THUCYDIDES' PENTEKONTAETIA AND OTHER ESSAYS

B. In the first edition of Baedeker (1883), a route (no. 27) leaving Elaious, ascending Mount Zavitza, and continuing to Ayios Petros, was the recommended way from Argos to Sparta. In the *Guide-Joanne* (no. 42, p. 244), the same route was described as "direct et plus court" between Argos and Sparta. Lolling noted several khans at the beginning of the route near Elaious. In *Topography* 7 chapter 7 ("A Road on Mount Zavitza"), I reported on this well-terraced kalderimi road over Mount Zavitza with a sketch-map in fig. 10 (p. 177) and photographs in pls. 168–173. There are two forks to the road on the Lerna side which converge about half-way up. One ascends from Verdelis' temple site at Elaious. The other ascends from the modern church of Ayios Georgios with an abandoned Turkish khan on the other side of the valley (pl. 166). In *Topography* 4 pl. 52, we offered what we believe is a continuation of this road on the southern side of the mountain, a stretch between Tsorobos (= Anthene) and Kato Doliana (= Neris). This paved and well-terraced road, traceable for many kilometers, is the most direct and shortest route between Argos and Sparta. The Ayios Petros-Sparta segment of the route is marked in red on Loring's end-map in *JHS* 15 (1895). He writes (p. 57), "We have abundant evidence for the use of the Arakhova route in connexion with military expeditions." On p. 62, he refers to "the ordinary route from Argolis to Sparta by the Thyreatid plain."[32]

[32]In Diodoros 15.64, three routes to Sparta are listed as being used after Leuktra for an invasion of Lakonia. The "middle" route was used by the Boiotians and led to Sellasia. This would seem to be the route leaving Tegea and using the valley of the Sarandapotamos and the Klisoura. West of this was one used by the Arkadians to invade the Skiritis. This would seem to be the Eurotas valley route. The logical candidate for a route which is east of the "middle" route is Pausanias' road. It was used by the Argives. Diodoros' text designates it as κατὰ τοὺς ὅρους τῆς Τεγεάτιδος. But Bölte, whose knowledge of the geography of the Peloponnesos was unrivaled, writes (*RE* s.v. Sparta [1829] 1304): "Diod. XV 64, 2, wo κατὰ τοὺς ὅρους τῆς Θυρεάτιδος χώρας statt

V. AETIOLOGY SANS TOPOGRAPHY 235

3. *Sites.* **A. Plain of Astros.** We can be certain that in Pausanias' day there were two prominent and inhabited sites.

1. AYIOS ANDREAS. On the coast at the southern rim of the plain was the heavily walled site of Ayios Andreas. Photographs of the walls are published by Papachatzes (2 p. 300 pls. 337 and 338).[33] In *Topography* 6 pl. 164, I offered a photograph of the wall on the landward side, and in *Topography* 8 pls. 103 and 104, photographs of the more impressive walls on the seaward side.[34] In *Topography* 7.95, we collected the opinions of those, including Phaklares, who had sherded the site. It was occupied from the late fifth century into Byzantine times. Moreover, the city was laid out with straight streets according to a "Hippodamian" plan. Just as several new settlements have been laid out today according to designed patterns, after the destruction of villages by earthquakes, the plan at Ayios Andreas suggests that in the last quarter of the fifth century, a new town was established at the site, which accords well with the masonry of the polygonal walls. Since the

---

Τεγεάτιδος wenigstens für Ephoros zu schreiben ist." Bölte's text would account for three main routes to Sparta, i.e. through the valleys of the Eurotas, Sarandapotamos, and Kelephina passing Arachova (= ancient Oinous). However, there are other sources, including Xenophon, for the invasion. In *Topography* 7.156–157 with pl. 159, we published remains of a kalderimi road, which we suggest was the mountain route (Polybios 5.18) from Tegea to Sparta used by Philip in 218 B.C. We note that Yanis A. Pikoulas, *H Notia Megalopolike Chora* (Athens 1988) 201–225, has now given us a report on the roads leading from Megalopolis and Asea to Sparta. He finds four carriage roads (= wheel-ruts) leading from southern Arkadia into northern Lakonia. He regards the Eurotas valley road which leads north to his site of Oresthasion on the western slopes of Mount Tsemberou, then northeast to Asea, as the chief military road.

[33] For other photographs, see Phaklares (1985) pls. 10–12; (1990) pls. 7–9.

[34] For photographs of the markings for the game of five-lines carved on the rocks of the akropolis of Ayios Andreas, see *CSCA* 1 (1968) pl. 6.

236 THUCYDIDES' PENTEKONTAETIA AND OTHER ESSAYS

town of Thyrea, located ten stades (= 1850 m.) from the sea (Thucydides 4.57.1), was burned by the Athenians in 424 B.C., the evidence of the sherds and the pattern of streets suggested to me that the inhabitants decided to relocate their city at a more easily defensible position a few kilometers away. It is important to note that in Pausanias' day, a polis of that name existed. In the fifth of the roads described by Pausanias as leading out of Tegea, he mentions (8.54.4), "The highway from Tegea to Thyrea and to the villages in the Thyreatis."[35] Moreover, a neglected funerary inscription, republished by Phaklares, *Archaia Kynouria* (Athens 1990) 90, proves that Thyrea was in existence in the third century A.C. Bibliography for the early travelers who referred to this route is given by Frazer (4.444–445). It followed the course of the river Garates, having the village of Doliana with its famous marble quarries high up on the mountain side. Phaklares (*Archaia Kynouria* [Thessaloniki 1985] 267–268) charts this route, noting that wheel-ruts have been reported at Καριούλα and ″Αγιοι Δέκα. Parenthetically, Robertson (196 n. 45), in his effort to dissociate the Thyreatic sites from any attested name, writes about the 8.54.4 passage, "Why mention the villages unless 'Thyrea' by itself was a doubtful indication?" Pausanias gives the names of poleis as terminal places for many of his routes. If one says that he drove from Philadelphia to Princeton through the towns of New Jersey, this does not mean that Princeton is a "doubtful" town. We can be sure that in Pausanias' day there was a town by the name of Thyrea and that it was the terminus of a road. Accordingly, I have suggested that Ayios Andreas is the site of the post-Thucydidean Thyrea.[36]

---

[35]For εὐθεῖα ὁδός, as a term denoting a "highway" and connecting cities, see *Topography* 3.337–338.

[36]For the suggested identification of the site as Methana, see *Topography* 6 chapter 4, esp. pp. 96–97. Following several other scholars, including E. Meyer, I believe that the name of Methana in Pseudo-Skylax was misplaced. It occurs

V. AETIOLOGY SANS TOPOGRAPHY   237

2. GREAT ESTATE OF HERODES ATTICUS AT LOUKOU. The second site in the plain of Astros is commonly denoted as Loukou after the monastery of that name. It comprises the great Roman villa of Herodes Atticus, the most sumptuous private estate in the Peloponnesos and probably on the Greek mainland. Phaklares, *Archaia Kynouria* (Athens 1990) devotes pls. 29–35 to photographs of the site. An elaborate Nymphaion and a large stoa have been excavated here. Many antiquities have been found, including sculpture and reliefs of the Roman period,[37] capitals of columns of the Korinthian and Ionic orders, fragments of mosaic pavements. Within a radius of a quarter of a mile, columns of grey granite and foundations of walls have been reported. An impressive Roman aqueduct from nearby springs, made of bricks, is part of the complex; see *Topography* 6 pls. 159 and 160. Chapter 3 of the same volume of *Topography* is devoted to testimonia about Loukou.[38] So impressive is the site that it has been included in the itinerary of the American School for their graduate students. The site eclipses all others in the region.

In 7.20.6, Pausanias refers to the magnificent building on the southern slopes of the Athenian akropolis as "built by the Athenian Herodes in memory of his deceased wife." In 2.27.6, he tells us that Herodes Atticus had adorned the temple of Poseidon at Isthmus. In 1.19.6, he refers to the stadion of Herodes in Athens as "wonderful to see." Arguments ex silentio are difficult to appraise in the case of Pausanias, who omitted many monuments

---

in the *Periplous* one entry removed from the Lakonian Epidauros. I believe that the text is sound, but the entry misplaced. In the record of Epidauros and Troizen in the *Periplous*, there is no listing of the city of Methana, where one would expect to find it. It is located on a striking rocky peninsula with a long history; see E. Meyer, *RE* s.v. (1980) 1375–1379. No one believes that there were two cities of this name. In any case, those who regard Ayios Andreas as Methana must account for Thyrea of Pausanias and the late inscription.

[37] Cf. Follet, *REG* 105 (1992) 446.

[38] Cf. Semni Karusu, *MDAI(R)* 76 (1969) 253–265 with pls. 81–87.

238 THUCYDIDES' PENTEKONTAETIA AND OTHER ESSAYS

from his itinerary; but in the context of a description of a region far from any large urban center, we prefer to believe that Pausanias would have visited this palace, the Versailles of its day.

B. Sites on the road from Lerna to frontier. Normally, one might take up the sites along Pausanias' road by starting with the epigraphically attested one, Eva. However, the two critics of my position about the sites in the Thyreatis have taken as the *point d'appui* a passage about the site Neris, i.e. a reference in Statius (not Kallimachos) to Neris and the Charadros river. All the testimonia about Neris, including that of Pausanias, accord well with a candidate on the Tanos river on the road between the walled towns of Eva and Tsorobos except for this one passage, which Winter and now Robertson have seized upon as being in conflict with my identification. One is reminded that after Rhys Carpenter had collected all the data, as he conceived it, to support his theory of the late introduction of the Greek alphabet, a student of his who excavated at Korinth produced a single inscribed sherd which she claimed was in an earlier context than that allowed by Carpenter. Carpenter (*AJA* 42 [1938] 59) replied with his usual wit and sleight-of-hand by re-examining the context of the lone inscription and invoking what he called the "Law of the Single Sherd," i.e. that there is one item which seems to fall outside the accumulated instances and this item is given precedence over the mass of the testimonia. There are actually three and possibly four sherds.

1. NERIS. With regard to the site of Neris, Robertson speaks out of both sides of his mouth in attempting to discredit our position. The main thrust of his argument is that Neris is on the Charadros river, a tributary of the Inachos, many miles removed from Pausanias' route. In the same breath, he alludes to a second Neris in the Thyreatis, the site of which he makes no effort to locate. Since he chastises those who did not recognize that Neris (i.e. of Pausanias) was on the Charadros, we take up his position

V. AETIOLOGY SANS TOPOGRAPHY   239

about this Neris as the only meaningful one. We limit ourselves to quoting from a passage on p. 190, which gives the gist of the argument:

> Callimachus used the name for 'an Argive mountain,' one that stood above a long river valley with a frightening torrent called Charadrus.[24] Details like these are precious to topographers, who have always looked for the village Neris beneath a steep mountain and beside a long dangerous river. But Neris the mountain belongs elsewhere. For the name has appeared once more, in the form Νῆρις, in a papyrus fragment of Euphorion, and the scholiast describes it as a place 'at which the Heracleidae encamped during their expedition to Argos.' Now we hear very little about the route of the Heracleidae after they entered the Peloponnesus, save that they passed through Arcadia without disturbing the inhabitants. ... But they would not go by way of the Thyreatis. It is safe to assume that they followed the main road north and struck at Argos by the shortest route, from Mantineia past Oenoe. And just here is a long valley with a dangerous torrent, now the Xerias, but anciently Charadrus. The steep mountain at its western end is therefore Neris. Our hopes of situating the village Neris are dashed.

In his n. 24, Robertson gives two references without citing the texts, as is his custom throughout. The only reference to a mountain of Neris is in a scholion to Statius *Thebais* 4.46, which refers to Kallimachos (frg. 684 Pfeiffer): 'Neris' montis nomen Argivi, ut ait Callimachus. Kallimachos' mountain is in the Argolid. The ancient Charadros, which drains into the Inachos, and Oinoa are securely fixed. The "steep mountain at its western end" is Artemision, well attested in the literature. Oinoa is not Neris. The "shortest route" from Sparta to Argos is by no stretch of the imagination through Mantineia.

Taking my cue from Pfeiffer's commentary on the Kallimachos fragment (no. 684), I repeated (*Topography* 6.93) his warning

240   THUCYDIDES' PENTEKONTAETIA AND OTHER ESSAYS

that Kallimachos uses Lyrkeia, Marathon, and Neris for places, mountains, and/or rivers. The usage signifies no more than Lyrkeia's river, Lyrkeia's mountain. Lyrkeia's river is the Inachos. Marathon's mountain is Pentelikon (or Brilessos). So. Neris' mountain is Parparos, certainly not Artemision. Robertson does not understand poetic usage, and ignores our better commentators.

In line 28, a papyrus fragment (*Ox. Pap.* 2085) refers to the *Chiliades*,[39] which is known as an epyllion of Euphorion of Chalkis (third cent. B.C.), who was characterized as writing poetry full of glosses and being "Homeric" (*Anth. Pal.* 11.218). The poem is said to have been written against certain persons who had defrauded Euphorion of money, and guaranteed their punishment by a recital of oracles fulfilled after the lapse of a thousand years, hence the title. Hunt titled the papyrus as "Scholia on Euphorion (?)": *Oxy. Pap.* 2085. It is republished by Lloyd-Jones/Parsons as *Supplementum Hellenisticum* (Berlin 1983) 430. Meanwhile, Lloyd-Jones kindly supplied me with the text of the critical lines, as published in *Topography* 4 (1982) 77.

The fragmentary opening lines of the papyrus seem to make reference to the Bacchantes and the struggle between Dionysos and Perseus, and do not concern us. In lines 23–25, we have a lemma, where reference is made to the *rivers* Neris and Inachos. For the Inachos, the scholiast makes reference to Orneai and Kallimachos' work *On the Rivers* (Pfeiffer frg. 457). For the Neris, he makes the statement that it was at this river that the Herakleidai encamped in their invasion of Argos. Robertson makes much of the Herakleidai reference in order to strike the historical record from account. We repeat the relevant part: "The scholiast describes it as a place 'at which the Heracleidae encamped during

---

[39]The phrase ἐν ταῖς Χιλιάσιν is explained by Lloyd-Jones/Parsons: "id est 'in commentariis ad Chiliadas'." What we have is scholia on a commentary to the *Chiliades*. Robertson writes, "Νῆρις, in a papyrus fragment of Euphorion"!

V. AETIOLOGY SANS TOPOGRAPHY   241

their expedition to Argos.' Now we hear very little about the
route of the Heracleidae after they entered the Peloponnesus,
save that they passed through Arcadia without disturbing the
inhabitants." In the first place, in the papyrus, the Neris is not a
"place," but a river. The Herakleidai encamped at Neris' river,
which we believe is the Tanos which empties into the Gulf of Astros. Secondly, who are Robertson's Herakleidai, who, he says,
were allowed passage through Arkadia to invade Argos? He gives
two references to F. Prinz and to C. Robert. Prinz in the pages
cited (*Gründungsmythen* [Munich 1979] 299–313) does not mention Arkadia or our problem in any way. C. Robert, *Die
griechische Heldensage* 2 (Berlin 1921) 660–662, gives the testimonia. In 7.9.1, Diodoros writes, "Practically all the peoples
throughout the Peloponnesus, except the Arcadians ($\pi\lambda\dot{\eta}\nu$
'Αρκάδων), were driven out on the occasion of the Return of the
Heracleidae" (Loeb tr.). In connection with this passage, Robert
cites Pausanias 5.4.1, where Oxylus, as leader of the Dorians, won
the kingdom of Arkadia by avoiding open battle and became king
of Elis. In Polyainos 1.7, a passage Robert believes is taken from
Ephoros, Kypselos, by a stratagem, reconciled the Arkadians and
Herakleidai and brought about an alliance. In Pausanias 8.5.6, we
read that when the Dorians came back to Peloponnesos, they
came not by the Isthmus, but in ships to Rhion, and Kypselos
married the son of Aristomachos and thereby secured Arkadia
from all risk.

Frazer, in the Loeb Apollodoros 1 p. 281, assembles the testimonia for two invasions of the Peloponnesos by the Herakleidai.[40] The second return, in conjunction with the Dorians, is
dated by Thucydides (1.12.3) and Pausanias (4.3.3).[41] All the ref-

---

[40]Frazer focuses on the record in Apollodoros. Smith's *Dictionary* (2.386–
387) enumerates five different expeditions in the saga. There are other classifications.

[41]It was in the first invasion under Hyllos, the eldest of the four sons of
Herakles by Deianeira, that Argos under king Tisamenos, son of Orestes and

242 THUCYDIDES' PENTEKONTAETIA AND OTHER ESSAYS

erences about the exemption of the Arkadians have to do with an expedition starting at Rhion/Naupaktos. Naupaktos is said to have derived its name from the Herakleidai having here built the fleet with which they crossed over to Peloponnesos: Strabo 9.426; Ephoros *FGrH* 70 frg. 121; Pausanias 10.38.10; Apollodoros 2.8.2. Cf. the scholiast on Aristeides *Panathenaikos* 11.8 (Dindorf). Aristodemos, son of Aristomachos and a descendant of Herakles, was killed at Naupaktos by a flash of lightning, just as he was setting out on his expedition into Peloponnesos. The association of the Herakleidai with Arkadia has to do with the second return, starting at Rhion and bound for Sparta, not Argos.

Who are the Herakleidai of our scholiast of the second century A.C.? C. Robert (p. 648) records that Herakles had about seventy sons, as well as a few daughters, who are attested in Peloponnesos, Thessaly, Rhodes, Kos, Lydia, etc. Frazer (Loeb Apollodoros 1 p. 285) observes, "According to the traditional genealogy, the conquerors of the Peloponnese were great-great-grandsons of Hercules." The early kings of Sparta were referred to as Heraklids. Aristodemos, Eurysthenes, Prokles, et al. are called Heraklids. Leonidas is called a Ἡρακλείδης in Herodotos 7.208.1. Before Plataiai, the Spartan heralds refer to Ἡρακλεῖδαι οἱ ἀπὸ Σπάρτης (8.114.2) At Plataiai, the Spartans made great offers to Tisamenos, the Elean soothsayer, to induce him to take command of their army "together with the children of Herakles, their kings" (Powell tr. 9.33.3, ἅμα Ἡρακλειδέων τοῖσι βασιλεῦσι).

Returning to the scholiast's statement that the Herakleidai encamped at Neris' river, we note, 1) In all the preserved varied accounts of the saga of the "Return of the Herakleidai," there is none which attests an invasion of Argos from Sparta. 2) If the scholiast knew of a version which is not in the preserved litera-

---

Hermione, was taken. This invasion started from the north and sheds no light on a road from Sparta to Argos. It appears from his references in notes 27 and 28 that Robertson is completely confused about the saga of the Herakleidai. He offers references which he has not digested.

V. AETIOLOGY SANS TOPOGRAPHY 243

ture, there is no reason to believe that the legend would not have conducted the Herakleidai along the normal military route from Sparta to Argos, i.e. through the Thyreatis. 3) It seems more likely that the scholiast applied the term for the royal family to a later attested invasion. Kourmeki, our candidate for Neris, is situated on the broad Tanos river near its mouth. Before Kleomenes sailed from Thyreatis to Nauplia and Tiryns (Herodotos 6.76), he must have encamped on Neris' river. Much earlier, the Lakedaimonians under king Nikandros invaded the Argolid to join with Asine in ravaging the land (Pausanias 2.36.4; 3.7.4; 4.14.3). Their route must have taken them through Neris. This invasion is supported by archaeological evidence and is dated before 700 B.C.[42] The route is not given; but any army bound for Asine and by-passing Argos would certainly take the Thyreatis route.

In the fourth book, lines 1–344, of Statius' epic poem *Thebais*, the poet gives a catalogue of the Argive host. In support of the Seven come men of Prosymna, Midea, Phleious, and Neris ("and Neris that quails at Charadros foaming down his valley's length," Loeb tr. lines 45–47). Neris is followed by Kleonai, Thyrea, Sikyon, Lechaion, etc. The idea is not geological. As noted in *Topography* 6.93 n. 4, Kahrstedt had observed that Statius' characterization of the river Neris could not apply to the Argive Charadros, flowing past Oinoa, which in any case is a generic name, concluding, "Die Wendung des Statius passt nur auf den Tanos," as I would agree, having traced both rivers to their source.[43] Just below in line 52 of our passage, Bölte, *RE* s.v. Hellison (1912) 94.51, observes that Statius' phrase "*anfractu riparum incurvus* ist nur eine Ausdeutung des Namens." Helm, *RE*

---

[42]See George Huxley, *Early Sparta* (London 1962) 21.

[43]Statius never visited Greece. We identify Neris with the plateau Kourmeki west of the town of Kato Doliana (see also Christien and Spyropoulos, *BCH* 109 [1985] 457); but most of the ancient town is probably buried under the modern town.

244 THUCYDIDES' PENTEKONTAETIA AND OTHER ESSAYS

s.v. Papinius 8 (1983), discusses the sources for Statius' *Thebais*, suggesting (col. 996) that Statius was using some mythological handbook such as that used by Diodoros. As noted by Bürchner in *RE* III.2.2113 and 2115, Χαράδρα and χάραδρος are generic terms, as χαράδρα is today. Smith's *Dictionary* (1.603) notes that it is the name of many mountain torrents, specifying our one in Statius.[44]

The most conclusive reason for rejecting the modern Xerias (anc. Charadros) as a candidate for Neris' river is that there is only one polis on the river, and that one securely identified as Oinoa. The river is short, and the district has been surveyed by many, including Colin Edmonson and myself, who have hiked its length. Neither Neris nor Eva, as we shall see in the next section, is on the Xerias. Robertson's repeated exhortation to the reader that sites "are to be looked for" means no more than that he has not himself looked either on the ground or in the literature.[45]

Since the evidence of Hesychius has elsewhere been invoked by Robertson, we note that Hesychius, using an accusative plural form, a common convention of citing nouns according to a textual form, annotates the word Νηρίδας as τὰς κοίλας πέτρας. Rising immediately above Kato Doliana, and clearly visible from the road, is a spectacular cliff honeycombed with caves

---

[44]A river might have two names, one in mythology and one in later authors, but there is no basis for suggesting this because of the Statius passage. The Acheloos had four, Thoas, Axenos, and Thestios. See Smith's *Dictionary of Greek and Roman Geography* 1.18. In the Pseudo-Plutarch *de fluviis*, many rivers, including the Acheloos, Inachos, Eurotas, etc., are given more than one name. Strabo (8.3.11.342) tells us that at Dyme in Achaia the river called Peiros by Hesiod was the Teutheas. See also 10.2.1.450. Furthermore, a long river might be given one name for the principal stretch, another for its upper tributary.

[45]Robertson's double-talk is illustrated by his note on page 196, "It does not help to smuggle in the name by whatever means, without a description of the site." Robertson gives no description of sites on the Xerias.

V. AETIOLOGY SANS TOPOGRAPHY   245

(*Topography* 3 pl. 81), called Σπηλιές, which are unparalleled for the Peloponnesos, the strongest of testimonia for the site. Cf. *LSJ*[9] s.v. νῆρις: "*hollow rock, cavern*, Hsch. (pl.)."

2. EVA. Robertson writes (p. 196 n. 43):

> Since Eva was in later days the chief settlement in the district, the discovery at Helleniko of a tile with this name, Εὐατᾶν, falls short of proving that the site was Eva. See Phaklaris, *Archaia Kynouria* (Salonica 1985) 120–1, 234–5, and *Horos* 5 (1987) 110. The coordinates for Neris have been sharply changed by Euphorion's mention of the name, as we saw above.

The object was not a tile, but the matrix of a tile, a tablet for stamping tiles, bearing in relief the reverse inscription Εὐατᾶν δημόσιοι, "public (tiles) of the citizens of Eva"; see Kalitses, *AE* 1960. Chr. 6–8; *SEG* 30.377. The matrix was found at the site of the temple illustrated in *Topography* 6 pl. 163. Except for Robertson, almost all scholars have accepted the identification.[46] Single tiles, single stones are taken as precious evidence for the identification of sites, unless convincing evidence can be adduced to the contrary. Even so, our object is not a tile, but a matrix from which tiles were made. It seems unlikely that the inhabitants

---

[46]On the basis of an alleged sanctuary of Polemokrates at Loukou and Asklepios reliefs found there, Kalitses suggested that Eva in Roman times had moved down the hill to Loukou. I accepted that theory in my early publication in *Topography* 3.125–126, but abandoned it when it became clear that Loukou was only the estate of Herodes Atticus, who had transported the reliefs from Eva, where there was a sanctuary of Polemokrates, or from Athens, and that Helleniko was inhabited in Roman times. Yvonne Goester, "The Plain of Astros. A Survey," *Newsletter Netherlands Institute at Athens* 4 (1991) 53, and *Pharos* 1 (1993), rightly criticized my initial position, but does not note that I corrected myself in *Topography* 6 chap. 3 once it was established that Loukou was the villa of Herodes Atticus.

246   THUCYDIDES' PENTEKONTAETIA AND OTHER ESSAYS

of Helleniko would have stamped the tiles of their temple with the name of a foreign city.

As to Robertson's phrase "in later days," Eva (= Helleniko) with its impressive circuit wall was inhabited from Mycenaean times until the third century A.C.; see the evidence collected in *Topography* 6.89–90. Phaklares, in his excellent study, *Archaia Kynouria* (Thessaloniki 1985) 82–99, offered a detailed catalogue. Subsequently, Y. Goester in *Newsletter Netherland Institute at Athens* 4 (1991) 55ff. and *Pharos* 1 (1993) 55ff. offered a report on the pottery on the surface. Following the excavation of two cemeteries at the site by Abadie and Spyropoulos, "Eva de Thyreatide," *BCH* 109 (1985) 385–454, Christien and Spyropoulos in the same periodical explained the prosperity of Eva as resulting from the fact that it was on the direct and shortest route from Argos to Sparta.

As to Robertson's effort to associate Eva with his "coordinates for Neris," this refers to his completely mistaken effort to place Neris miles removed on the Xerias river, a tributary of the Inachos, where we have only one site and that securely identified as Oinoa. Since Robertson wishes to place Pausanias' site for the Battle of Champions in the plain of Astros, it is difficult to conceive how Pausanias got from Astros to Oinoa on his way to Sparta. More importantly, in spite of his repetitious comments about the defects of all topographers who have studied the region, Robertson has failed to tell us how and why the matrix was transported to Helleniko from the valley of the Xerias. Or, did the citizens of Helleniko whimsically make a matrix with the name of an unattested town? Unless other evidence is adduced, Helleniko is Eva.

3. HERMS AT LAKONIAN FRONTIER. In *Topography* 3.127–134, I reported on Rhomaios' two excavations of three rubble mounds on the old dirt road, now completely abandoned, which led from Sparta to Ayios Petros. The site seems originally to have been an archaic mountain shrine of Artemis beside a road. In *Topography*

V. AETIOLOGY SANS TOPOGRAPHY 247

6 chapter 6, I located the site after some difficulty and published pls. 167 and 168. The herms are taken to mark the boundaries of Lakonia, Tegea, and Argos (Pausanias 2.38.7). Frazer (3.310) wrote, "It is tolerably certain, at least, that Pausanias, going to Sparta, must have passed this way." The site is on the crest of a ridge which forms the watershed between the waters flowing to the Thyreatic Gulf, to Tegea, and to Sparta. When Pausanias (13.10.6) resumes his itinerary from the herms, it is clear that he is on his way from Tegea to Karyai and Sparta, and any route from Helleniko must have taken him this way. Lolling (*Baedeker. Greece*[4] 361), too, gave his opinion that the boundaries must have been at this point. Loring (*JHS* 15 [1895] 55), who worked on the roads of Lakonia before the days of the automobile, likewise concluded, prior to Rhomaios' excavations, that the three heaps of stone were at a position which marked the common boundary of Argos, Tegea, and Lakonia.

4. ANTHENE. The walled site of Tsorobos (Τσιόροβος) on the southern slopes of Mount Zavitza is about two kilometers below the watchtower illustrated in *Topography* 3 pls. 67 and 68 and three kilometers above the town of Kato Doliana. On my first visit, I estimated the distance by pedometer on a winding trail as eight kilometers from the river to the watchtower. Phaklaris (*Archaia Kynouria* [Athens 1990] 90) gives the distance as three kilometers from Kato Doliana to Tsorobos.[47] Photographs of the

---

[47]Y. Goester, *Newsletter Netherlands Institute at Athens* 4 (1991) 55, writes, "Tsorovos and Kato Doliana (Kourmeti) are lying very close to each other on the same bank of the Tanos. This can only have been possible if very few people lived there," and in *Pharos* 1 (1993) 53, "It (Neris) could be the replacement of Tsorovos when times were safer." Abai and Hyampolis were poleis which were closer together (a little over a mile) than Tsorobos and Kato Doliana, as were many other villages, ancient and modern. Phaklares, *Archaia Kynouria* (Athens 1990) pl. 27, offers a photograph of Tsorobos taken from Helleniko. Kato Doliana is not in the picture, but the distance is considerable.

248 THUCYDIDES' PENTEKONTAETIA AND OTHER ESSAYS

walls at the site were published in *Topography* 3 pls. 76–79.[48] Although the wall is much overgrown, we picked up traces of it running for some four hundred yards. Touchais in the *Chronique* of *BCH* 103 (1979) 561, reported: "Sur le flanc Sud du Mont Zavitsa, parmi les ruines de *Tsorovos*, presque entièrement recouvertes aujourd'hui, on a cru déceler les traces d'un mur d'enceinte de 1 000 m de long." Frazer (3.308) commented that the stones are almost unhewn and regarded them as very ancient. On different occasions, I have sherded the site with archaeologists, as reported in *Topography* 3.121 and 4.75–76. In addition to many classical sherds, Phaklaris reported Hellenistic, Roman, and Late-Roman. The requirements for the site of Anthene are that it be a polis in Thucydides' day and a kome in Pausanias', that it be beyond the site of the Battle of Champions by a road leading up and inland, continuing on to Neris, Eva and Sparta.[49] All of these conditions are met by assigning Tsorobos to Anthene. No other site meets these conditions.

5. BATTLE OF CHAMPIONS AND THE CENOTAPH INSCRIPTION. Jacqueline Christien, well-known for her explorations in the Peloponnesos, has recently written (*BCH* Suppl. 22 [1992] 158):

> Je suis de l'avis de K. W. PRITCHETT, *Studies in Ancient Greek Topography*, III (1980), p. 116 et IV (1982), p. 75–79, concernant l'emplacement d'Anthana, mais je récuse l'idée que l'inscription trouvée en ces lieux soit liée au cénotaphe. Il s'agit d'un inscription

[48]See also Phaklares, *Archaia Kynouria* (Thessaloniki 1985) pl. 42, and *Archaia Kynouria* (Athens 1990) pl. 27. The town of Kato Doliana and the bridge carrying the road are shown in *Topography* 3 pl. 81; but Tsorobos is higher up the mountain out of view. In turn, pl. 83 is taken from below Tsorobos with the town of Kato Doliana in the center and Loukou at the bend in the road at the upper center.

[49]For the road, see *Topography* 7 chap. 7 with pls. 167–173. There is no other way to get to Tsorobos except by ascending from Kato Doliana.

V. AETIOLOGY SANS TOPOGRAPHY 249

éginétique venant du site même d'Anthana: cf. la lecture de Ch. KRITZAS, «Remarques sur trois inscriptions de Cynourie», dans *BCH* 109 (1985), p. 709–716. De même Eua romaine aussi bien que classique est à placer à Helléniko, en encorbellement au dessus de la plaine, de l'autre côté du Tanos.

The inscription, stipulating that no one harm the κενεάριον and no one harm the ὀχετός, was first published (in part) by Rhomaios (*PAE* 1950. 237). I published photographs of what remains of the stone (subsequently broken and partly lost), now stored in the apotheke of the Astros museum, in *Topography* 6 pls. 156–158. Following Rhomaios, I (6.79–83) took the word κενεάριον as another form of the attested noun κενήριον, a cenotaph, following in this respect *SEG* 13.266 ("sepulcrum"), the editors of *LSJ*[9] Suppl. p. 82, and E. Meyer, *Der kleine Pauly* 4 (1972) 528.[50] However, Kritsas, as cited by Christien, noting that the adjective κενέαρος, glossed by Hesychius as κενός, ἐλαφρός, takes the noun as meaning a cavity for conducting water, emphasizing that the other noun in the inscription means waterpipe.[51] Kritsas has been followed by Dubois, *REG* 100 (1987) 416 no. 621, and 103 (1990) 514/5 no. 418; and by Christien. Robertson (pp. 184–187) rejects both interpretations, claiming that κενεάριον is synonymous with βήλημα, a word attested for an aqueduct at Andania,[52] but βήλημα is defined by Hesychius as

[50]There is difficulty with the text, since it is necessary to assume that, although it is cut in monumental style, the engraver or the copyist added a superfluous omicron in line 6. A teacher in the gymnasium at Astros insisted that he had accompanied an Oxford professor to copy the unbroken stone, but the copy has never come to light.

[51]As indicated in fig. 10 of *Topography* 7, there are two powerful springs on the watchtower ridge, from either of which a water-channel might have conducted water to the natives of Anthene.

[52]The impressive aqueduct of Andania has left massive remains (*Topography* 5 pl. 14), although in a populated area. What is called an ὀχετός

250 THUCYDIDES' PENTEKONTAETIA AND OTHER ESSAYS

κώλυμα, φράγμα ἐν ποταμῷ, i.e. a "barrier, fence" and cannot signify something κενός, ἐλαφρός.

We offer the following observations about the κενεάριον inscription: μεδεὶς ἀδικεῖτο τὸ κενεάριον· τὸν ὀχετὸν <ο> μὲ ἀδικεῖτο.

1. We have two separate injunctions in the inscription, not two objects connected by καί as would be the case if the reference were to two parts of the same object. The two separate sentences can be explained if a water channel was laid in a place where it ran past a cenotaph.

2. Since the adjective κενός is obvious from the first part of the word κεν-εαριον, the part to be accounted for in Hesychius' gloss is ἐλαφρός. The adjective "light" carries no connotation to support an unattested noun meaning a cavity or a barrier. The supporters of this meaning offer no etymological explanation of the second part of the compound-εαριον. To invoke Hesychius' adjective is meaningless. Rather, a meaning for some part of a water channel has been hypothesized to accompany ὀχετός.

3. Nouns compounded with the first component of κεν-ός are common, and the compound κεν-ηριον is attested. Etymologists attest that the root of ἠρίον has a digamma (w, v). For Indo-European forms, see Frisk s.v. ἠρίον. For the variation (w)ηριον/(w)εαριον, we have an exact parallel in the common word meaning "of spring," (w)ηρινός, (w)εαρινός. Variant spellings occur in the same author in prose or verse.[53] So also ἦρ and ἔαρ, of which Frisk writes, "ἔαρ, ἔαρος auch ἦρος, ἦρι

---

on Mount Zavitza has left no remains, although it is in a sparsely populated place. Presumably, it was a water channel such as that published in *Topography* 1 pl. 10a, carrying water across the sandbar at Pylos. The latter could easily have been broken by foot-traffic. There is no comparison between the two.

[53]In Euripides *Hipp.* 76, the text is read as ἠρινή; the scholiast has ἐαρινή. Barrett says that Attic uses ἐαρ in the nominative and accusative, ηρ in other cases. In poetry, the scansion of εα is often with synecphonesis.

V. AETIOLOGY SANS TOPOGRAPHY 251

(att., auch ion. und Alk.)" etc. Latin *ver* is a cognate, with a root in digamma (v, w).[54] So with ἠρίον, we find Fηρίον in Homer with a root in V (w). The parallel is exact except that one word is much more common and the form ἐαρίον has not hitherto been attested: ἠρινός or ἐαρινός, ἠρίον or ἐαρίον. Differences in vowel contractions are numerous: κῆρ and κέαρ is a parallel (ἤν, ἐάν; the imperfect forms of εἰμί [ἦ and ἔα], possibly the interjections ἦ and ἔα). For ἠρίον from the root uer, Pokorny in his index to *IEW* refers to page 1161; for ἔαρ from the root ues-r to p. 1174. See also Schwyzer, *Gr. Gram*. 1.251. ἠρινός and ἐαρινός, ἦρ and ἔαρ, ἠρίον and ἐαρίον, κενήριον and κενεάριον, κῆρ and κέαρ are the same. Schwyzer (518 n. 5) adds Ζέαθος and Ζῆθος, κέαθοι and κηθοί. Compare also νεᾶνις and νῆνις, the latter in Anakreon and on a vase; see *LSJ*[9]. ὄρεα equals ὄρη, etc. Kühner-Blass (1.202, 203, 210, 471) offer many examples under different categories, of which we select the following: στέαρ and στῆρ, φρεατία and φρητία, δέλεαρ and βλῆρ (Aeol.); φακέα and φακῆ, ὄρη and ὄρεα, Καρνήδας and Καρνεάδης, Στρατῆς and Στρατέας, χαλκῆ and χαλκέα, ἐπεάν and ἐπήν, ἀλέα and ἀλῆ. The name of the goddess 'Ρέα occurs as a monosyllable in Homer *Il*. 15.187 and Sophokles *OC* 1073, but as 'Ρῆ in Pherecydes *Syr*. 9. The first person imperfect is ἐτίθεα in Herodotos. In an inscription from Eretria (*IG* XII.9.191.A line 26), the genitive form of ἔαρ is spelled as ἦρος. For an early use of ἠρίον (ἐρίον) as a cippus sepulcralis, see *SIG*[3] 11. The indices to the four-volume *Grammatici Graeci* will lead the reader to many references to the coalescing of εα into η. In 4.372.23, we have κέαρ κῆρ κέαρος κῆρος. Herodian (320.25) writes, τὸ κῆρος καὶ ἦρος ἐκ τοῦ κέαρος καὶ ἔαρος συναλήλιπται, ὁμοίως καὶ αἱ δοτικαὶ κῆρι καὶ ἦρι. It seems not to be a matter of dialects, as I sug-

---

[54]Cf. Latin vernifer, but Greek ἐαροτρεφής; Walde-Hoffman, *Lateinisches etymologisches Wörterbuch* s.v. ver. See also R. Maltby, *A Lexicon of Ancient Latin Etymologies* (Leeds 1991) 635 s.v. ver, citing Servius, *Aen*. 1.292 (ut digammos sit adiecta, sicut ἦρ ver) and others.

252 THUCYDIDES' PENTEKONTAETIA AND OTHER ESSAYS

gested in *Topography* 6.81–82, but a regular rule for the contraction of unlike vowels. Our inscription refers to a cenotaph, as the editors of *LSJ*⁹ Suppl. 82, recognized. Thus, we have two separate injunctions about two distinct objects.[55]

Writing with contumelious ignorance of the literature, Robertson questions the practice of a cenotaph, "One would like

---

[55]Robertson devotes pages 197–199 to another inscription, one of a tiny bronze bull, the best photographs of which are published in *ADelt.* 26 (1971) Chron. pl. 70b. The object measures only 0.066 x 0.04, although it has twenty-one letters. Phaklaris (*Horos* 5.115) published the correct text, after it was misread by the original editor, Kritsas, and Dubois, as Ηελικὶς ἀνέθεκε Παρπάρο<ι>. He collected a number of early inscriptions where the iota was omitted from the dative form, including Jeffery, *LSAG* p. 408 nos. 26 and 27. For other Lakonian inscribed dedications of miniature bronze animals, some to mountain deities, see Jeffery, *LSAG* p. 200, and *Topography* 7.183. In *Topography* 7.171, I reported on my repeated visits to the Nauplia museum to inspect the object, but it was always reported as misplaced. Cf. *SEG* 41.295. It is clear on the photographs that the engraver crowded the letters at the end of the text by superimposing the letters alpha-rho, then inscribed a small omicron on the upper part of the leg of the bull, omitting the iota, I would suggest, because the lower part of the tiny leg was too fragile, although Phaklaris' observation is sound. Robertson (p. 199) now alleges that the text should be read Ἑλικὶς Παρπάρω ἀνέθεκε, claiming that one reads the part on the sides of the bull before one reads the top. This is absurd. The word ἀνέθεκε is between the two proper nouns, the customary order in all dedications. He cites no parallel for a person named after a mountain or a festival, nor accounts for the omission of a dedicatee. The one example cited (Πέρπερος) is neither a mountain nor a festival, and is found only in late Roman times. Robertson's effort, as we shall take up, is to dissociate the site of the temenos where the bull was found from any connection with a mountain cult. We do not know the god for whom the Parparonia was celebrated; Jacoby (Note to 595 Sosibios p. 373) suggests Apollo. There is no reason to question the cult of a mountain deity Parparos at the temenos near which the bull was found. The temenos, however, does not mark the site of the battle.

V. AETIOLOGY SANS TOPOGRAPHY
253

to hear more of the practice." Part of the enormous bibliography on cenotaphs was collected in *War* 4.257–259. The vocabulary varies: κενοτάφιον, κενήριον, κενὸν ἠρίον, κενεὸν τάφον, σῆμα κενόν, μνῆμα κενόν, or simply a μνῆμα. The practice is found in Homer. For heroes, cenotaphs were common; Pausanias reports many. Archaeologists have noted burials where the whole rites of burial were carried out, but the bones, ashes, or bodies are missing. An excavated cenotaph at Salamis on Cyprus was for a single family who died in a holocaust of the palace. At Athens, an empty bier in the *ekphora* represented the "unknown soldier" (Thucydides 2.34.2). In naval battles, many would be lost. The lion monument at Amphipolis was judged by its excavator as a cenotaph. In the early literature, scholars were lavish in adorning the Kerameikos with cenotaphs. Xenophon attests the practice in the *Anabasis* (6.4.9). Plutarch (*Mor.* 770E; cf. *AP* 7.250) refers to a military κενοτάφιον at Isthmus. I suggested that our κενεάριον had to do with warfare, but there are other possibilities. Christien suggests the inscription was set up by Aiginetans of Anthene.[56] One always thinks of the missing in action, but Aristotle erected a cenotaph for his intimate friend Hermeias, and Pausanias saw the cenotaph of Euripides beside the road from Peiraieus We do not know in what context Hesychius found the adjective κενέαρος, but when he defines it as ἐλαφρός, I do not believe that the adjective was applied to a part of an aqueduct.

Herodotos (1.82) says that the Lakedaimonians were in possession of Thyreatis at the time of the Battle of Champions, hence the battle must have been at the frontier. Lerna and Elaious north of the northern base of Mount Zavitza were Argive. The watchtower on the ridge of Mount Zavitza above, with its panoramic view of the Argive plain (see *Topography* 3 pl. 70), was clearly controlled by the natives of Tsorobos, and the ridge would be a logical place for the battle. A photograph of the tower

---

[56]Dubois attaches significance to the "blue" chi. It was used at Aigina as well as in many Dorian cities.

254 THUCYDIDES' PENTEKONTAETIA AND OTHER ESSAYS

was published in *Topography* 3 pls. 67 and 68. The broad plateau is illustrated in pl. 74, as seen from the watch-tower, as well as in pl. 75. The ridge extends east-west. To the west of the spring-house marked on fig. 10 of *Topography* 7 is a large threshing-floor in an absolutely level area. The ridge qualifies for a battle-field on the frontier regardless of what depth we assign the combatants.

Entirely apart from the matter of the cenotaph inscription, Pausanias' route requires us to assign the Battle of Champions to a position before (i.e. north of) Anthene. This is the primary qualification. The broad plateau is on the border, before Anthene, and suitable for a battle. Thus meeting all the conditions.

In the course of discussing the topography, Robertson makes general statements, of which we extract the following.

PAGE 197: For our site for the Battle of 300 Champions, Robertson writes, "It is disconcerting to be told that this was a mountain top. The sole warrant is the kenearion inscription — which we have disposed of."

The top of Mount Zavitza is several kilometers removed from the watch-tower ridge, as we have made clear in descriptions and photographs. We have not visited it, but were told that there were many sherds near the monastery. The road up Zavitza from Elaious and the site of Anthene are the key factors in confirming Pausanias' site of the battle.

PAGE 188: Of the plain of Astros, Robertson writes, "The plain of Thyrea is not a feasible place for a hoplite battle."

This statement is incredible. The author has no conception of the topography or of Greek battle terrain. We offered in *Topography* 3 pls. 47 and 48, photographs of part of the plain, which is about five miles in length and half that in breadth. Phaklares, *Archaia Kynouria* (Athens 1990), offers excellent photographs of different parts of the plain in pls. 1, 2, 3, 7, 10, and 19. It is much more level, for example, than that of Plataiai

V. AETIOLOGY SANS TOPOGRAPHY   255

and could have accommodated any battle of the Greek world. In *SEG* 13.261, a late tombstone of the Athenian L. Gellius Carpus refers to him as the πραγματευτὴς τῆς Θυρεατικῆς χώρας. It is critical for Robertson's mythological theory that he have Pausanias mistake a hypothetical tomb of Othryadas as the burial place of the champions; so he posits that a battle could not have taken place in the Thyreatis, and thus converts Pausanias' polyandrion into a burial mound for Othryadas.

PAGE 204: "In Pausanias' time the Thyreatis was a backwater, and the very town of Thyrea had disappeared."

In 8.54.4, Pausanias writes: ἡ δὲ εὐθεῖα (ὁδὸς) ἐπὶ Θυρέα καὶ κώμας τὰς ἐν τῇ Θυρεάτιδι ἐκ Τεγέας ("the high road from Tegea to Thyrea"). See also 8.3.3. Pausanias does not give terminal points for places which had disappeared. Both Tegea and Thyrea were in existence. As to being a backwater, the Thyreatis contained the palatial chateau of Herodes Atticus with its monuments and sculpture, its nymphaion, stoa, and aqueduct — the Versailles of the Greek world. It never occurs to Robertson to account for excavation reports, survey teams, walls and pottery, and the reports of investigators, nor to visit the place himself.

PAGE 195: "The stadium and hippodrome must be sought in the plain."

On p. 188, we have seen that Robertson condemned the plain of Astros as unsuitable for a battle. Now, we find that seven pages later, in assigning the festival of Parparonia to this same plain, he apparently realized that this festival requires various games, and that boys' foot-races and a horse-race are attested for the Parparonia in a fifth-century inscription (*IG* V.1.213), although he

256 THUCYDIDES' PENTEKONTAETIA AND OTHER ESSAYS

does not mention the evidence.[57] Thus, a plain which cannot accommodate the Battle of 300 Champions becomes one with both a stadium and a hippodrome. As to the phrase "must be sought," it seems not to occur to him to give us the benefit of his own autopsy.

To summarize Robertson's position on the topography of the sites and roads mentioned by Pausanias: He disposes of the matrix for Eva, found at Helleniko, by saying that it "falls short of proving that the site was Eva," referring rather to his "coordinates for Neris." His "coordinates for Neris" are on a river Charadros, tributary of the Inachos, with its only attested site Oinoa, many miles from Thyreatis and reached by a different road. The Anthene of the Pausanias 2.38 passage is not sited at all. Rather in n. 32, he dilates on the restoration of the word in the lacuna of 3.16.4, which was discussed in *War* 4.162, and is irrelevant to our topography. Thyrea is disposed of by saying that it did not exist. The name of Herodes Atticus does not occur in thirty-eight pages of text. His map of Thyreatis in his fig. 6 is the most meaningless in topographical history without the name of any city of Thyreatis, ancient or modern, with no rivers, with contour lines of 200, 500, and 1,000 (meters ?), and finally, without any roads. Robertson is sure that there is no lacuna in the text of Pausanias, and the impressive road ascending Zavitza is ignored, as well as the reports of travelers who went from Argos to Sparta via Elaious. He concludes (p. 197), "To sum up, the received text of Pausanias is our best guide to the festival site." Declining to identify any of Pausanias' sites with walled remains in Thyreatis, he nonetheless has Pausanias be the guide to the site of a festival which is not mentioned at all by the Periegete.

---

[57]Damonon as a boy won the στάδιον καὶ δίαυλον (line 63). His son Enymakratidas won the boys' stadion, the diaulos, and the long race. The horse-race was won at the same time (44–48).

V. AETIOLOGY SANS TOPOGRAPHY

AETIOLOGY

We saw in the case of Hysiai that Robertson posits that by hypothesizing an imaginary statue of Argos and an imaginary hippodrome as part of an imaginary festival of Hermes at Kenchreai, he has created an "aetiology" for a "legend" of the Battle of Hysiai. About how this evolved, he is completely silent; the word "aition" is enough.

With the Battle of Champions, he has much more material out of which he creates a veritable jungle. On p. 184, he makes the pronouncement, "All the details of the battle have the appearance of aetiology." Instead of a statue, he posits an isolated and imaginary tomb of Othryadas in Thyreatis and an attested festival of Parparonia.

The tomb for Othryadas is postulated on the basis of late epigrams, which Robertson claims were grave-markers. Hellenistic poets created and published epigrams, which, though brief and direct, like inscriptions, were never meant to be carved in stone. As collected by Gow and Page, Thermopylai and Spartan heroism were favorite themes. There are several for the Battle of Champions. One is written for the tomb of Leukas (Gow and Page, *Hellenistic Epigrams* Chaeremon 2). *HE* Chaeremon 3 (= *AP* 7.721), of which the first line is corrupt, speaks from the grave, but the verbs are in the plural with the dual ἄμφω as for a common grave of the combatants. One is a dialogue between two survivors (*HE* Dioscorides 31). Another is an inscription for the Spartan tomb, the words of which are put into the mouths of the dead (*HE* 'Simonides' no. 5 = Page, *FGE* 'Simonides' no. 65). *HE* Damagetus 3 is for the tomb of the Spartan Gyllis; the editors suggest that an imaginary exploit has been bestowed on an historical figure. *HE* Nicander 2 describes the heroic behavior of the Spartan Othryadas. There are other references to the Champions, but they are not pseudo-epitaphs. Clearly, none of these is ascribed to a tomb of Othryadas, although he and Thyrea are prominent in the contexts.

258   THUCYDIDES' PENTEKONTAETIA AND OTHER ESSAYS

Without informing the reader about the ascriptions of the epigrams or discussing the Hellenistic genre of pseudo-epitaphs, Robertson affirms (p. 200), "The epigrams are intended for a monument of Othryades on the battlefield." This statement is completely false, and is accompanied by interpretations which badly misconstrue the texts, as the reader may deduce from the fact that he does not give the Greek or translations in their totality. Without continuing into his analysis of the various accounts of the Battle of Champions, we remind the reader that he has earlier assured us that the Battle of Champions, attested in Herodotos, Thucydides, Sosibios, etc., was pseudo-history, that no such battle took place. He now alleges that Pausanias mistook the tomb of Othryadas, the only Spartan who survived the battle, for the graves of the Champions, and that, topographically speaking, no battle could have taken place at the site of his tomb. He then claims that the tomb and the Parparonia festival comprise the aition of the legend about the battle and so has proved that the battle is not historical. If the tomb is the aition of a legend which did not exist before the erection of the tomb, its Othryadas must be a proto-Othryadas, a Dark Age figure who gave rise to the legend, one who was interred long before the "Battle of Champions." Moreover, for Robertson he can hardly be a military figure, at least he was not buried on what he allows to be a battlefield. To return to Robertson's text. "The battle of champions was invented by festival observers." "The games began as funeral games." "Somewhere at the festival site a memorial of a person, often a grave was displayed." He assures us that the memorial grave was that of Othryadas. "When the festival was in their (i.e. Argive) hands, they spoke of Othryades as an enemy overthrown ... When Sparta seized the district, Othryades too was appropriated." By this scenario, we have a grave of an overthrown enemy Othryadas, and, since the funeral games in his honor were begun by the Argives, they celebrate at the tomb of the enemy — a very non-Greek custom. Robertson dilates over several pages on a very fanciful and completely undocumented

V. AETIOLOGY SANS TOPOGRAPHY 259

reconstruction of the legend in the cults of Argos and Sparta,[58] but he offers no clue as to why this isolated tomb of his non-military, proto-Othryadas was erected in the plain of Astros as one descends from the Anigraia, as he would place it. Be Proto-Othryadas Spartan or Argive, why was he buried so far from home; what was the occasion for his death? "The tomb of Othryades must be early, being presupposed in both the Spartan and the Argive versions of the contest" (p. 205). We can be reasonably certain that Proto-Othryadas did not speak from a Mycenaean tomb in the fashion of 'Simonides'; Phaklares' survey would have turned up such a conspicuous tomb. Herodotos dates the battle about 545 B.C. when presumably Robertson's "legend" was fully developed. How Proto-Othryadas informed passers-by, Spartans and Argives alike, who he was is not clear; tombs in the Dark Age carried no inscriptions.

More importantly, why did the Argives institute a festival earlier than the Battle of Champions in the area between the mouth of the Tanos and the exit of the Anigraia? According to Herodotos, the Thyreatis was held by the Lakedaimonians at the time of the battle. Whereas the Thebans celebrated funeral games at one of the gates of the city in honor of the children of Herakles (Pindar *Isth.* 4.61 (104) ff.), we have no record of any games for Proto-Othryadas. What we regard as legendary figures gave rise to elaborate family-trees, as found in Apollodoros, but our imaginary being has eluded the treasure-house of Greek mythical and legendary lore. There is no record of semi-divine or heroic honors to Proto-Othryadas; he has no pedigree either at Argos or at Sparta. There is no trace in the literature or in Argive inscriptions of a Parparonia or of any athletic or festive activities assigned to such a festival. We are left completely in the dark about this Argive ur-festival of the Parparonia.

---

[58]All of the Hellenistic epigrams were composed on the assumption that there was a historical battle of champions. A proto-Othryadas cannot be extrapolated out of these contexts.

260 THUCYDIDES' PENTEKONTAETIA AND OTHER ESSAYS

Parparonia. The literary sources for the Lakonian festival of the Parparonia are Pliny *NH* 4.17; Hesychius (Πάρπαρος· ἐν ᾧ ἀγὼν ἤγετο καὶ χοροὶ ἵσταντο); Anecd. Bekker 1408 (Πάρπαρος· τόπος ἐν ᾧ περὶ Θυρεῶν ἐμαχέσαντο Ἀργεῖοι καὶ Λακεδαιμόνιοι); and Athenaios 15.678bc = Jacoby, *FGrH* 595 Sosibios frg. 5. The fifth-century agonistic inscription of Damonon (*IG* V.1.213, lines 44–49, 62–64) names boys' foot-races (στάδιον καὶ δίαυλος) and a horse race at the Parparonia.[59] The evidence for the Parparonia was collected by Bölte (pp. 130–132) in his important article on Spartan festivals in *Rh.M.* 78 (1929). He believes that the victory was celebrated at the site of the battle, but that features of the festival were transferred to the Gymnopaidiai after Thyreatis was lost.

For the site of the Parparonia, which must be before Anthene on Pausanias' itinerary, my candidate is the long watch-tower ridge on Mount Zavitza where the kenearion inscription was found. A possible candidate for χοροί is the large level area which today has a threshing floor in the center. The long stretch of what I first took to be the ancient road from Lerna with a retaining wall on either side (*Topography* 3 pl. 71) could be a candidate for a race course. Subsequently, in tracing the road up the northern side of Zavitza (*Topography* 7 chap. 7), I found that this road comes out at the spring marked on fig. 10, and that the road with retaining wall of *Topography* 3 was not part of the Lerna road. It could have accommodated two racers abreast.[60]

The alternative candidate is that of Phaklares, *Archaia Kynouria* (Athens 1990) 183–185, at Xerokampi (Marmaralona), where the bronze bull was found. See his figs. 55 and 113, and for the landscape pls. 39 and 41. There may well have been a sanctuary of the mountain deity here, but the site, near modern Ayios

---

[59]For the date, see Jeffery, *LSAG* 196–197.

[60]The artifact published in *Topography* 3 fig. 72, I took to be from some shrine. A goatherd said there were others. See *Topography* 3.119 n. 37 and 120 n. 38. There are many sherds around the watchtower.

V. AETIOLOGY SANS TOPOGRAPHY 261

Ioannis, is entirely outside of the Astros region and could not have been on a road through Anthena and Eva.

The Parparonia at the time of Damonon was a national festival. One needs concrete evidence as to why the Argives would have earlier instituted such a festival so far from the city at the site of the tomb of Proto-Othryadas. In connection with his hypothetical ur-festival which resulted in the invention of the legend of the Battle of Champions, Robertson (p. 207) cites an incident at the time of King Echestratos, who, according to the Kings' list, is dated in the middle of the eleventh century B.C. (so Niese, *RE* s.v. [1905] 1915), when the Spartans befriended the Argives by expelling freebooters from Kynouria. He also cites Apollo killing Python, the Abantes, festivals in Messenia, festivals to Hera and to Zeus, the Gymnopaideia at Sparta, etc. — a veritable hodgepodge of mythology without anything approaching an explanation for his Proto-Othryadas and this ur-festival, all completely unrelated to Mount Parparos.

Granted that the Greeks believed in legends about wars, including the Trojan War and the Seven against Thebes, and about the exploits of Herakles and the Herakleidai, it does not follow that by using the 'buzzword' aition we can hypothesize as pseudo-historical any battle attested by Herodotos and Thucydides on the basis of a festival commemorating the event. After Plataiai, the Greeks instituted the famous Eleutheria (Plutarch *Aristeides* 2.1; Thucydides 3.53). It would be foolhardy to argue that the Eleutheria was the aition for a pseudo-battle at Plataiai. The Athenians commemorated Marathon and Salamis by various festivities; it would require convincing arguments to relegate these battles to mythology. Epitaphia and epinikia are well attested; see *War* 3 chap. 5, with bibliography. J. and L. Robert, *REG* 77 (1964) no. 227, have a long catalogue of athletic festivals in honor of those who fought. Wade-Gery, *CQ* 43 (1949) 79–81, has argued that festivals were sometimes instituted in the hour of defeat to rebuild morale, specifically the Gymnopaidiai at Sparta; this may be right, but is harder to prove. Taking my cue from

262   THUCYDIDES' PENTEKONTAETIA AND OTHER ESSAYS

Herodotos (τὸν δὲ οἶδα αὐτὸς πρῶτον ὑπάρξαντα),[61] I would draw a distinction between what the Greeks of the fifth century remembered about events of the period of Kroisos and Polykrates and thereafter from their traditions about events of the Mycenaean and Dark Ages. I certainly do not believe that Spartan girls made an all-day hike from Sparta to Thyreatis to put on wreaths called Thyreatic crowns resulting in the creation of a story about the Battle of Champions out of these head-pieces while they danced around the unmarked tomb of Proto-Othryadas.

The Thyreatis has suffered greatly at the hands of Canadian scholars. On page 55 of her survey of the plain of Astros, Y. Goester, *Pharos* 1 (1993), writes, "I would like to express my thanks to Professor F. E. Winter who kindly helped me by giving his view on the matter. He suggests an itinerary of Pausanias, however in his own words far-fetched," a judgment on Winter's article in *EMC* 205–222, with which we would warmly concur, having reviewed Winter's position in *Topography* 7.205–222, noting that he takes Pausanias' Sparta-bound traveler over impassable gorges and cliffs. Robertson's work, in turn, displays even less understanding of the topography of the Argolid, written in a Canadian chimney-corner without benefit of oil-lamps, but replete with disparaging remarks about those of us who have worked on the topography.

3. PHIGALEIA AND THE ORESTHASIANS

In chapter 11, N. Robertson gives us another long mytholiterary jungle — this time about Phigaleia. The upshot is (p. 249), "We conclude that the story of those hundred Oresthasians is the *aition* of a pre-existing hero cult." Pausanias (8.39.3–5) tells us that the Phigaleians recovered their city from Sparta with the

---

[61]Cf. *The Liar School of Herodotos* 55–56.

V. AETIOLOGY SANS TOPOGRAPHY

help of one hundred picked men from Oresthasion,[62] and, when he comes to the agora, writes (8.41.1), "In the agora of Phigaleia is a polyandrion of the picked men of Oresthasion, and every year they sacrifice to them as to heroes."

After a selective review of the early history of Phigaleia and Sparta,[63] independent of modern authorities, N. Robertson assures us that the two cities were not embroiled against each other in early days and that Pausanias' story is pure invention attributable to some written source. He invents a scenario in which at the time of the founding of Megalopolis after Leuktra, a body of Oresthasians crossed over the mountains to Phigaleia to assist against possible Spartan encroachment. "If ever there was a time when a body of Oresthasians came to Phigaleia, it was surely in the early or mid 360's" (p. 243). This assistance resulted "in vehement patriotic literature which reconstructed the past in the light of the present." This "version is taken from a writer whose penchant was for reinterpreting ancient cults and providing pedigrees replete with Delphic oracles" (p. 244).[64] N. Robertson has assured us (p. 238) that "Pausanias himself was not gulled. He was aware, however, that there is a very large class of readers, and of listeners and observers too, who actively want to be deceived, for whom delusion is one of life's chief pleasures. He wrote with them in mind, as do many other ancient writers," with a footnote referring to D. Fehling's "exposure" of Herodotos. Thus, Pausanias used some undesignated source which concocted an early

---

[62]For the oracle, see H. W. Parke and D. Wormell, *The Delphic Oracle* 1 (Oxford 1956) 97.

[63]For a history of Phigaleia, see E. Meyer, *RE* s.v. (1938) 2065–2085, and Suppl. 14 (1974) 383–384.

[64]N. Robertson (p. 236) writes of Pausanias, "This phrase, 'the Phigaleians say,' denotes a book about Phigaleia."

264   THUCYDIDES' PENTEKONTAETIA AND OTHER ESSAYS

battle at Phigaleia out of Oresthasian assistance in the mid-360's and passed it on to his readers who wanted to be gulled.[65]

One might think that this scenario would settle the matter for N. Robertson. He has what he calls "that book on Phigaleia" (p. 244), which has projected an alleged event of the mid-360's into the recovery of the city of Phigaleia with Oresthasian assistance in early times. Instead, he launches into a review of the placement of hero cults in Greek agoras, concluding, "the agora, the muster-ground of citizen-soldiers, was never the obvious place for burial: not at the beginning, and not as a later development. The Greeks were therefore wrong in their belief that the hero cults of the agora arose from the burial of great men" (p. 247). In accordance with his theory of aetiology, he announces, "Ritual precedes and begets belief." An early ritual at Phigaleia which involved the shedding of the blood of oxen resulted, he says, in the need for a "single founder-hero" (p. 249). Thus, having assured us that the Phigaleians were mistaken about their hero cult in the agora, he begins a new section with the announcement, "We conclude that the story of those hundred Oresthasians is the aition of a pre-existing hero cult" (p. 249), whereupon he has the Phigaleians evolve a ceremonial procession in re-enactment of "the capture of Phigaleia by the Spartans" (p. 250),[66] for which "the starting-point must be the temple at Bassae" (p. 252),[67] ending in a ceremony "for enrolling young men as citizens." By this scenario, we have in order, 1) a Phigaleian ritual in the agora, 2) the estab-

[65]In this chapter (n. 3), Robertson double-speaks concerning another scholar that he "builds a massive edifice of conjecture," in an article whose work was examined seriously by Wade-Gery in the V. Ehrenberg Festschrift.

[66]Robertson cites 6.27.2, an epitome of Polyainos, lost from the original work, which refers to Spartans, transformed, however, into Argives.

[67]The procession sounds easy on paper, but it required three and a half hours for Frazer (4.393) to go from Phigaleia to Bassai over steep slopes. As the crow flies, Bassai is about four miles northeast of Phigaleia at an altitude of 1140 m. By today's road, the distance is thirteen kilometers.

V. AETIOLOGY SANS TOPOGRAPHY 265

lishment of an heroon, a cult for the founder-hero, about which, however, they were mistaken, 3) this hero-cult becomes Pausanias' polyandrion, which in turn becomes the aition of the fictitious story of the hundred Oresthasians.

Our interest is solely in the role assigned to the Phigaleians, their polyandrion, and the topography. The chapter is one of double-talk. Up to p. 244, we are assured that Pausanias took the account in 8.38.3–5 about the Phigaleian recovery of their city with Oresthasian assistance from "that book on Phigaleia." From 244–end, Robertson has it that the Phigaleians evolved the same account as an aition to explain what was mistaken for a heroon of their founder-hero in the agora, which becomes a polyandrion. "That book on Phigaleia" is the source for an apocryphal account in Pausanias 8.38.3–5, whereas the Phigaleians evolved the same story, which they accepted and amplified with ceremonies, as the aition for their mistaken hero-cult. The Phigaleians themselves regarded the account as true, but "that book on Phigaleia" invented the story as an expression of vehement patriotism. Thus, we have two distinct sources for the "legend."[68]

Fortunately, topography helps to resolve the dilemma, at least in part. Robertson's distortion of the topography is even greater than that of his aetiology. He writes, Oresthasion "was moreover a strategic site, guarding the approach to Arcadia ... So whereas many people were brought into Megalopolis, it is likely that a few were sent the other way, to Phigaleia ... The main district near the centre of the plain was Oresthasium/Oresthis ... If there ever was a time when a body of Oresthasians came to Phigaleia, it was surely in the early or mid 360s."

Whether one adopts my early candidate for the site of Oresthasion or that, more recently, of Yanis Pikoulas, i.e. whether

---

[68]If I read him aright, Robertson even attributes to the Phigaleians an armed festival of hoplites, which the Phigaleians created in honor of their visiting Oresthasians.

266   THUCYDIDES' PENTEKONTAETIA AND OTHER ESSAYS

the site is east or west of a pass over Mount Tsemberou,[69] Oresthasion was not by any stretch of the imagination in the center of the plain of Megalopolis.[70] For any Spartan army advancing up the Eurotas, Oresthasion was within easy reach. To date, no walls have been reported for either candidate. Pausanias came to Phigaleia by way of Lykosoura. Phigaleia is situated miles away from Oresthasion on a high plateau above the right bank of the Neda about halfway between its sources and the mouth, bounded by ravines and deep glens, north of the Messenian frontier, and cut off from the rest of Arkadia by the mass of Mount Lykaion.[71] The circuit of the walls measures about three miles (Frazer), and the remains are very extensive and have been described by many travelers. The remoteness of the city is familiar to the traveler who today visits Phigaleia's most famous monument, the temple of Apollo at Bassai. It was the Oresthasians, not the Phigaleians, who would need aid against a potential invader. If ever there was a time when a body of Oresthasians would *not* have left their families to assist the well-fortified Phigaleians on a mountain frontier, it was in the 360's.

[69]See *Topography* 4 chapter 2; 5.73–74. E. C. Drakopoulos, *AC* 60 (1991) 29–41, defends the candidate I proposed, which seemed to have the advantage of being near the great kalderimi road from Megalopolis to Asea; but there is no ceramic evidence on the surface, whereas there are many sherds of good quality as well as a wheel-rutted road at Pikoulas' site. Pikoulas (*Horos* 8/9 [1990/91] 201–204) replied vigorously to Drakopoulos. Earlier, in *H Notia Megalopolitike Chora* (Athens 1988), Pikoulas reported in detail on his site of Oresthasion at Ἀνεμοδούρι (102–112 with pls. 46–53) and what he regards as the chief military road from Sparta, up the Eurotas, through Oresthasion, to Asea (203–218).

[70]Pausanias (8.44.2) sites Oresthasion on the road from Megalopolis to Asea.

[71]For a plan of the region, see Cooper, *AAA* 5 (1972) 359. N. Robertson refers to Phigaleia as "small."

V. AETIOLOGY SANS TOPOGRAPHY   267

What of the polyandrion which Pausanias (8.41.1) reported that he saw in the agora at Phigaleia? N. Robertson, in his entire chapter, uses the word but once (p. 244),[72] but, according to his scenario, the monument must be in the opinion of the Phigaleians the grave of the hundred Oresthasians, from which he derives various military rites. For him, sometime before the mid–360's, a heroon for a pseudo-hero in the agora was transformed into the polyandrion. As to what the site of the monument was originally, before the Phigaleians mistakenly identified it as the heroon of their founder, we are given no clue. We add that the position of the agora of Phigaleia has been determined by the discovery of the statue of the pancratist Arrhachion (Pausanias 4.40.1), now displayed in the museum at Olympia.

That the Phigaleians would convert their alleged heroon for a founder-hero into a polyandrion for the Oresthasians defies credibility. As W. H. D. Rouse, in his *Greek Votive Offerings*, attests, the shrines of heroes were often marked with tablets, dedications, even statues, as well as many offerings. By the mid-fourth century, the accumulation may well have been large and hardly to be relegated to dismantlement. The cult required sacrifice, libations, and offerings of food. The hero was at times the guest of honor at a feast, a scene frequently depicted in art. To use a favorite phrase of Robertson, "We would like to hear more about" how the Phigaleians swept away their hero cult in the agora and replaced it with a polyandrion, after which they created a legend as an aition, instituted a military procession and all in the mid-360's B.C.

We question that Pausanias would have mistaken a polyandrion for anything but what it was. Some historical polyandria are in the form of mounds heaped over the remains of the dead. Since according to the preserved record the Oresthasians died fighting for the city at Phigaleia, it would be not inappropriate in

---

[72]Robertson lapses into such phrases as hero cult, tomb, grave. But a polyandrion is distinct from the tomb of a hero.

268   THUCYDIDES' PENTEKONTAETIA AND OTHER ESSAYS

an early period for them to be buried at the site of the battle. We can only guess about the extent of the early agora. On the other hand, by the mid-fourth century, polyandria were often marked by tablets with the names of the dead. If this were true at Phigaleia, when the Phigaleians are alleged to have converted a heroon for their hero into a polyandrion, apparently as a gesture to visiting Oresthasians, the visitors would be supplying the names of fictitious warriors on a cenotaph commemorating a fictitious battle. In an earlier chapter, N. Robertson has said that he would like to hear more about the practice of a cenotaph; but he sheds no light on his own creation. Finally, it seems to have escaped Robertson that his monument has been the aetiology of his military procession and rituals, not the reverse, as his thesis throughout his book requires.

The theory of the dismantlement of a hero shrine and this rewriting of Phigaleian and Spartan history lacks any credibility.

4. THE ITHOMAIA AND THE MESSENIAN WARS

Few scholars doubt that the Lakedaimonians waged two Messenian wars in the period starting about 740 B.C. (or 690, Parker). Pausanias in book 4 gives the only complete account of the wars. Book 4 is unique; twenty-nine of the thirty-six chapters are devoted to history and only seven to the sites. He tells us that he drew material from two third-century sources, Myron and Rhianos. Myron was a professional historian, of sufficient standing to be quoted side by side with Hieronymos of Kardia in the Lindos Temple Chronicle. Rhianos wrote an epic poem on the Second Messenian war,[73] which Polybios (4.33.5) called the Aristomeneion war, in which Aristomenes was the hero, like Achilleus in the *Iliad*, as Pausanias complains (4.6.3); a figure also like the

[73]In addition to the bibliography on Rhianos in *Topography* 5.10–11, add *Lustrum* 21 (1979) 24–25; M. M. Kokolaki, Φιλολογικὰ Μελετήματα (Athens 1976) 129–162, reviewed in *REG* 98 (1985) 181.

V. AETIOLOGY SANS TOPOGRAPHY   269

Klepht of the Greek War of Independence. Pausanias (4.14.7; 4.32.3) tells us that in his day Aristomenes was worshipped as a hero, and this fact is confirmed by *SEG* 23.207.13 (ἐναγισμός), where in Augustan times, Kraton is recorded as making a donation for the sacrifice of a bull to Aristomenes.[74] C. Habicht, *Pausanias' Guide to Ancient Greece* (Berkeley 1985) 36–63, summarizing the excavations of Orlandos, has given us an excellent review of Pausanias' itinerary at the site, confirming that as an eyewitness Pausanias can be trusted.[75] The excavations have been resumed under the direction of P. Themelis who has found many new inscriptions and buildings.

As to the topography of the battles, we have noted that Derai, the site of the first battle of the Second Messenian war (4.15.4), is attested epigraphically: *Topography* 7.179–181. Following in the wake of the travelers, we offered a candidate for Ampheia (4.5.9–10. 6.6), captured in the first battle of the First Messenian war: *Topography* 5.33–46; G. A. Pikoulas, *H Notia Megalopolitike Chora* (Athens 1988) 240–241. Our candidate for the Kaiadas (4.18.4–7), we believe is secure: *Topography* 5.58–60; cf. Pikoulas, *Horos* 6 (1988) 85. The account of the third and last battle of the Great Dike in the Second Messenian war (4.17.2–10), we believe has found strong confirmation in Tyrtaios' taphros in *P. Oxy.* 3316 (1980), which we have discussed at length in chapter 1 of

---

[74]In 4.32.3, Pausanias writes of the tomb of Aristomenes, οὐ κενὸν δὲ εἶναι τὸ μνῆμα λέγουσιν. His bones had been brought from Rhodes; cf. J. and L. Robert, *REG* 79 (1966) p. 375.

[75]Pausanias made errors. We know that the town of Ithome, which Pausanias (4.9.2) says was mentioned in the Homeric catalogue (*Il.* 2.729), is not in Messenia, as he has it, but at the foot of the Pindos mountains. One could cite worse mistakes in the notes of P. Levi's Penguin translation. It may be noted that Pausanias twice states and contrasts two contradictory stories (4.4.2; 4.5.1).

270 THUCYDIDES' PENTEKONTAETIA AND OTHER ESSAYS

Topography 5 (pp. 1–68; "The Topography of Tyrtaios and the Messenian Wars").[76]

The use of Kretan mercenaries by the Spartans in the third battle of the First war (4.8.4) has found confirmation in A. M. Snodgrass' study, *Antichita cretesi, Studi in onore di Doro Levi* 2 (= *Cronache di Archeologia* 13 [1974] 196–201). By comparing Tyrtaios and Pausanias, we have defended the style of fighting portrayed by the two authors in *War* 4.37–44, and *Topography* 5.12–15. The fact that the Great Dike was chosen for the site of a battle also lends credence to the Platonic and Aristotelian record that it was necessary to use compulsory measures to get the Spartan λαός to fight at the time of the Second Messenian war (*Topography* 5.17–18). These are important items, because it suggests that where it can be tested, the tradition about the warfare was sound. The difficulty is that Pausanias' narrative is rich in oracles,[77] manteis, portents, dreams, and visions, elements which lend themselves to folktales and legends. On the other hand, we know that such features were common in early times. Moreover, scholars believe that elements can be attributed to pro-Delphic,

[76]See also *Topography* 7.181. Independently of our study, K. Tausend treats the same papyrus in *Tyche* 8 (1993) 197–201. Much progress has been made since the criticisms of L. Pearson, *Historia* 11 (1962) 397–426, and C. G. Starr, *Historia* 14 (1965) 257–272, which in our opinion have lost a great deal of their credibility. V. Parker is of a differing opinion. He begins his article, "The Dates of the Messenian Wars," *Chiron* 21 (1991) 25–47, with the statement, "It has long been recognized that Pausanias' history of the First Messenian War is hardly any history at all. Lionel Pearson has effectively discussed his 'sources', and there is no need to go through that here again." The testimonia for the date of Tyrtaios and the Messenian Wars is collected and studied by A. A. Mosshammer, *The Chronicle of Eusebius and Greek Chronographic Tradition* (1979) 204–209.

[77]The oracles are rejected as unhistorical by both H. W. Parke and D. E. W. Wormell, *The Delphic Oracle* 1 (Oxford 1956) 248–253, and J. Fontenrose, *The Delphic Oracle* (Berkeley 1978) 103–107.

V. AETIOLOGY SANS TOPOGRAPHY 271

pro-Spartan, pro-Messenian factions. It is important to emphasize that Pausanias quotes five passages from Tyrtaios, whom he names in eight different places: 4.6.5, 4.13.6, 4.14.5, 4.15.2, 4.16.2, 4.16.6, 4.18.3. In 4.15.2, he expressly tells us that he searched through the poems of Tyrtaios.[78]

In accordance with his theory that early battles can be explained by aetiology, N. Robertson finds the action of the Messenian wars in the festival of Ithomaia. His focus is only on creating an ur-festival. He achieves the remarkable feat of condemning the historicity of the Messenian wars without a single reference to Tyrtaios, even in the notes, not to mention other sources besides Pausanias. For the historian, his work might as well be thrown into a shredder.

Aetiology. N. Robertson begins his chapter (10) on the early Messenian wars with the statement, "The festival of Zeus at Mount Ithome is mentioned in the legends of the early Messenian wars, and on closer inspection it emerges that the festival business has helped to shape the legends ... Almost everyone agrees that these legends, even when they are popular tales, have no value as a record of events." In his concluding page, he states,

> These picturesque details are taken from the youthful hunters who joined in the festival on Ithome. In early days the festival was chiefly theirs, and the "Hundred-slaughter" was a thank-offering for the hunting season of spring and summer. Hunting and warfare are similar and related activities; it was easy for a festival that celebrates the hunt to become a festival that celebrates war.

Robertson adduces the following "details" to support his thesis that the Ithomaia was a cult of hunters from which the legend of the Messenian wars arose.

---

[78]For the origin of Tyrtaios, see *Topography* 5.28 n. 44 (Athenian?). Bons (*Mnemosyne* 44 [1991] 253) suggests Sparta, following *CHCL* 1.130.

272   THUCYDIDES' PENTEKONTAETIA AND OTHER ESSAYS

1. He claims that the early Messenians were hunters, not warriors. "In earlier days, however, the worshippers were not warriors, but hunters, the way of life in rural Messenia ... Hunting was always feasible in the region of Ithome, and the ritual was of interest to hunters ... Despite the legends of the Messenian wars, warfare can hardly have been a normal or staple enterprise for Messenians of say the eighth or seventh centuries BC — at least in this area, which is the focus of the legends. The legends, however, allow us to glimpse another form of livelihood more suited to the area, namely hunting."

2. In 4.12.9, Pausanias relates that a number of Lakedaimonians entered Ithome, including Oibalos who carried in a bag a hundred clay tripods which were to be dedicated to the god to fulfil an oracle. Oibalos disguised himself as a hunter (ὡς ἀνὴρ θηρευτής) by carrying hunting-nets (δίκτυα). In *Kyn.* 2.5, Xenophon describes δίκτυα which were to be used in catching hares.[79]

3. In the Messenian order of battle in the fifth year of Aristodemos, Pausanias (4.11.3) states that the Messenians and their allies had breastplates and shields, but some were protected by animal hides. Pausanias specifies that the armor of hides was particularly true of the Arkadians. Robertson's conclusion is, "They are virtually hunters."

4. "Aristomenes is a hunter of Spartans." It follows for Robertson that Aristomenes was originally a hunter of game, and he adds that the song of Messenian women recorded in 4.16.6 "honours a hunter returning with his kill." The song, not quoted by Robertson, reads (Loeb tr.), "To the middle of Stenyclerus' plain and to the hilltop Aristomenes followed after the Lakedaimonians."

[79]Robertson has missed one "picturesque detail." In the *Kyn.*, Xenophon, after describing various hunting-nets, turns his attention to dogs to be used in hunting. In 4.13.1, Pausanias relates, after a series of portents and a dream, that all the dogs gathered in one place and howled all night.

V. AETIOLOGY SANS TOPOGRAPHY 273

These four items are the "picturesque details" which Robertson gives on pp. 230–231 to substantiate his theory that the Ithomaia was an ur-festival of "youthful hunters."

Topography suggests that the primary pursuit of the inhabitants of Ithome was not hunting. The Stenyklaros plain, one of the largest in Greece (7 x 3 1/2 miles), is described by Baedeker (1909 English ed., p. 383) as follows, "This fertile and well-watered expanse, sheltered from the N. and E. winds by screens of lofty hills, is covered with luxuriant groves of orange-trees, fig-trees, olives, and mulberries, interspersed with a few date-palms. The vineyards and corn-fields are surrounded with impenetrable hedges of cactus, and in the villages the aloe attains the dimensions of a tree." W. G. Loy, *The Land of Nestor* (Washington 1967) 144, says that the plain contains "57 square kilometers of prime alluvial land." Diodoros (8 frg. 7) says that a wealthy Messenian Polychares had many flocks and herdsmen, which the Spartan Euaiphnos took over. The same story with variations is also in Pausanias 4.4.5. After the Spartans were victorious in the third and last battle of the Second war, the Messenians conducted raids against the Lakedaimonians, when σῖτος, βοσκήματα and οἶνος were taken. The Spartan government then ordered that the Stenyklaros plain was to be uncultivated (ἄσπορος) by the farmers (γεωργοῦντες): Pausanias 4.18.2–3.[80] More importantly, Tyrtaios (frg. 5 West: 4 Prato), writing in the seventh century B.C., states (Loeb tr.): "Messene so good to plough and so good to plant, for which there fought ever unceasingly nineteen years, keeping an unfaltering heart, the spearmen fathers of our fathers, and in the twentieth year the foeman left his rich lands and fled from the great uplands of Ithome." Another fragment [6 West] of Tyrtaios strikes a similar note: "Like asses worn by their great burdens, bringing of dire

---

[80]For the Spartan impoverishment and a demand for redistribution of land in Lakonia, see Aristotle *Pol.* 5.1306b.38, and Newmann's commentary.

274   THUCYDIDES' PENTEKONTAETIA AND OTHER ESSAYS

necessity to their masters the half of all the fruits the tilled land (ἄρουρα) bears."

If one wishes to hypothesize an ur-festival of the Ithomaia, we have substantial grounds for positing one of agriculturists, but none of hunters. When the Spartans coveted the land, it surely was not for the purpose of hunting hares.

Pausanias (4.33.2) tells us that in early times, the festival of Zeus Ithomatas was a musical one: τὸ δὲ ἀρχαῖον καὶ ἀγῶνα ἐτίθεσαν μουσικῆς. He deduced this from two lines of the epic poet Eumelos, whom he quotes, and other sources. Eumelos is dated by A. Lesky, *A History of Greek Literature* (English tr. 1966) 106, and *The Cambridge History of Classical Literature* 1 (1985) 108, 168, 588, 726, in the eighth century B.C. The lines were studied by M. Bowra, "Two Lines of Eumelus," *CQ* 57 (1963) 145–153, in connection with a cult of music and song. In this earliest reference to the Ithomaia, there is nothing to support the theory that it was a festival of "hunters."

Again, in 7.24.4, Pausanias states that there was a statue of Zeus at Aigion made by Hageladas of Argos (fl. 432, Pliny); see Meyer, *RE* Suppl. 15 (1978) 154.19–42. Pausanias says this image was a παῖς. Frazer, on the 4.33.2 passage, explains:

> Now Aegium lay directly opposite Naupactus, the town for which, when it was occupied by the Messenians, Ageladas made the image of Ithomatian Zeus. Thus the two towns, separated only by an arm of the sea, had both statues of Zeus by the same artist. Moreover both statues were worshipped in the same way; each year a priest was chosen, who kept the image in his own house. Again, the Messenians had a tradition that Zeus was born and brought up in Messenia, and that one of his nurses had given her name to Mt. Ithome (Paus. iv. 33. 1). Similarly the people of Aegium had a legend that the infant Zeus was brought up by a she-goat at Aegium (Strabo, viii. p. 387). From all these coincidences Brunn thought it highly probable that the Zeus of Ithome, like the Zeus of Aegium, was represented as a child, which would further explain

V. AETIOLOGY SANS TOPOGRAPHY 275

why the priest, acting as a sort of foster-father, kept the image of
the infant god in his house.

Again, we have no suggestion that the cult of the παῖς Zeus
was one of "hunters."[81]

Topography refutes Robertson's theory which stipulates that a
legend arises from the grave of a hero and funeral games at the
site. At Messene, the tomb of Aristomenes with his marker in the
form of a column was in the lower city (4.32.3), whereas the festi-

---

[81]In 4.32.1, the word ἱεροθύσιον of the exemplar is often emended to ἱεροθέσιον, suggested by E. Rohde, *Psyche* (English tr. 1972) 554 (= 1925 ed. II. 343), on
the basis of the name given to the burial place of King Antiochos of Kom-
magen. For ἱεροθέσιον, "mausoleum" (*LSJ*), see also *SEG* 32.1383, and 33.1214
and 1215. Papachatzes retains ἱεροθύσιον. He identifies the building as one
outside the southern side of the Asklepieion, no. 28 on the plan in his vol. 3 p.
116. Pausanias says that the building contained the *agalmata* of the Greek gods,
a bronze *eikon* of Epameinondas, and ancient tripods. Robertson (221 n. 2 and
229–230) translates hierothesion as "Ritual depository" and claims that the
tripods were used for sacrifices at the cult of Zeus on the summit of Mount
Ithome, and then the meat was brought down in these "tripod cauldrons,"
because there was no room on the mountain peak, and consumed below at
leisure, all of which is wide of the mark. The manuscript reading of ἱεροθύσιον
is now defended against Rohde's ἱεροθέσιον by J. Winand, *Les hierothytes*
(Mémoires Acad. Royale de Belgique, 68 [1990] fasc. 4) 174–181. The ἱεροθύτης
is a cult official, widely attested in inscriptions, but with different functions; see
Stengel, *RE* s.v. (1913) 1590–1591. At Histiaia, he was an eponymous official; see,
for example, Cairns, *ZPE* 54 (1984) 135 and 140. At Messene, he is mentioned in
agonistic inscriptions as subordinate to the agonothetes: *IG* V.1.1467–1469. His
duties at Messene are studied by Winand. The discovery of new inscriptions
shows that the priest of Ithomian Zeus was eponymous at Messene: see *SEG*
41.334–336, 338, 374. There are many references to this official on the island of
Rhodes, including the philosopher Panaitios: *SEG* 39 (1989) 1821. All of this
copious material has escaped Robertson.

276   THUCYDIDES' PENTEKONTAETIA AND OTHER ESSAYS

val of the Ithomaia was on the summit of Ithome (4.33.2). The top of Ithome forms a ridge or narrow plateau running from south-east to north-west. The ridge is made up of four peaks, but the depressions between them are so small that the summits coalesce into one ridge. On the highest peak, the second from the northwest end of the ridge, is a ruined monastery. On the third from the northwest is a paved threshing-floor of the old monastery. Frazer (3.437) notes, "The threshing-floor is now the scene of the annual festival of the Panagia, at which the peasantry dance crowned with oleander blossom." On his sketch-map, Papachatzes (3.113) marks the monastery and the temenos of Zeus Ithomata, with photographs of walls and monuments on the ridge in pls. 81–86. The rites to Aristomenes involved the sacrifice of a bull.[82] The annual festival of Ithomaia was of a different order and had nothing to do with funeral games.

Finally, a compelling reason against regarding pre-historic Ithome as a town of aboriginal hunters is that their patron deity was not Artemis, but Zeus. Artemis was the huntress among the immortals, the goddess of the flocks and the chase. She is called the stag-killer (ἐλαφηβόλος), the lover of the tumult connected with the chase (κελαδεινή), and ἀγρότερα. Restricting my search to W. H. D. Rouse, *Greek Votive Offerings*, s.v. "Hunter's dedications," I find no example of a dedication to Zeus by hunters. "The huntsman paid his devoirs to Artemis Agrotera, or Pan, or other deities of the woodland" (p. 50). For characteristic figures of Artemis with animals of the wild woodland, see Rouse p. 305.[83]

[82]As to how his "youthful hunter' of the Dark Age got buried near the fourth-century Asklepieion Robertson sheds no light.

[83]Pausanias tells us in 4.31.7 that there was a statue of Laphira at Messene. Laphira was an epithet of Artemis, as Pausanias explains in 7.18.8. However, the cult was not indigenous, but adopted from Kalydon when the Messenians were at Naupaktos.

V. AETIOLOGY SANS TOPOGRAPHY

Foundation of Messene. Both Pausanias (4.27.5) and Diodoros (15.66) attribute the building of Messene to Epameinondas. Diodoros dates it under the year 369/8 B.C., and says (15.67.1) that the Thebans built it in eighty-five days. To achieve such a feat must have required a very large work force; cf. A. W. Lawrence, *Greek Aims in Fortifications* (Oxford 1979) 384. Pausanias (9.15.6) quotes the inscription in elegaic verse which he says was on the statue of Epameinondas to the effect that because of Epameinondas Messene took back her children and "thanks to Thebe's weapons, Megalopolis was girt with walls." The first line of the inscription was earlier quoted by Cicero, *Tusculan Disputations* 5.17.49. One might think that the same Theban work-force was employed in constructing the impressive walls and public buildings of two cities not far removed and directed against Sparta. According to Pausanias (8.27.8), the foundation of Megalopolis took place in 371/0 B.C. The Parian Marble (*FGrH* 239. 73) places the event in 370/68 B.C. According to Diodoros (15.72.4), the city was not founded until 368/7 B.C. Frazer preferred the evidence of Pausanias, a conclusion recently advocated by Hornblower (*BSA* 85 [1990] 71–77) citing Dusanic. Niese and Meyer think that the Proxenos who raised 300 darics at Magnesia on the Maiandros for the walls of Megalopolis was not the same as the Proxenos of Xenophon: see Hiller, *IG* V.2 p. xviii.15-20. Ziegler (*RE* s.v. Proxenos 7 [1957] 1033) disagrees. Hornblower also rejects the idea of different men, but does not mention the inscription. Messene, Megalopolis, and Mantineia (refounded in 371 B.C.) half-encircled Sparta, their common enemy. Xenophon (*Hell.* 6.5.5) states that the walls of Mantineia were built with the aid of labor contributed by other Arkadian cities and three talents of money given by Elis. When Epameinondas withdrew from his invasion of Lakonia in 370/69, Diodoros (15.67.1) says he left a garrison in Messene. At the time of the invasion, Epameinondas' army numbered 40,000 hoplites with many light-armed (Plutarch *Agesilaos* 31.1), while Diodoros puts the combined force at more than 50,000 men (15.62). Plutarch

278   THUCYDIDES' PENTEKONTAETIA AND OTHER ESSAYS

Pelopidas 24.2 and *Mor.* 346B has the figure 70,000. Some of this force may have been deployed to construct walls and buildings of Messene. Both Pausanias (9.14.4) and Plutarch (*Pelopidas* 25; *Mor.* 194B; cf. Nepos 15.8.5), in explaining that Epameinondas with Pelopidas had retained their command as boiotarchs four months longer than the legal expiration of their term, place the establishment of Messene as a city after the invasion of Lakonia. Endorsing the chronology of Pausanias, we have the sequence (371-spring 369), Mantineia, Megalopolis, Messene. Of the three cities, Messene is the one unlikely to have been able to afford heavy expenditure, nor do we have any evidence of a subsidy from elsewhere, in contrast to Megalopolis and Mantineia. In the nine kilometers of the fortification which included the summit of Ithome, some scholars (F. Winter, *Greek Fortifications* [1971] 165 n. 46) have suggested different dates for sections of the enceinte. There is no record of the city being taken. In 316, Kassander won over all the cities of Messenia except Ithome: Diodoros 19.54.4. In 315, he relinquished his plan to besiege it: 19.64.1. In 295, Demetrios Poliorketes besieged the city and was wounded by a missile from a catapult: Plutarch *Demetrios* 33.3. New evidence relating to this event is published in *SEG* 41.322. Following W. M. Murray, I believe that we have firm evidence at Akarnanian sites that different styles were used in the same building program: *Topography* 8.121. Meyer, *RE* Suppl. 15 (1978) 138–142, has provided an excellent summary of the bibliography about the date of the walls, likewise concluding that they were completed in 369. At Messene, some of the impressive public buildings must have been part of the original program, but we need further clarification.

The only proper method for the defense of the position that the combination of a Dark Age (or later) hero plus funeral games at the site resulted in legends which Herodotos and/or later sources reported as historical is first to adduce well attested examples recognized by all. Robertson has presented not even one, but simply invoked the buzz-word *aition*. Nor do we confuse myths about Mycenaean and earlier deities with legends about

V. AETIOLOGY SANS TOPOGRAPHY 279

later "heroes." His fictitious history has been presented in a topographical framework, which either visits to the various sites or inspection of published photographs would have corrected.[84] For the student of history, Robertson's book makes no contribution.

[84]With regard to the first half of his book which is concerned with the festivals of Athens, Robertson writes (p. xiv): "From the festival sites, we see how the city grew, from southeast Athens to the old agora, then to the new Agora and the northwest sector." We see how the city grew by plotting the findspots of the deposits from the neolithic period, bronze age, 10th, 9th, 8th centuries B.C., etc., on a city plan, and not from the festival sites, many not located. We find out about the secular history of a city by coordinating the information from the written sources and the archaeological evidence. And why limit oneself to festival sites? Why not study the sanctuaries and find out what the earliest evidence is for each one? I am told by my Agora friends that the distribution of sanctuaries by age will tell a very different story from that of N. Robertson.

Printed in the United States
By Bookmasters